Titles by *Langaa* RPCIG

Francis B. Nyamnjoh
Stories from Abakwa
Mind Searching
The Disillusioned African
The Convert
Souls Forgotten
Married But Availabale

Dibussi Tande
No Turning Back. Poems of Freedom 1990-1993

Kangsen Feka Wakai
Fragmented Melodies

Ntemfac Ofege
Namondo. Child of the Water Spirits
Hot Water for the Famous Seven
The Return of Omar
Growing Up
Children of Bethel Street

Emmanuel Fru Doh
Not Yet Damascus
The Fire Within
Africa`s Political Wastelands: The Bastardization of Cameroon

Thomas Jing
Tale of an African Woman

Peter Wuteh Vakunta
Grassfields Stories from Cameroon
Green Rape: Poetry for the Environment
Majunga Tok: Poems in Pidgin English
Cry, My Beloved Africa

Ba'bila Mutia
Coils of Mortal Flesh

Kehbuma Langmia
Titabet and the Takumbeng

Victor Elame Musinga
The Barn
The Tragedy of Mr. No Balance

Ngessimo Mathe Mutaka
Building Capacity: Using TEFL and African Languages as Development-oriented Literacy Tools

Milton Krieger
Cameroon's Social Democratic Front: Its History and Prospects as an Opposition Political Party, 1990-2011

Sammy Oke Akombi
The Raped Amulet
The Woman Who Ate Python
Beware the Drives: Book of Verse

Susan Nkwentie Nde
Precipice

Francis B. Nyamnjoh & Richard Fonteh Akum
The Cameroon GCE Crisis: A Test of Anglophone Solidarity

Joyce Ashuntantang & Dibussi Tande
Their Champagne Party Will End! Poems in Honor of Bate Besong

Emmanuel Achu
Disturbing the Peace

Rosemary Ekosso
The House of Falling Women

Peterkins Manyong
God the Politician

George Ngwane
The Power in the Writer: Collected Essays on Culture, Democracy & Development in Africa

John Percival
The 1961 Cameroon Plebiscite: Choice or Betrayal

Albert Azeyeh
Réussite scolaire, faillite sociale : généalogie mentale de la crise de l'Afrique noire francophone

Aloysius Ajab Amin & Jean-Luc Dubois
Croissance et développement au Cameroun : d`une croissance équilibrée à un développement équitable

Carlson Anyangwe
Imperialistic Politics in Cameroun: Resistance & the Inception of the Restoration of the Statehood of Southern Cameroons

Excel Tse Chinepoh & Ntemfac A.N. Ofege
The Adventures of Chimangwe

Bill F. Ndi
K`Cracy, Trees in the Storm and Other Poems

Kathryn Toure, Therese Mungah Shalo Tchombe & Thierry Karsenti
ICT and Changing Mindsets in Education

Africa's Political Wastelands:
The Bastardization of Cameroon

Emmanuel Fru Doh

Langaa Research & Publishing CIG
Mankon, Bamenda

Publisher:
Langaa RPCIG
(*Langaa* Research & Publishing Common Initiative Group)
P.O. Box 902 Mankon
Bamenda
North West Province
Cameroon
Langaagrp@gmail.com

Distributed outside N. America by African Books Collective
orders@africanbookscollective.com
www.africanbookscollective.com

Distributed in N. America by Michigan State University Press
msupress@msu.edu
www.msupress.msu.edu

ISBN:9956-558-62-1

© Emmanuel Fru Doh 2008
First published 2008

DISCLAIMER
All views expressed in this publication are those of the author and do not reflect the views of Langaa RPCIG.

*To the memory of my father, Philip Doh Awah,
and for my mother Theresia, who always lamented the days of old.*

Praise and Glory To God Almighty

Acknowledgement

As this work progressed, a number of people read the manuscript at various stages and offered valued critical insight and encouragement. In particular, I should like to thank Professor Milton Krieger, a distinguished Cameroonologist, and Professor Tatah Mentan for spurring me on. Drs. Dominic Awahmukalah and Augustine Enow Bessong, like Mr. Clement S. Gwanyama, became very committed to the venture; they made themselves available at all times when I needed help with ideas and facts. I am grateful to you all. I am indebted to my dear friend Susan Sandoval who has functioned almost like a private secretary of mine, one with great editorial skills and challenging ideas. Dee Klagstad of Century College's writing lab also read this manuscript. I thank her for her perception. I am grateful to the staff of Century College's library, especially to Cathy Adams who was so graceful in ensuring that I got on my desk whatever book I needed from wherever. To all those scholars whose works I read as I worked to put my ideas in perspective, I am appreciative. I am particularly indebted to my spouse and our children for bearing those lonely hours when I could not be with them. However, whenever we could afford time together, our challenging discussions, as I bounced ideas off of them, gave me an overwhelming sense of purpose in this venture. I am, above all, most grateful to God almighty for giving me back my life, without which I could not make this contribution.

Contents

Preface   p.vi

Note to the Reader   p.xi

1. Imperialism and Postcolonial Africa in Perspective   p.1
2. Ahmadou Ahidjo, Independence, and the Hidden Agenda   p.19
3. Government and the Status Quo in Cameroon   p.32
4. The Cameroonian People: An Abused Blessing   p.59
5. Cameroonian Resources and the Exploitation of the Masses   p.74
6. Of Uniformed Officers and the State of Anomy   p.115
7. Towards a Renaissance: What Must Be Done   p.136
8. Conclusion   p.162

Notes   p.177

Works Cited   p.183

Preface

I barely made it back to Cameroon alive after a gruelling apprenticeship at the University of Ibadan, Nigeria, that left me gasping for breath because of the rigorous nature of the academic atmosphere I experienced on that campus. It was with enthusiasm, then, that I returned to my native country, Cameroon, excited to begin serving a rich and ambitious student population by practising and imparting on to them what I had learned from some of the very best Africa could offer. I have always loved teaching and still do. However, my search for a position in the country's university system, at the time, 1990, exposed me to another side of life in Cameroon—the nasty—as I came to realize that things were not what they should be, at least as I had grown up experiencing and expecting. I grew up happily during the Southern Cameroons and West Cameroon days, and became an adult full of hopes during the United Republic of Cameroon era, only to be frustrated by the ongoing epoch of The Republic of Cameroon.

My years away as a university student had deprived me of opportunities of being initiated into the chaotic, corrupt, and totally tragic administrative structures that climaxed years after the demise of the Ahmadou Ahidjo regime. Thanks to a few altruists I met upon returning home, especially Professors Linus Asong and Ba'bila Mutia, and the late Engineer Charles Fofang, I was navigated through the maze of corruption and man-made hurdles until somehow I got recruited into the university system as faculty. It was the beginning of my education into the uncharted waters of a nation's shameful labyrinthine alleys of disorganization and mismanagement—dysfunctionalism. There was absolute turmoil from the ministries down to the chancellery. Shocked, because of the order I had seen within the educational set-up on Nigerian university campuses, I managed to serve the university for seven years before throwing in the towel. It was that or lose my mind in an effort to survive, transformed into a sycophant, where it was my right as a qualified and devoted professor to exercise my duties freely.

In April of 1997, I left Cameroon for the diaspora, abandoning an otherwise burgeoning career as a university professor because of the stifling conditions under which one was working. It was frustrating, an atmosphere that was further exacerbated by government policies that destabilized the mind by adding financial woes to already stress-warped thought processes as one worried about the direction in which one's career and even the nation were headed. Nobody, apparently, from the minister of higher education to the vice chancellor, seemed to care about anything, not even for the students that one was supposed to be serving; it was all politics and a dirty game of survival in usually shady positions of power and wealth.

Away from home, I had to begin afresh, painfully aware of how much I could have achieved already were my country—Cameroon—a sane society instead of the wasteland that, like most of Africa south of the Sahara, it was being turned into by a corrupt club of banditti masquerading as leaders. The beginning was not easy, of course, like every beginning, but with God, and a programmed society with a sacred constitution designed to serve its population,

I was able to begin a new life, even with a heart throbbing for Cameroon, for my people. I had to survive.

From beyond the national boundaries, and having had contact with different societies around the world, I have come to consider it a duty to review my homeland in an effort to see how far down the drain it has gone. The idea is to jumpstart our loving and hardworking citizens out of a state of stupor, orchestrated by heightened corruption, into realizing what procrustean leadership has done to a once thriving nation. This effort is all the more urgent as the vast majority of young adults today were born during this era of social decay within the country and so know no better. Cameroonians born in the seventies and after, have never known a local police force, for example, that was not prone to corruption; they have never known that there was a time when a person went to prison for giving a bounced check. To this generation, therefore, supposedly the future of this nation, all the citizens think they need is a job and some money to keep finding their way through the maze of sleaze and professional ethical squalor that marks social life in Cameroon today. My idea, therefore, is to let Cameroonians know that there could be better, that there had been better, and that corrupt practices need not be the way of life. In a corrupt society, only a few — the conniving and powerful — continue to enrich themselves even as others think they are making it too. But in a law-abiding nation, I have come to realize that the vast majority make it; yes, all who can afford to discipline themselves and seek gainful employment. This is the case because everybody benefits from the social, economic, and political stability of the nation, which are the ingredients that fertilize the environment and lead to lush existence instead of the haphazard efforts at survival that characterize Cameroon under Mr. Paul Biya's regime; a regime, like most in Africa, fashioned, guided, and still being influenced by unpatriotic despotic zeal along with imperialist whims.

Because this is an honest effort at bluntly diagnosing a nation's woes in a bid that somehow Cameroonians, and Africans as a whole, may begin working towards a better tomorrow, personal names have often been intentionally left out and only mentioned where the deeds of the individuals amount to common national knowledge. Names are also mentioned where it is believed individuals deserve recognition for their effort, in one way or another, towards improving upon the situation anywhere in the country. Our frustration and dissatisfaction are with the system and those people who through selfishness and neglect of their duties and responsibilities have fuelled the collapse of our nation, or else looked the other way while mayhem established itself as a system in a nation that has known better days. Most petty individual perpetrators of the ongoing state of anomy are themselves only victims of the system. They are the debris of a national disaster, drowning men and women clutching at straws of corruption and chaos for survival even though their niggling actions, comparatively speaking, have helped fan the flames of national destruction by raising corruption in Cameroon, and Africa as a whole, to shocking heights. Some individuals, accordingly, are bound to have their pride wounded by this effort, and so frown at it, but one has no choice. The plight of the suffering masses, and not a powerful but corrupt minority, is our concern here, and so this venture is more of a duty to us than otherwise. This is especially the case because being able to look at Cameroon from beyond, has brought to the fore so many unhealthy practices in the face of which one cannot afford to remain mute. After all, it is said one needs a mirror to see oneself better. Accordingly, by looking at other systems overseas a reflection of the chaos in most countries within the mother continent slaps one in the face.

Accordingly, a "true" portrait of Cameroon is a combination of what it is when experienced both from within and from without, especially when cultural and socio-political values are compared and contrasted with the situation in other nations. In this regard, it is a painful fact that Cameroonians are made to dream that there is cooperation between the Cameroonian government and certain Western governments, such that people even dare to hope the West will bring about positive change in Cameroon. How often have Cameroonians hoped, for example, that by getting involved and working with either the government or the opposition, the United States will help in bringing about the end of certain political malpractices in the country? Cameroonians were to realize belatedly, that Cameroon, at best, was only a blip on the radar scope of the State Department which did not even feature on the agenda of the particular United States government at the time? As Alex Thomson has rightly pointed out, after the cold war, "Apart from a desire to spread liberal democracy and capitalism across the globe, African affairs troubled few within Washington DC's circle of foreign policy makers" (151). Equally devastating to these hopes is the fact that not even Britain's government seems to remember Cameroon, its former protectorate, else how does one explain the Baroness of Asthal's blunder when in her capacity as Britain's Under-Secretary of State in the Foreign and Commonwealth Office she referred to Cameroon as a Francophone country (Jua 92), thereby displaying her ignorance of the bilingual nature of the Cameroon nation which her country once colonized. In this light, Cameroon, in the main, has been examined against the backdrop of imperialist activities within Africa in the past and today. The idea is to see if one can agree with those who think it is time Africa be held responsible for her plight today instead of being continually accorded the role of victim in the hands of Western nations, organizations, and their activities on the continent.

We, as Africans, especially those south of the Sahara (we are always carved out thus, as if we are that other Africa), are at a point in our history when the truth must out in a forceful and more direct manner. Our concerns now must transcend petty individual egos as we take stock in an effort to see how we can salvage a continent that was bastardized by colonialism only to be repeatedly abused by irresponsible leadership, and one dares to say the citizenry also, as people have now fallen so low as to condone corruption by doing whatever it takes to make ends meet. The result is the collapse of order as African states are reduced into veritable political wastelands.

This then is a continental stock-taking, done through the Cameroonian experience, in the main, provoked by the denigrating images encountered abroad of a hospitable and hardworking people—Africans. Many African countries can be used effectively to portray the tragic political wastelands characteristic of Africa today, but Cameroon is ideal for at least two main reasons. Primarily, the continent of Africa is too complex, and more so are the problems and their causes, for any one volume to make claims of attempting to address the happenings in each country within the entire continent. For this reason, a country considered significantly representative is used as an example for addressing the pulverizing crisis situation in Africa today. Cameroon fits the mould. Secondly, Cameroon is the choice because this is a country that became independent with minimal crisis, comparatively speaking. It was nurtured by Ahmadou Ahidjo, albeit dictatorially, into a thriving economic bastion in Africa, only to be completely bastardized by a parvenu, Paul Biya. This choice of Cameroon notwithstanding, when it is appropriate, illustrations are taken from other African countries.

It is unfortunate indeed that the damning portraits of Africa, somehow, rarely make it back to the continent such that Africans can react to them accordingly. As a result, many Africans sit back thinking so-called advanced countries are truly out to help them, even as conniving African leaders bleed their countries dry with the help of armed forces that only obey without thinking. It is common knowledge that it is more complex from a soldier's standpoint than this may reveal, but then, too much is too much. Africans, especially those from African countries still dangling from the reversed umbilical cords gripped by their colonial plunderers, must stop dreaming, wake up, and face the truth about how African nations can survive without Western superintendents breathing behind them for whatever reason. Freedom and development are qualities that are never handed to a people; they must be wrenched out of the hands of the oppressors, be they from within or without. But first, in the vein of the Igbo saying alluded to by Chinua Achebe, we need to know where the rain beat us so we may begin thinking of knowing where to dry our national bodies ("Role of the Writer" 157).

At best I am a social critic and not a political scientist as such. Even then my love for the subject is natural, such that as a boy of about five I remember asking my father what it took to be Ahidjo. Ahidjo had been in power for so long that his name became synonymous to "head of state", a position that looked like the highest form of success to a child. It was no surprise then that I nursed thoughts of reading political science in college. Alas when the time came, Ahidjo was still head of state and had established a notorious reputation for himself as a bloody dictator such that it did not require any effort for me to be dissuaded from my dream career. It was a turf permanently scanned and purged by Ahidjo after the manner of the biblical Pharaoh who went as far as to kill all children under a certain age in the hope of eliminating the newborn king. Rumours confirmed that Anglophone Cameroon had only one Political Scientist at the time, Mr. Samuel Fonyam, and it was said his every move was closely monitored by the regime. Accordingly, I ended up, after other interesting twists of fate, studying in the Department of English at the University of Ibadan, Nigeria. The program, however, was such that beyond the department, one was able to follow lectures by guest speakers and also take courses in other departments like Philosophy, History, and Classics. Subjects like African Political Thought, and Modern Political Thought, to name two, nursed my interest in politics, and so have events in the world, especially Africa, but more so Cameroon. Though somewhat fretful about my competence to delve into a territory outside my area of professional expertise as such, the will to educate, highlight, and redirect my suffering compatriots was overwhelming. Along with my confidence in the training given me at Ibadan, to dare and master, I set to work, emerging with this venture: *Africa's Political Wastelands: The Bastardization of Cameroon*. My goal, however, was to produce a work that the professional and the lay person alike, the latter especially since they form the baulk that needs conscientization, could read, enjoy, and benefit from without being weighed down by heightened professionalese as is typical of works by scholarly experts intended for their peers. Accordingly, if the least I have achieved is to highlight our problems as Africans through the Cameroonian experience such that we can begin questioning and examining our daily actions and how they impact upon Africa's image and welfare as a whole, I would have succeeded.

To those who feel that because some of us left Cameroon when we did we betrayed a struggle, my answer is that I knew where it pinched the most, and so it was better for me to keep running while continuing the struggle, than to have stood my ground and ultimately fallen without a fight. To retreat, regroup, and then do battle is the strategy of many a successful warrior, and to learn from the masters is not a sign of weakness.

This book is, therefore, not an attempt to insult anybody; rather, it is an honest examination of the Cameroonian national conscience, as a microcosm of the continent of Africa, in the hope of transforming us all into national prodigals willing to make amends, for we have all erred in one way cr the other against the image of our nation and continent as a whole. Accordingly, every Cameroonian must sit back and review his or her lifestyle, and answer to his or her own conscience if he or she can call himself or herself a responsible citizen. If not, then we must begin changing as individuals by charting new social, political, and ethical courses, and subsequently broaden out in the way we apply these trends in the face of other Cameroonians, and before long, we would be serving Cameroon and Africa better. We are a noble people by our traditional ways, and so we must revert to our ways or perish aping others along paths charted for us by alien values and experiences as the trends today indicate.

Note to the Reader

To avoid confusion, some clarification as to the usage of certain terminologies needs to be made. The orthography for "Cameroon" is as fluid as are the nation's problems and this is due to Cameroon's historical background.

Mainly the Portuguese, Germans, the French and the British have romanced Cameroon, and the result is a plethora of terms of reference and even spellings for the name of this nation. The situation is exacerbated by the fact that Cameroon is today a bilingual nation, with English and French as the administrative languages; the result is "The Republic of Cameroon" and "La République du Cameroun" as officially accepted terms of reference. Beyond these, the spelling of the country's name as was used by each of the former colonial nations is still being used in different contexts. Accordingly, there is the Spanish "Camarões", the German "Kamerun", the French "Cameroun", and the English "Cameroon". Even then, other terms of reference are used in this book depending on the point in history to which one is referring. Before reunification, when today's Cameroon had been split between the French and the English, the English-speaking part of Cameroon at that time was referred to as "Southern Cameroons", and the French-speaking part as "La République du Cameroun". After reunification, when both the English and French colonized parts came back together to form a federation, the terms "West Cameroon" and "East Cameroon" respectively, came into existence for the English and French speaking parts of the nation respectively. After these appellations and the attendant political structure, came the "United Republic of Cameroon" when Ahmadou Ahidjo eliminated the federation in his effort to annex English-speaking Cameroonians. Today, the name of the country has returned to "La République du Cameroun" in French and "The Republic of Cameroon" in English. However, English-speaking Cameroonians refer to their country as "Cameroon" since the present name — The Republic of Cameroon — has political implications to the effect that the former West Cameroon of the federation has been annexed by the former La République du Cameroun of the same era, and this is not the case. Or better still, the French speaking part of Cameroon has seceded from its union with English-speaking Cameroon.

In a nutshell, therefore, the time one is referring to, and the linguistic perspective from which one is coming all determine which term of reference this country is given. Accordingly, English-speaking Cameroon will occasionally emerge under names such as "British Cameroons", "Southern Cameroons", "West Cameroon", "English-speaking Cameroon", "Anglophone-Cameroon", and "Cameroon", whereas French-speaking Cameroun will be encountered as "La République du Cameroun", "French Cameroun", "East Cameroon", and "French-speaking Cameroun". "Cameroon", will, however, be used for the entire nation in this text.

Chapter One
Imperialism and Postcolonial Africa in Perspective

Africans, like other peoples around the world, "are innately no more violent, no more corrupt, no more greedy, and no more stupid..." (Thomson 2); in fact, they are generally speaking, simple, friendly, hospitable, trustworthy, and hardworking, even while still being human. These sterling qualities notwithstanding, this is not the picture of the continent being painted in the West; it is mostly one of sloth as hatchet men lambaste and ridicule the continent and the peoples of Africa, especially those south of the Sahara. As Paul Bohannan and Philip Curtin confirm, "Africa has for centuries been seen by Europeans and North Americans through webs of myth. The myths change from time to time and place to place, depending far more on the needs and prejudices, even ignorance, of the myth-makers than on the facts in Africa" (6). Bohannan and Curtin go on to add as a way of illustrating their point, that in the popular mind, Africa is still associated with lions, and lions with jungles, hence the primitiveness of the continent. Yet it is true that lions do not live in the rain forest, but in open grasslands, and only about 5 percent of the African landmass can be classified as "jungle", if jungle means rain forests. The point that becomes obvious is how facts are distorted and everything done to present Africa in a demeaning manner. Yet when one looks back in time, while questioning oneself if any people, especially those of Africa, deserve this, the truth dawns on one that Africa is where she is today—tormented by socio-economic malaise—mainly because of her encounter with the West. This, of course, is not a new observation for as Alex Thomson points out,

> Indeed, imperialism or 'neo-colonialism' has been cited by many Africanists as the major governing force behind Africa's poor economic and political performance in the post-colonial era. The ways in which foreign governments, international organisations and transnational companies have interacted with African states and civil society groups have certainly been influential.(5)

This is the case in spite of those arguing today that Africa should now take full responsibility for her plight, as so much time, enough for Africans to have turned the tide of events, has gone by.

This venture, however, is not an effort to present Africa as a victim, yet it is common knowledge that most of Africa is independent only in principle while being ridiculed for refusing to progress. Indeed, most African leaders are mere puppets and those daring enough to reject this role are dealt with differently. Remember Nkwame Nkrumah of Ghana, Sekou Touré of Guinea, Patrice Lumumba of today's Democratic Republic of Congo, and Pascal Lissouba of Congo-Brazzaville to name a few? They were all betrayed by meddling imperialist regimes. For struggling to free the rest of Africa from other colonialists, beginning with Rhodesia, and for exposing too much about imperialist covert activities in Africa, Nkrumah was overthrown in a military coup which left fingers pointing at Britain, West Germany, and the CIA above all; for choosing to be totally free at the time of his country's independence instead of remaining a French puppet, the French stripped Sekou Touré's country of everything they had installed there before totally abandoning Guinea; Patrice Lumumba, the first Prime Minister of the Congo, was assassinated, it is believed, with the connivance of the CIA for he was considered a communist; lastly, the struggle between the US and French imperialists for influence over the affairs of Congo-Brazzaville, led to the ousting of Pascal Lissouba. Yet Africa must forge on even while the architects of her woes continue to damn her as she struggles to survive.

In the world today, especially in Africa, there are many countries that are presented as very poor nations, otherwise referred to as "developing nations", and at times derogatorily as "underdeveloped nations" or the "third world". It is not surprising then that people say and write whatever they want about these nations without giving them the respect they deserve, all else notwithstanding. It is this sense of frustration that drove Célestin Monga to declare along the same lines:

> When it comes to Africa, one can afford to indulge in approximations, generalizations, even illiteracy. Africa's overall image is so negative that only the most pessimistic types of discourse conform to the logic that governs understanding of the continent. Publications as 'prestigious' as the *Financial Times, Der Spiegel,* or *Time* can publish cover stories and surveys built upon falsehoods and factual errors without stirring up a storm of protest, no doubt because 'experts' on Africa know that rebuttals will not damage their professional reputations (*Anthropology of Anger* 39).

Academic and scholarly dishonesty along these lines conjured not by genuine error but bias and intentional nonchalance, is not only unfortunate but has led Monga to hold up to question so much that is written about Africa. It is no wonder he see Africa as "the final frontier for those who like to tinker with ideas; ... the Luna Park for lovers of ideological orgies" (40). The perpetrators of this unfortunate trend do this simply because, according to them, they are from societies that are more successful. They fail to realize that it is only their economies and attendant bastions of consumerism that are thriving and hardly much else. And so they assume they are in a position that gives them the right and might to disrespect others, especially Africa south of the Sahara, through deprecation and vilification. Consider, for appetizer, G. Pascal Zachary's piece on Cameroon in which he describes an encounter between a group of possible protesters and the officials of "American utility giant AES" in Douala:

> – The gods were displeased.
> That was beyond the question to the delegation of chieftains and shamans who gathered one blistering afternoon in 2003 in front of the offices of American utility giant AES in Douala, the largest city in Cameroon, a western African nation of 16 million. The rains had failed to come. Rivers had run dry. Locusts were moving in from the north. Lethal gases had suddenly boiled up from a placid lake in the highlands, killing

dozens of villagers.

It was also abundantly clear to the delegation that AES was a target of this divine ire, and most likely its prime cause. AES runs Cameroon's electric system, and the drought meant no water to operate hydroelectric dams, which in turn meant a plague of power outages. So chiefs had arrived, beating drums and leading a menagerie of goats and dogs and chickens, with a proposal: They would slaughter animals and recite the incantations needed to get AES right with the gods, in hopes that the rains would come and the lights would return.

This is the very beginning of Zachary's article, which goes on to scoff at Cameroon and Cameroonians in a manner redolent of Joseph Conrad in *Heart of Darkness*. Most interesting is how Zachary has combined a series of sporadic events scattered along Cameroon's historical and geographical landscape into a dramatic series of ideologically and temporally connected acts and scenes climaxing in his bizarre and equally primitive portrait. This notwithstanding, besides upholding Conrad's approach to Africa, in the 21st Century, and despite how often he writes about Africa, Zachary is yet to know that only for a god within the traditional pantheon of genuine Cameroonian fondoms or chiefdoms will an authentic traditional leader—fon, chief or any other—lead an animal for sacrifice. True to how these African countries are usually misrepresented and ridiculed by such sensational writing, Zachary, after echoing Transparency International's ratings of Cameroon as a most corrupt nation, ends up by saying Cameroon "now places better than Iraq". Zachary is the person who does not only bite the finger that feeds him, but will, in the process, mangle his own tongue if need be. He fails to ask himself why Cameroon is where she is today, or better still a nation like Iraq which Zachary today declares the only place on earth worse than Cameroon. In his vitriolic article, characteristic of Western insulting rhetoric when it comes to other cultures, especially those of Africa, Zachary fails to ask himself why AES is in Cameroon today, and who their true predecessors were, or why Iraq is the mess he himself declares it is today. He must still believe that AES is in Cameroon to help those "natives" by bringing light to a darker part of the "heart of darkness" itself. This kind of thinking and writing in the 21st millennium is certainly disturbing, yet it is barely on the wane in certain countries because it boosts shrunken and misguided national egos. In the same vein, I cannot help wondering why the heat in Africa is "blistering" or "deadening" in Zachary's words, a man from whose world temperatures sometimes climb to over 100^0 F" only to turn around and drop to 0^0 F" and below in other parts, sometimes leading to heat and cold waves that bring about deaths. But that is Africa and so even things that would be praised elsewhere must be scorned. Yet when this is done by a writer of Zachary's calibre, then one realizes how far away the affairs of Africa are from dispassionate and stereotypical representations, in spite of claims that the world long left such dispositions behind.

Again, poverty, which has been transformed into the Achilles heel of these countries, since it renders them incapable of reacting to foreign insults about their cultures and ways, is relative as it depends on what one is focusing on—economics or morals. After all, economic poverty might not necessarily be as devastating as moral destitution even in the ocean of material wellbeing. As if to corroborate my view, Fuabeh P. Fonge, in a lesson to the African child exposes the failings of supposedly civilized and economically successful societies:

> In order for the African child to fulfil his role in the African society that is in dire need of economic development today, he must avoid falling into the temptations of embracing elitism, individualism, bribery and corruption, materialism, alcoholism, and any form of excessive pleasure that might demean and deaden his spirit. History teaches us how these shortcomings have played havoc in the Western child, polluted his psyche and distorted his sense of social justice, equality and equity. Africa, in fact, has no place for the manipulated modern legal systems that seem to reward criminals today. No, Africa has still not come to the stage where lawyers will convince juries that murderers are not responsible for their crimes because they were victims of abuse twenty or thirty years ago. It is still unthinkable in Africa that a wife would cut off her husband's penis while he lay asleep and be supported by a women's liberation movement simply because she claims to have been abused by the husband, not on the day of the ugly incidence but some time ago in their marriage....It is still a mortal sin in many African clans for children to talk back at their parents; and unthinkable that men in their twenties could murder their own parents—the very parents who gave them life—for the sake of their money and that lawyers would twist the legal system to make the dead parents look like the criminals. Neither would you find parents in Africa abandoning their children or giving them up for adoption by total strangers, no matter how desperate such parents might be. Even an insane African mother never hurts her baby. (302)

Fonge warns though that Africa is catching up with these foreign practices very fast and something must be done to stem the tide. He reveals in a powerful manner that given current trends, when people talk today about poverty, or of their countries being the most successful nations on earth, their focus is on nothing else, but the economy, materialism, consumerism in other words. Economic affluence is that which accords the baton of command in today's world even when all else reeks. In this guise, some of the leading so-called poor nations are in Africa. For this reason, should anyone, especially people from these "developing countries", venture to read what has been written by foreigners about their nations, the first word of advice is for them to develop a thick skin.

Aware of this distressing and equally misleading practice, of writers deliberately presenting Africa's problems as typical and unprecedented, Patrick Chabal and Jean-Pascal Daloz observe in their book, in a universalizing manner, about the occurrences in Africa:

> Much of what we discuss has already happened elsewhere in the world in earlier periods and could well happen again in those parts of the world which now view Africa with such distaste—as the ghastly recent history of the break-up of Yugoslavia makes perfectly plain. (xx)

What those self-declared authorities and maestros of so-called third world countries, who constantly pour scorn on Africa do not realize, even with all their claims of being knowledgeable, is that despite the degree to which they believe they have understood these cultures, their knowledge, as some of the very best and well intentioned writers themselves will profess, is only peripheral. Anyone with good sense knows, for sure, that it is certainly over-assuming for an outsider to think he or she has mastered a people and their values so well simply because of a number of years spent with them. Yet this is the attitude of many writers around today, such that they easily become judgmental and normative about other cultures, those in so-called "third world" countries, especially those countries in Africa south of the Sahara.

It is not surprising that most of the writers condemning and writing condescendingly about these "poor" African nations, especially, are Westerners whose sole goal is to berate and present African nations as failures without—in most cases—frankly considering why these nations are in such socio-economic throes. The truth, in any case, is that some of these writers have a reasonably good understanding of the goings-on in these nations. The vast majority, on the other hand, are only outsiders whose understanding of the reverberations in Africa comes, at best, after a few short visits down the years, or from books written by others who have only visited briefly, and are themselves biased. Those amongst these writers who have visited Africa did so with, all else notwithstanding, a tilted mindset—to authenticate established notions—and so could never be objective enough to emerge with a dispassionate insight into the plight of the continent. Hence my conviction that only those belonging to a culture and its plight, and a handful of rare scholars, who can truly detach themselves from cultural prejudices, can best present the plight of a people or foreign culture even if along with damning vitriol; after all, one has to feel it to know the pain.

Whatever the case, the fact remains that many African countries today pass for poor not because they are poor indeed, but because of age-old world politico-economic trends otherwise referred to nowadays as globalization. The result is that virtually every African nation—especially those south of the Sahara—is a sorry tale of socio-economic anguish. How is this the case, when in terms of natural resources Africa is the richest continent on earth, with "… 50% of the world's gold, most of the world's diamond and chromium, 90% of the cobalt, 40% of the world's potential hydroelectric power, 65% of the manganese, millions of acres of untilled farmland as well as other natural resources"? (Mentan, *Recolonisation* 9). Even though some of those writers who are too angry or disappointed with the status quo to be objective would disagree with me, the truth is that the present situation is the climax of a historical tragedy with acts and scenes ranging from slavery through colonialism, neo-colonialism, and today, globalization. The consequence of these holocausts is what we see in today's Africa, the nightmarish leadership notwithstanding, as it amounts to just one more spice in the tragic broth, the encounter of the West and Africa, put on the fireside of time.

One can imagine some already echoing the protestations that it is wrong to continue blaming the past and the West for Africa's wretchedness today, given that it is decades already since independence. This school's argument is based on the fact that many years have gone by since the theoretical ending of colonialism; and so, were Africa a better place and Africans reasonable people with a sense of purpose, the continent should have recovered from the atrocities of colonialism by now. They go on to argue that other countries like Australia, Canada, New Zealand, the United States, and Hong Kong were colonies but are already thriving and so they wonder how different colonialism was in these countries as opposed to what obtained in Africa which is unable to flourish decades after the colonial encounter. The truth, however, is that there are indeed a number of strategic factors unique to colonialism in Africa as opposed to these other colonies. Primarily, the cultural differences between these colonies and their colonizers did not run deep as was and still is the case with Africa with the exception of Asian countries. Another significant point is the colonialists' disposition towards these non-African colonies. The colonialists did not approach these colonies with the same racist prejudice, disgust, and condescension that characterized and is still typical, even today, of their relations with independent nations of Africa. That is why even the terms of the Atlantic Charter in 1941, drafted by Franklin D. Roosevelt and Winston Churchill, were not intended to apply to the colonized peoples of Africa. It was the realization of this conniving spirit that led twenty-eight Africans, under the leadership of the African National Congress (ANC) to publish a point-by-point response to the Atlantic Charter demanding that colonized people in Africa and elsewhere "...shall not be excluded from the rights and privileges which other groups hoped to enjoy in the post-war world" (Chidester). Again, besides the fact that "Almost everywhere, the African was engaged in a constant struggle with a harsh environment..." (Tordoff 24), it is true that "These powers differed, often widely, in their specific policies and overall approach to colonial development" (Tordoff 27).

The discrepancies between African scholars on the consequences of colonialism in Africa vis à vis other colonies notwithstanding, it remains a fact that of any scenario or case study, the beginning is as important as the end; the causes are as important as the effects. One must, therefore, never stop picturing where Africa came from, where she is today, and where she is headed, without acknowledging the thriving nature of Western covert and overt political and economic actions in this part of the world. Victor T. Le Vine's observation about early colonialist activities and the results they had on the continent of Africa strengthens my argument that one cannot afford to neglect the very beginnings of Africa's anguish, triggered by her encounter with the West, simply because so much time has gone by. Time, in fact, has little to do here as, along with neo-colonialist activities, it has only helped in shaping and strengthening the current trend by giving vistas for the proliferation of typical evils originated during this encounter of Africa and the West. Le Vine writes:

> The immediate effect of the establishment of a *pax Europea* was the substitution of one set of authority figures for another. In a deeper sense, it involved a displacement of traditional authority symbols by a European administrator, the creation of a 'king' or chief from a senior notable or councillor (Ardener suggests that the spate of Bakweri and Douala 'kings' stems from just such arrangements), or by the removal of

one chief and the substitution of another more amenable to his conquerors. Once the authority systems of traditional societies had been breached, other forces began to accelerate the process of disintegration. (*The Cameroons* 45)

Like it or not, today's Africa, in all its monstrosity, therefore, is the brainchild of those Western nations that were involved in the colonization of the continent and have continued manipulating and [mis]guiding the strides of the continent hitherto. It is these Western nations that structured and later decided on Africa's leadership and the direction towards which these leaders were to pilot their countries, mindful of already existing conflicts between the East and the West— Communism and Capitalism. It is now common knowledge that the interest of these new African nations was never an issue; from the beginning, they were mere pawns in an East/West game of power and influence. In the words of Naomi Chazan et al,

> The United States and the former Soviet Union shared an important attribute in common in African affairs. They were both relative newcomers to the continent....Each approached the continent in the light of their mutual rivalry: neither was particularly attentive to African realities, and both interpreted African interests in terms of containing the other. (431)

The drop in the interest displayed by the US, the sole surviving super power upon the collapse of the Soviet Union, towards African nations confirms this further, had anyone any doubts left. Chazan et al. also bear out that the end of the bipolar era had many consequences for Africa's role in world politics. According to them, "With no East-West strategic chessboard left on the table, external powers reevaluated their interest on the continent....Certainly the 1990s represented a period of relative disengagement from Africa by the major powers—with the exception of France" (451-452). Despite these withdrawal gestures, the truth is that, via other routes, pressure is still being put on Africa today as to the direction in which her leaders must sail their state-boats, instead of leaving an already wrecked people to figure out how events, along with their cultural values, differences and similarities notwithstanding, might guide them back to a state of socio-political wellbeing. In the same vein, after confirming that nation-building in Africa south of the Sahara is at an early stage, of course being mindful of nation building along Western lines as imposed on the continent by the colonialists, Victor T. Le Vine emphasizes a fact which highlights further Western influence, in the case of "Cameroun" which has culminated today in the bastardization of the nation, like most of Africa south of the Sahara:

> Nation-building, whether Africans wish it or not, involves the creation of an entity whose models are implicitly Western and whose construction therefore involves the use of ideas, institutions, and methods explicitly borrowed or adapted from the West. Consequently, it becomes necessary to examine in detail some aspects of the so-called Westernization process as it affects or affected the Cameroun. (*The Cameroons* viii)

Although the cold war and colonialism theoretically, are over, not all colonizing nations, as they would like the world to believe, have indeed left their former colonies. The French are the greatest offenders here. They are still everywhere in Africa influencing government policies while benefiting in many ways, especially from the natural resources of those nations to which they are clinging parasitically, while giving the world to think they are helping these nations as they flaunt about their post-colonial mantra of "coopération". Consider the latest atrocities in Cote d'Ivoire and see how a once stable African country was destabilized because of French influence there. Yet Western writers will look the other way, only to turn around later when Cote d'Ivoire will be struggling with the consequences of French atrocities in that country, to damn the nation as another African disaster.

Obviously a victim of the same frustration that has characterized my readings in the West about African countries and their political unrests, Boubacar Boris Diop opens his paper on the recent, yet simmering, crisis in Côte d'Ivoire thus:

> There is a widespread belief, never clearly formulated, that the culture of violence is deeply rooted in Africa. The underlying assumption is racist: that power struggles in the continent are the expression of secular ethnic hatreds.
>
> Unsurprisingly, Western media have persisted in imposing their clichés and preconceptions upon the conflict in Ivory Coast, presenting the head of state, Laurent Gbagbo, as a wily but brutal visionary, the rebels as good communicators and the shouting masses as young patriots.
>
> Two weeks after the rebellion broke out in September of 2002, France's then foreign minister, Dominique de Villepin, explained to the Senate in Paris: 'The present crisis is the result of traditional tensions. Ivory Coast, with its north-south split, is an ethnic and religious patchwork that has been in crisis since the death of Houphouët-Boigny' (1). What he meant was: 'here's another fine mess Africa's got itself into.'

Diop goes on to argue:

> It is a convenient way of looking at things: one side is as bad as the other, armed rebellion becomes legitimate and the rest of the world can sit back and watch a country split into two. The devastation caused by ethnic attitudes in Ivory Coast is appalling; we cannot condone it but we have to look beyond it. The present mess has not arisen simply because the Dioula and Bete tribes (2) have realized that they cannot live together any more. France is a central, and increasingly open, player in the crisis, and any understanding of the conflict depends upon an awareness of France's role.
>
> French interests represent 33% of foreign investments in Ivory Coast and 30% of its gross domestic product. Since Ivory Coast's independence in 1960, French companies have used one-sided contracts to repatriate 75% of the wealth generated there. President Henri Konan

Bédié, Houphouët-Boigny's constitutionally designated successor, tried to correct these anomalies in 1994 by granting coffee and cocoa export contracts to major United States companies and by licensing another US company, Vanco, to prospect for oil. At the end of 1999 he was overthrown in a military coup.

In this way Diop succeeds in showing how one example of a former colonial nation has not only exploited its former colony, but has gone on to do everything possible to maintain a state of economic dormancy and political and civil unrest, since the former colonialist nation remains to benefit under such a climate. Even then, Côte d'Ivoire should be blamed for failing to make progress, according to those who think Africa should stop blaming the West for her plight. Yet we see France, still in Diop's words, typical of this so-called world power, engraving further Africa's unfortunate backwater portrait in the mind of the world. In the process, however, this former colonial power exposes an example of Western activities on the continent of Africa, which continues to estrange, alienate, and antagonize Africans while hammering further the image of the continent as a political wasteland without a sense of purpose and direction:

> The present crisis began on 6 November when the government attack on Bouaké also killed nine French peacekeepers. The French president, Jacques Chirac, ordered the destruction of the Ivorian air force. In Abidjan Gbagbo's supporters promptly turned on the expatriate French community.
> None of this settled anything, but it did clarify the nature of the conflict. This was the first time in 40 years of postcolonial apprenticeship that the lives of French citizens in Africa had been so threatened. Everyone had been happy to watch Africans kill each other, but television images of tearful French evacuees stepping off planes outside Paris were another matter – almost enough to make viewers forget that French forces had killed Ivorian civilians and destroyed a sovereign state's air force to reassure 15,000 compatriots and to avenge the deaths of nine soldiers.
> Even the most sceptical were forced to recognize that France was closely implicated in the power struggles in its former colonies. Paris usually worked behind the scenes, but events in Abidjan forced it to show its face.

Again, consider French involvement in the Central African Republic (CAR) as reported in a Cameroonian newspaper—*Eden*. The French are said to have clashed with rebels in the central African nation where they are present, supposedly, "to provide logistics and intelligence to CAR in their struggle against rebels who have recently seized several towns" ("French Army Clash" 11). As usual, the French claim to have reacted in self-defence. Yet here we are again with the citizens of a sovereign nation struggling to set their nation "right", and in between the feuding factions is France. One cannot help wondering who provided France with logistics when the Bastille was being stormed by disgruntled, hungry, and livid French citizens who, by the way, have never been called "rebels" the way Africans rising against corrupt Western backed regimes of theirs are frequently branded. Africa's tragedy today could never be divorced from Western deeds on the continent, from their very first contact with Africa to what they are doing there today.

In the 1950s and early 1960s especially, the French alongside the Francophone Cameroonian authorities with whom they were "cooperating", would not let Cameroonians determine the direction in which their independence struggle was to unfold. Ahidjo, for example, was manipulated into power by the French, because he was one the French believed would listen to them as well as maintain French interests in Cameroon. It is also widely believed that even until today, the French will not let anyone be president in Cameroon unless he meets their standards, which, of course, requires such a candidate to transform himself into a French stooge instead of the leader of his own people. Elsewhere in Africa, French troops were responsible for restoring Léon M'ba to Gabon's presidency after a military coup. Most interesting is the fact that the French Foreign legion is said to have arrived in Libreville, Gabon's capital, some 24 hours *before* M'ba officially requested assistance (Thomson 148). Similar examples of direct French military intervention include: Zaire, where incursions from Angola were thwarted; Chad, as a counter-measure to Libyan attentions; the Western Sahara, to help the Mauritanian government against POLISARIO rebels; and the Central African Republic, protecting President Jean-Bédel Bokassa's circus of a regime (Thomson 148). In then Zaire, fed up with the failing Mobutu administration, Katangan rebels routed the Zairian armed forces from the South of the country only for the dying nation to be returned to its state of stupor by French intervention as they flew in Moroccan troops who ended up winning the First Shaba War. A repeated attempt at ousting the unpopular Mobutu government was snuffed by the notorious French foreign legionnaires and Belgian paratroopers before the entrance of a pan-African peacekeeping force. Again, when the army seemed poised to oust Mobutu, a corrupt leader without any vision for his country, in 1991 and 1993, the true "owners" of then Zaire—France and Belgium—once more sent in troops that helped maintain a totally hopeless, unrepresentative, and therefore illegitimate regime in power simply because their nations benefited from it. Why is this the case, yet many a learned and savvy writer has wondered out loud what is wrong with those Africans in Cameroon, Zaire, and Côte d'Ivoire, to name a few, that they cannot take control of their governments and nations? Is this Western meddling not responsible for the apathy characteristic of most of these nations today since it is common knowledge that France, at least, will always send in troops to maintain its African stooges in power come what may and in spite of the plight of their citizens? Interestingly, in the case of Cameroon, Jean-Germain Gros has made some rather troubling observations that need to be addressed even if it means digressing a little.[1]

In a simplistic and rather nonchalant manner Gros dismisses the far-reaching influence France has over Cameroon's affairs by pointing out that:

> Cameroon has been very close to France, but it is too simplistic to argue, as disgruntled Anglophones are wont to do, that Cameroon's diplomacy is hostage to France's. France may still be Cameroon's most important

partner but French interests and Cameroon's are not identical. This reality has at times created foreign policy difference between the two states. As in other African countries that make up the historical *pré carré*, Franco-Cameroon relations are developed through and shaped by personal contact between the heads of states and the politico-economic elites of the two countries. ... (18)

Is Gros saying he is unaware of how much influence France has in the affairs of her former colonies? And why is it necessary for two countries to have similar interests in order for the one to be interested in the affairs of the other, especially when the one considers itself a world power and former colonial authority? Alternatively, how else could the relationship between two countries be established to convince an observer that they could, in the process, be unfair other than through "personal contacts between the heads of states and the politico-economic elites of the two countries"? Any other approach is likely to qualify as an invasion politically, and smuggling economically. By the way, when the entire continent of Africa was being invaded and plundered during the so-called era of colonization, what similarities were there in the interests of the people of the Congo and those of Belgium other than that King Leopold II saw a source of incredible wealth he could exploit for his people even while painting a philanthropic front? What similarities were there in the interests of the people of Algeria and those of France, or the people of Nigeria and Britain? And then Gros qualifies a people with a genuine national concern "disgruntled", thereby conjuring a patronizing portrait of his approach to Anglophone problems, as his diction connotes a bunch fomenting unnecessary unrest in an otherwise "stable" country. Gros knows better, but would rather people believe otherwise. In the extreme, one can only suspect that Gros was misled by some Francophone politicians and scholars alike who tend to want to convince themselves that the Anglophone problem is fomented by a few Anglophone elites who were ignored during the sharing of rewards at one time or the other. After all, Paul Biya himself accepted in a dismissive manner in January 1999, that the Anglophone problem exists, but he considered it a minor problem caused by only a handful of hotheads (Jua and Konings "Anglophone Nationalism").

Equally misleading is Gros' description of Cameroon's relationship to France as one between partners; indeed, they may be partners, but the former is a junior and subservient partner. It is President Biya himself who declared on April 13 1991, that he was François Mitterrand's best pupil. Mitterand was French president at the time. Beyond this embarrassing confession from a presidential counterpart, how often has anyone seen the president of France and another of a Francophonie state relating as equals? Not with all the imposition France brings to bear on Francophonie nations. Usually, even in pictures taken during their Francophonie jamborees, these African presidents are positioned around their French counterpart like governors surrounding their president. No, these relationships with France are hardly those of equals. After all, it is common knowledge that African presidents who have gone contrary to French expectations in serious matters were virtually committing political suicide at the very least. Gros, himself, substantiates my point by observing about this relationship as far back as the dawn of independence thus:

Close ties between Cameroon and France were assured at independence. In 1960 there were more experienced and talented political, business and civic leaders than Ahidjo, men such as Douala Manga Bell and Paul Soppo Priso in Francophone Cameroon and Foncha in West Cameroon. However, Ahidjo, hailing from the north and less educated that many of his urbane compatriots, *was thought to be malleable and conservative.* (18 emphasis mine)

One cannot help wondering who was doing this thinking and believing Ahidjo malleable. Of course it was the French thinking, and by being "malleable" and "conservative", Gros' euphemism does not escape notice. The French, in other words, found Ahidjo one that they could manipulate (malleable) and one who would maintain and protect French interests in Cameroon (conservative). This was not the only time the French placed their interests before those of their colonized "partners". Jennifer Cole points out that when the French granted Madagascar independence, the departing colonial administration handed power over to a regime that ensured French military, economic, and cultural interests would be protected (13). Partners do not relate in this manner, else at the very least, the choice of a president for Cameroon would have been a Cameroonian affair in the main. But it is common knowledge that what Cameroonians wanted on the eve of their independence was of little consequence; French "manoeuvres facilitated his ascension to power in 1960..." even if they "did not exactly handpick Ahmadou Ahidjo to be Cameroon's first president..." (Gros 18). This is what politics and diplomacy is all about it would seem to me. Facts are facts irrespective of the language in which they are phrased. France "maneuvering" and facilitating his ascent to power instead of "handpicking" Ahidjo and making him Cameroon's president brought the same results to France—they had a candidate of choice at the helm of affairs in Cameroon. Since these are partners, is it possible for Cameroonians, on the other hand, to determine or influence who is to be president in France, bearing in mind Cameroon's interests as the determining factor?

Gros, once more, supports his argument that France is not holding Cameroon's diplomacy hostage by pointing out how Ahidjo went contrary to French wishes by supporting Nigeria during the Nigerian-Biafran crisis. Gros believes this guaranteed Nigeria's support in the event of a similar crisis since Anglophones in Cameroon had no less of a claim to sovereignty than Biafrans in Nigeria. If this is the case, then Gros, intentionally or otherwise, is only confirming the fact that Ahidjo, from the very onset, at the beginning of the federation, had a hidden agenda to annex West Cameroon ultimately as that is the only scenario that could have led to Ahidjo already trying to court Nigeria's support in the future. However, in defence of the idea that France does not hold Cameroon's diplomacy hostage, this observation limps as it is commonly believed that because of Ahidjo's sporadic truancy towards the French, he later paid with his presidency. As Joseph Takougang and Milton Krieger observe,

> While it is generally agreed that Ahidjo's exit from power was due to his failing health, there are those who argue that his retirement may also

have been precipitated by other factors, including a lack of support for his administration by the newly elected socialist government of French President Mitterrand.... The rift with the French president was not only the result of ideological differences between Mitterrand and Ahidjo, who had never concealed his admiration for Charles De Gaulle and regimes like his in France, or his disdain for the Socialist Party there. It could also be traced back to the 1950s and that party's support for the UPC against Ahidjo's government. The conflict between the two leaders was also exacerbated by the refusal of Ahidjo's administration to grant an entry visa to a French socialist lawyer who had volunteered to defend Ernest Ouandié, the militant UPC leader who was captured in August 1970. (63-64)

Accordingly, in spite of domestic unrest, the truth is Ahidjo's administration died because he fell foul with French authorities, hence the control the French have over their Francophonie "partners". Biya's joining the commonwealth can easily be dismissed as a cheap ploy to placate "disgruntled" (according to Gros) Anglophones; a manoeuvre, which even France can easily support as it is of little or no consequence indeed to either of these "partners". Yet Gros goes on to point out only what Cameroon stands to benefit in this "partnership" with France for he writes: "In sum, the relationship between France and Cameroon is clearly asymmetrical and points to the dependency of the latter on the former" (19). But is this dependency not what French idea of cooperation with her former colonies is about? As Richard Joseph had lamented as far back as the mid seventies,

> ...the vice in which France has kept its former African territories appears all the more remarkable. 'Neo-colonialism' seems too general a term to convey the degree of economic, fiscal, political, diplomatic, and cultural dependency *France has imposed* on its former African territories by means of the so-called Cooperation agreements signed with the newly independent countries... (3 emphasis mine)

The picture of Cameroon's dependence on France, as painted by Gros, amounts to philanthropy beyond the reach of even much better Western economies. Hardly is there such a nation that beyond its own economic woes will gladly take on those of another nation for free and for decades on end. To claim thus is to declare oneself not in sync with world trends and tendencies. Yet one can see in the words of Joseph how Gros was easily misled:

> As the 1971 Gorse Report Demonstrated, France has also succeeded in entrenching the dependence of its post-colonial periphery in Africa. This dependence has been noticeably reflected in the close personal relationships between the metropolitan and peripheral Gaullist leaders. *Yet as in the case of a magician's performance, a peep behind the scenes may reveal the hidden supporting structures, whose presence appears all the more remarkable because our attention has been so distracted by the oratorical display.* (27 emphasis mine)

Gros' observation about these African countries being dependent on France only confirms what French colonial policy, Gaullist especially, is all about—ensuring that the former colonies are dependent on France, even as she (France) drains them of their resources. This was so effectively done by de Gaulle's special advisers and agents such that, as Joseph effectively puts it, these colonies could risk breaking away from France only at their own peril. In the process, France benefited in many ways. For example, French soldiers who were stationed in different African countries, at once transformed these states into French strategic military bases while reinvigorating France's global defence network. Some of these soldiers were even present in the local armed forces as was the case in Cameroon. These "cooperating soldiers" were not paid from the French treasury and so brought back foreign exchange in the guise of their salaries, which they deposited in French banks. Are there any doubts that these soldiers earned much more than their local peers? So while being paraded as security forces for the local puppet's French-backed regime rather than strategic support for French global defence network, France found employment for French citizens who otherwise might have been jobless in France, or whose salaries would have been exerting further pressure on France's treasury. It is not surprising that for decades there were large numbers of French military personnel serving as technical advisers in different African nations and Cameroon in particular. Is anyone surprised then at the level of secrecy that has always shrouded this atmosphere of cooperation?

It is obvious that France stands to benefit greatly from these cooperation agreements with her former colonies. From another perspective, by these former French colonies belonging to the Franc CFA zone, French inflation is automatically transferred onto these countries which then act as buoys to French economy. By requiring that the foreign currency earnings of these former French colonies be held in French treasuries, France is given infinite opportunities in the use of the foreign earnings of the former colonies even without any consultation (Joseph 19). Again, the terms of trade between France and its former colonies with which it is "partnering", are, to say the least, disgustingly revealing; they are unfair. As Joseph points out again, not only have these African "partners" been denied real control of their political economies owing to French domination of their monetary policies, the reciprocal so-called duty-free arrangements between these "partners" has led to the flooding of African markets with high-priced French goods protected in many ways from external competition (Joseph 21-22). That France benefited from these relationships was obvious even to Americans, for which reason The Secretary of State, Warren Christopher, made his acerbic comments in late 1996 about France continuing to try and monopolize relations with its former colonies. According to Christopher, "the days are over when Africa could be carved into spheres of influence and when outside powers could view whole groups and states as their private domain" (Tordoff 37). According to Gros' reasoning, these powers must have been disagreeing thus to squander their money on Africa for nothing in return? Interesting!

A common saying about the partnership between the right and left hand is relevant here. It points out that the one hand washes the other for both to coexist; the French are not fools to tolerate the colonies as mere parasites on the French, that is if indeed it came down to that. If the colonies were just parasites draining France, then why did it require blood for Cameroon or Algeria, in particular, to gain her independence from France? One would have thought France would only have been glad to let go such nations sucking dry her lifeblood like the English abandoned Southern Cameroons when, erroneously, they considered it a burden without any economic value. But how would that have been possible when it is remembered that even until today this philanthropic "partner", (France), for example, is supplying 25% of Cameroon's import needs, thereby enjoying a surplus in her trade with Cameroon? (Mentan, "Political Economy" 123). Summarily, that France required its African pro-consuls to agree to satisfy the bulk of their countries' educational requirements from France, to obtain their military supplies and advisers only from France, to consult with France before international conferences, and to exercise the same financial policies towards other countries as France did, best spells out the nature of this "partnership" and "cooperation" between France and her former colonies. One can argue that the tide is yet to change. No, France stands to benefit greatly from these "cooperation" agreements with her former colonies, even as it appears that African states are dependent on France; this is the illusory nature of the "cooperation" existing between the "developed" and the "underdeveloped" world, especially within *La Francophonie*.

At the peak of Cameroon's national cataclysm—1994—was the devaluation of an already weak currency, the Franc CFA. Then it must be remembered that even before devaluation, the government "decided to implement two draconian salary reductions of respectively 30 per cent in January 1993 and 50 per cent in November 1993 (Konings "Post-Colonial State" 254) for no reason other than that the government had to obey ultimatums from international monetary organizations. As a result, employees' allowances were radically reduced, while others went for months without their salaries and had to spend weeks in Yaounde trying to get things rolling again. How it is that a worker's salary is discontinued while he is still in place working, while those of people already away from the country were still being paid, remains a mystery that only this regime can answer. And so, rendered completely ineffectual, some Cameroonians who just could not find a way out crashed mentally and started holding monologues, with others conversing with their cars. Others, daring enough to start afresh somewhere else after all they had put in to be where they were in Cameroon, transformed themselves into migrant labourers willing to work even in humiliating circumstances in foreign countries just to make a living for their families. Mr. Biya could not care less; all that mattered to him was he had to be president.

Mr. Biya has not suffered the consequences of his maladministration because of how rich he has become since becoming head of state. He has a fleet of cars at his disposal; a private mansion for which he, being head of state, certainly does not pay any bills; a private jet and helicopter attached to his office, with pilots paid at the expense of the nation; and he has his private businesses all over the place. Mr. Biya goes on vacation anywhere in the world whenever he feels the urge to leave behind the squalor he has created, but this is not the case with the rest of his compatriots about whom he cannot care any less. Except for those who have and are benefiting from high positions in the Biya regime, the bulk of Cameroonians, the ordinary hard working people on the streets on whose shoulders the nation rests, have found their lives virtually destroyed as a once thriving nation has been mismanaged into a veritable socio-economic wasteland. The result is that Cameroonians who, even as late as 1988, would have laughed at anyone for daring to suggest that they leave Cameroon and settle elsewhere, have had to rush out of the country as they saw themselves economically emasculated by the failures of the Biya regime. And remember, Paul Biya himself might not be that bad; his chequered administrative machinery may be the problem. But that Biya lacks the guts to take positive timely steps to save Cameroon from a kleptocratic bureaucracy he is heading makes him the foremost traitor of the Cameroonian nation yet. Let us reiterate the fact that most citizens have nothing against Mr. Biya as a person. However, Cameroonians detest what he has done to them and their beloved country in the name of governance as he continues to [mis]manage the nation as if it were his private estate, even as the country degenerates into a source of instability instead of the bastion of security and economic success it was during the Ahidjo era.

Anyone who visited Cameroon in the sixties, seventies, and very early eighties, left impressed, so that many foreign nationals, Africans included, dreamt of settling there. Today the story is different: Cameroon is a sorry sight with a reputation that leaves once proud Cameroonians ashamed of their fatherland as in the international arena diatribes are heaped upon a nation and peace loving people struggling against evil forces just to survive on a daily basis. Something needs to be done before Cameroon is wiped off the face of the earth by an idiotic leadership that has been incapable of realizing that governance means leading a nation to prosperity, or at least maintaining a thriving nation where it was when power changed hands. At the very least, good leadership means being able to acknowledge failure by leaving office so another leader might emerge and try his/her hand at guiding the nation into prosperity. After all, Cameroon has many sons and daughters armed with the basic good will, a pre-requisite for wanting to manage any institution, more so when that institution is one's fatherland.

The least that can be done then is to look Cameroon's leaders in the face and tell them they have failed, and that they should leave before they start another war on a continent already notorious for wars that could easily have been averted, but for selfish and unpatriotic leaders. And the people of Africa must be exonerated of this guilt—the problem is the leadership which, when not selfish and thieving, must struggle with different alien theories of leadership, none of which seems suitable for governing their people given the rather peculiar roots of those communities passing today for African states and nations. In the case of Cameroon, beyond just chanting democracy, the country at independence chose political structures based on democratic principles heavily influenced by French and English versions, even though the latter recognized traditional leadership while the former created quasi-chieftaincies based on nothing but the whims of the colonial administrator and the colonial policy in place. The leadership today all chant multiparty "democracy" without questioning its values with relation to the historical and cultural structures of their "nations", without giving it the necessary bent to suit their ways if need be. They are mainly puppets primarily mimicking their former colonial administrators even while being summarily controlled from abroad, to the advantage of former colonialist nations. In the process these mostly moronic African puppet heads of states zoom around purposelessly in expensive cars and suits satisfied that they are in power even if their nations are running aground like ships without sailors.

Cameroon ought not to be where she is today because of the resources the nation has and because it was already on solid economic footing by the time Ahidjo left office. Cameroon was a thriving nation and the citizens happy, even though some with political ambitions lived in fear of Ahidjo's gestapo. Notwithstanding, there was prosperity and security, with Cameroonians realizing that somehow their labour was productive in terms of the money they earned, and the standard of their lives. Those were the days when being a civil servant meant being reasonably well off; those were the days when civil servants saw their salary increments every December; those were the days when going to school meant good chances of becoming somebody within the country upon graduating. Cameroonians who lived then will certainly agree with me that paradoxically, and as shamefully enfeebling as it sounds, it is better to have lived in Ahidjo's Cameroon with the "fear" than to live in Paul Biya's travesty of a democracy that has only bred poverty, instability, and above all insecurity. Given the trend of things, Cameroon is another war in the making unless Biya hands over the country to a true and nationally approved patriot who can then begin the long and challenging journey towards bringing her back to where she was thirty years ago under Ahmadou Ahidjo. Cameroon's socio-economic decay is a true example of the African odyssey today—an alien colonial foundation, irresponsible and unpatriotic leadership, the abuse of power, victimization, a woeful judiciary system, indiscipline, with bribery and corruption running wild in a wilderness loaded with heavily uniformed officers but without any security, as all too often some of the officers are themselves Ali Babas—patrons of marauding gangs. It is not news in Cameroon to hear of security officers equipping thieves who then go out and murder people in the process of stealing, and then bring back their share of the booty.

Cameroonian literary minds, for years now, have swathed their messages about a tormented nation in different literary pieces across all the genres, but to no avail. This then is an effort to reach all and sundry as, by looking at certain key areas in our society, an attempt is made to paint a blunt picture of the nation, as it is today. The hope is to jolt consciences that are feared already cataleptic, asphyxiated by an overdose of corrupt practices that are now being mistaken in Cameroon, and the rest of Africa, for the norm. Without the potentially blinding literary veil, it can be hoped that some might begin thinking as to how to salvage a once beautiful and thriving nation today in an advanced stage of decay. This is because of the neglect Cameroon, in particular, like many other nations south of the Sahara, is suffering at the hands of a bunch of people who think of nothing else but how much they can steal for themselves while rendering lip service to the nation. The outcome has been a slow but sure transformation of Cameroonians, Africans, by their leaders, into a beggarly bunch, desperados, doing all to survive right in the midst of affluence which seems, somehow, always to loom beyond the reach of the common folk. Yes, Africa, as a whole, is in trouble because of the activities of mostly unpatriotic leaders. Even then, their numerous blunders notwithstanding, it is hard to think one can ignore all what the West has done and is still doing on the continent and focus the blame of the continent's predicament on Africans and their leaders only. That would amount to discussing the *effects* of a situation while neglecting the *causes* because one considers them no longer relevant given the length of time that has transpired; certainly illogical and shrouding instead of rational and revealing as expected of such pursuits.

Chapter Two
Ahmadou Ahidjo, Independence and the Hidden Agenda

The once-upon-a-time twin yellow stars on the Cameroon flag told the tale of a nation, and so does the now lone star—the dilemma of a people: Anglophone and Francophone Cameroonians disagreeing over the kind of government to have—federation or otherwise—and the level of influence each faction should have in the management of the nation and its resources. The situation has led to Anglophones threatening to secede because of what they consider their second class status in their own country. This impasse ought not to exist but for the love of some people to foment trouble for absolutely no reason other than that they are egoistic, evil, and myopic, or at best easily manipulated by forces outside of themselves. Otherwise, there is absolutely no need to manipulate Cameroon's history, as has been and continues to be the case until today by imperialists and quisling forces within the current national territory.

The groups of people later to be identified as Cameroonians, with the emergence of the modern state, were a quiet, peace-loving people living in smaller communities, and sometimes organised states and kingdoms ruled by monarchs with as much rights to their crowns and positions as their European counterparts (Nyamnjoh *Africa's Media* 101). Above all else, they were held together by ethnic bonds. These communities were no doubt expanding as the members ventured out into other territories for different undertakings. Their activities ranged from hunting, trade, and subsequently socializing, but things were to change with the entrance of Westerners. Since then, Cameroon's history has been tormented by the presence of different Western nations relating to Cameroon in different capacities. The Portuguese, however, sometime in 1472, were the first to surface in this territory, with its foundation in the Atlantic Ocean, the map of which looks today like a triangle with a hump. The Portuguese, it is reported, also gave the country her name. Because of the prawns they saw up one of the estuaries, the Wouri estuary, they called the country they had come to, Rio dos Camarões, "River of Prawns". The name, with time, metamorphosed into "Cameroon", and has since been spelled differently depending on the language of the Western nation romancing the country at the time, starting with the Portuguese themselves. From their arrival until the end of the 16th century, Portuguese navigators and traders scoured the coasts of Cameroon, even as the trade in slaves and other valuables was going on. In 1841, Joseph Merrick and Alfred Saker were two of the first Protestant missionaries to arrive in Douala, Cameroon. This was the socio-political climate of Cameroon, when the Germans entered the scene, and on July 12, 1884, signed a treaty with the Douala chief of Akwa, making Douala a German protectorate. The Germans called the country "Kamerun;" they were, however, not to be around for long. Not having fared well during World War I (1914), the Germans, who had already begun establishing themselves in the country, were flushed out by the victorious allied forces.[1] This defeat of the Germans led to the sharing of Cameroon between France and Britain as a way of compensating them for their roles in the War. Whereas France received the larger part of the territory, Britain was placed in charge of what is today the English-speaking part of Cameroon, which is smaller in territory and population.

These two Western nations established their cultures in these parts of Cameroon and at once went to work exploiting the territories for their benefits. Whereas France treated her part of Cameroon (which they spell "Cameroun") as France overseas, and did a lot to develop it, Britain's legacy in the Southern Cameroons is shameful, comparatively speaking. Although the British established a firm system of governance to help them control the territory, there was absolutely nothing else done to develop it. It is said in Cameroon today that if Britain did any work that looked like development, it was intended to facilitate her draining of the region involved. For example, the dangerous winding tracks put in place for roads, and the railways, served the transportation of raw materials to the coast, for subsequent exportation overseas, and hardly anything else. This exportation of Africa's surplus subsequently resulted in underdevelopment. Small wonder one can point out, even today, numerous German structures in the former Southern Cameroons, but hardly anything by the English. To be fair though, there is an Alfred Saker Memorial in Limbe, and the girls' secondary school, Saker Baptist College, in the same town, erected by an English missionary. But this, for all the years as Britain's protectorate, while tons and tons of raw materials were carted out of Cameroon by Britain, with Cameroon's sons fighting for Britain in wars with which they had nothing to do, nor from which they benefited directly, is certainly embarrassing. Dervla Murphy is saying the same thing:

> Under the League of Nations the Cameroons became mandated Territories, five-sixths going to France and one-sixth to Britain....
> The French were intent on developing their Mandated Territory, by fair means or foul. Hospitals, schools, administrative buildings, hotels, churches, office-blocks, telegraphic services and shopping-arcades proliferated; roads and railways were maintained or extended. Meanwhile the British Cameroon regressed; apparently Britain regarded its mandate as a genuine White Man's Burden, to be shouldered uncomplainingly but unenthusiastically. (13)

This was the situation of things until then British prime minister, Harold Macmillan, noticed the "wind of change" blowing in Africa as Africans began clamouring for independence. With so-called independence, the English dropped what was then Southern Cameroons, not caring whether the nation they claimed to have been preparing for independence had the relevant structures in place. The English simply withdrew everything they had in the territory, packed their bags and left Southern Cameroons floundering, while the French, on the other hand, nurtured their part of the country into a potentially domineering state in the future Federal Republic of Cameroon that was to emerge.[2] Consequently, there is a consensus amongst Anglophone-Cameroonians that Britain failed to fulfil her obligations towards this part of Cameroon — seeing to it that the territory segued into a functioning independent nation instead of the oppressed lot that the citizens are today. This, of course, is the case thanks to British neglect on the one hand and on the other, France's continued tenacious presence and influence in Cameroon even after her part of Cameroon is said to have gained its independence on January 1, 1960. French presence in Cameroon and its role in the activities of the government of Cameroon, even today, is hardly any secret. But where is Britain, which, like France, a former colonial "mentor", ought to bring its weight to bear behind Anglophone-Cameroonians? The answer is blowing in the wind, as Cameroonians would say in their frustration at Britain's display of "windy" diplomacy towards its former colony.

Towards the Federal Republic of Cameroon

The road to Cameroon's independence was not as simplistic as it is likely to sound in this synopsis, being that in its entirety it is material for another volume, a goal which several writers have already achieved. However, for our purpose in this volume, the core of the situation remains that during the scramble for Africa different imperialist European nations had acquired control over parts of Africa and had subsequently agreed amongst themselves to respect the different possessions as such. Accordingly, the partitioning of Cameroon after WWI, as established above, which gave the bigger half, four fifths to France and the lesser part, one fifth, to Britain (Konings and Nyamnjoh, *Negotiating* 23), was ratified by the Versailles Peace Treaty of 1919. Under the auspices of the new world governing body, the League of Nations, the partitions became mandated territories administered by the English and the French respectively. With the emergence and subsequent end of World War II (WW II), the United Nations (UN) replaced the League of Nations as a world governing body, the League of Nations having failed in its goal to maintain world peace. With this new world order, Germany's former possessions in Africa, which had been seized after her defeat in WWI, became UN Trust Territories. Hence, there was the British Trust Territory of Cameroon that had been divided into Southern and Northern Cameroons for administrative purposes, and the French Trust Territory of "Cameroun".

This was the situation when, after decades of colonialist abuse, Africans started demanding independence from colonial governments. The Trust Territories of British Cameroon and French Cameroun were no different in their pursuit of freedom from the yoke of colonialism, even as the colonialists struggled to maintain the status quo. There is the need to recall here though, that some of the citizens, especially the very old today, still nurse nostalgic feelings for their days as one people under the Germans. Small wonder then, when these Trust Territories were seeking independence from France and Britain, some political leaders, especially Francophones who were resident in British Cameroon, nurtured the idea of a return to the Kamerun days. This was the case until then Premier E.M.L. Endeley declared his preference for British Cameroons to stay with Nigeria from where it had hitherto been administered; the British also preferred this option. This, however, led to the tasteless alternative accorded British Cameroon as a *sine qua non* for independence — to gain independence by joining the Federal Republic of Nigeria or by joining La République du Cameroun. The popular choice of gaining independence on its own merit, which the citizens sought, was denied British Cameroonians.[3]

In French Cameroun, meanwhile, France went to work trying to secure its place as a colonial presence, come independence or not. France quickly banned the only true nationalist party that it considered a threat to its exploitative colonial presence and policies—the Union des Populations du Cameroun (UPC)—before granting French Cameroun independence on January 1, 1960. The French, however, had in 1958 appointed Ahmadou Ahidjo—a stooge of theirs whom they had ascertained would protect French interests in Cameroon—prime minister of La République du Cameroun. Ahidjo, even though not as sympathetic to Pan Kamerunism, was goaded into adopting the pro-unification goal of Pan Kamerunists in French Cameroun. The intention of this manoeuvre was to deflate the appeal of the UPC in those parts of French Cameroun where unification was a cherished objective, just like it later was in Southern Cameroons with John Ngu Foncha and his party, The Kamerun National Democratic Party (KNDP). With Ahidjo leading the theoretically independent state of La République du Cameroun, British Cameroons became the point of focus as it grappled with its own independence struggle.

Foncha, who was pro Pan-Kamerunism, worked with Ahidjo in response to the U.N.'s request for constitutional proposals from both Nigeria on the one hand and La République on the other. It has been said that whereas Nigeria emerged with a complete constitution, Ahidjo's government presented only broad outlines of a potential constitution. Nevertheless, this was Pan-Kamerunism emerging, or so it seemed to the leaders of Southern Cameroons, who were yet to learn that politicians can be deceptive. Trusting Ahidjo, Foncha went on to sensitize his public as to the wisdom of joining La République du Cameroun. In a plebiscite on February 11, 1961, Southern Cameroonians voted to join La République du Cameroun. The northern part of what was British Cameroon voted to join Nigeria.

When Cameroon gained her independence, it was agreed, amongst several other things, that the nation would be a federation of two states—East and West Cameroon. It is also held, it was agreed under the auspices of the United Nations, that this union of East and West Cameroon would be revisited after a decade to see if it was working and if both arms of the federation were willing to continue co-existing as one nation called the Federal Republic of Cameroon. However, according to Piet Konings and Francis B. Nyamnjoh this belief came about as a result of the confusion that was created by the outcome of a conference organized in London in November 1960. The idea behind this conference was to get Britain's approval that the United Nations grant Southern Cameroons her independence in her own right. Britain, which showed sympathy at the onset towards this course, eventually rejected the proposal. Either because of inadequate information or half truths even, the failure of this conference led to confusion in the minds of Southern Cameroonians who emerged interpreting the options the United Nations had given Southern Cameroons towards attaining independence—either by joining Nigeria or La République du Cameroun—differently. Most significant was the view that Southern Cameroons had come out with a promise that if reunification with La République took place, the union would be revisited ten years later to see if Southern Cameroonians were satisfied in the union of East and West Cameroon (*Negotiating* 37). Therefore, whereas Southern Cameroonians lived, hoping to see how the union would work out, the astute Ahmadou Ahidjo went to work to put in place an agenda today referred to in Anglophone Cameroon, thanks to Nfor N. Nfor, as "the Hidden Agenda".

Ahidjo and France were quick, it is believed, to smell Britain's cold feet from the distance[3] and knew it was only a matter of time and Southern Cameroonians would be on their own, and so absorbing them into the larger French-speaking population, with French backing, would not constitute a challenging task—big mistake!

Ahidjo, first of all, solidified his base in East Cameroon by hunting down all those who were against his government. These were the distinguished leaders of the Union des Populations du Cameroun (UPC), or more fondly remembered as the UPCists. These were Cameroon's patriots who had seen that "cooperation" with France would lead Cameroon to her own Waterloo, even without a war, and were determined to trim France's claws off Cameroon. Unfortunately these prophets and heroes, after their political party the UPC was accused by France of communist leanings (the standard cold-war-era excuse for atrocities committed in Africa and elsewhere) and subsequently banned, were branded terrorists and hunted down to the last man by Ahidjo and his dreaded gestapo with obvious support from his French gurus. As Martin Z. Njeuma puts it,

> The UPC challenge to French rule had necessitated a direct French military build-up in the territory. The new Cameroon government largely depended on French aid to maintain stability and peace (Bayart 1979: 240). Also, Ahidjo had signed secret military and intelligence pacts with France which would increase reunified Cameroon's dependence on France.

The last of these UPC heroes, Ernest Ouandie, Raphael Fotsing, and Gabriel Tabeu alias Wambo Le Courant, were shot by a firing squad in Bafoussam in the Western province in 1971. With Ahidjo at peace now that he had either killed or chased into exile all who could oppose him, he turned his attention towards the re-colonization of West Cameroon, this time not by France, but by another former colony, East Cameroon.

Before the gullible politicians of West Cameroon could wake up to the game of politics, Ahidjo already had in place a gestapo which was used as an intimidating force to coerce West Cameroonian rivals into submission. For fear of losing their lives in the hands of Ahidjo's bloodcurdling gestapo or rotting in jail, many Anglophone politicians stayed mute in the face of Ahidjo's atrocious coup against the state of West Cameroon and his subsequent attempts at annexation. The indefatigable and fearless Albert Mukong, now of blessed memory, was one of the few who could stare at Ahidjo in the face and disagree with him, and he did just that. The result was that, like Mandela in South Africa, Mukong became Cameroon's most "notorious" political prisoner for years because he kept fighting, even while in prison, against Ahmadou Ahidjo and his tactics as president.[4] The other brave West Cameroonians who, like Mukong, could stand their ground in the face of Ahidjo, and they were numerically not up to the number of fingers on one hand, went to an early grave. The eccentric Professor Bernard N. Fonlon is, possibly, the only one who defied all the odds to die naturally.

But Ahidjo's plan to overrun Southern Cameroons was already in place, and so he outsmarted Southern Cameroonian politicians at the Foumban

Conference of July 17-21, 1961. At this conference, it was believed that under the aegis of the United Nations, Southern Cameroonians would decide if they wanted to return and be together as a nation with La République. If so, they were, together, to structure the constitution to guide the emerging federation. However, the choice given Southern Cameroonians in this conference has always been interpreted to amount to one between a "Yes" and an "Oui" (a "yes" and a "yes"); it was not a choice, in other words. Ahidjo had manipulated Southern Cameroonians to a point where they had no choice but to vote in favour of remaining with La République du Cameroun.

The pace towards the final realization of the "horizontal colonization" of Southern Cameroons by La République du Cameroun had thus picked up great speed, yet the plan remained subtle as its realization called for the tact of a master at political manipulation.[5] Ahidjo was up to the task as slowly, yet with brutish conviction and precision, he displayed his real colours as a true disciple of Machiavelli. Gradually, yet in a most calculated fashion, Ahidjo started dismantling everything that gave Southern Cameroons her ability to be independent: the political structures, as the leaders of government were being toyed with and made to distrust each other; administrative offices, as documents were shipped off to Yaounde and left to rot in corridors, with public servants being transferred all over the nation, even into French-speaking zones, despite their lack of knowledge of the French language; the economy, as not only was the currency changed from the British West African currency to francs CFA, the financial structures of West Cameroon were also overrun with inexperienced, pilfering Francophone Cameroonians; the educational system, as Francophone structures, programmes, and methods were introduced. West Cameroon was deliberately abused in the hope that it would die as its citizens were being slowly, though tentatively, transformed into second generation Francophones by the conniving and treacherous government of La République du Cameroun.

Another major political blow to West Cameroon came when on May 6, 1972 Ahidjo informed the National Assembly that he had decided to hold a referendum which would help determine whether Cameroonians preferred the unitary system of government he had conceived, as opposed to the existing federation which he considered uneconomical, as it entailed a lot of duplication. Interestingly, this was not reviewing the question of Cameroonians wanting to remain together, but a question of the kind of government under which they were to continue their political marriage. West Cameroonians, who were uninformed about the implications of such a move, had only two weeks to ruminate over the idea of a referendum. Accordingly, there was hardly any time to educate the masses as to the implications of such a move. Meanwhile, Ahidjo's government campaigned overwhelmingly for a "yes" vote as it promised relief to West Cameroonians who were already suffering greatly from the consequences of the subtle steps taken to eliminate the state of West Cameroon. Many English-speaking Cameroonians, for example, lost their entire savings when the change in currency from the British West African currency (the pound sterling) to the Franc CFA took place owing to miscalculations in exchange rates. This led to much suffering, and so the English-speaking Cameroonians hoped Ahidjo would come to their help as he had promised. The results of the referendum showed 99.9 percent voted for the United Republic even though only 98.7 percent of the electorate voted.

West Cameroonians, whose voices alone mattered in this structural transition, since they were the ones whose status was at stake, were manoeuvred into voting for a United Republic of Cameroon in a referendum for which they were ill-prepared. Without realizing it, they had stretched their hands out to be shackled in a union that would cost them more than they could have dreamt of at the time — their integrity as citizens of a potential sovereign nation.

The United Republic of Cameroon and Thereafter

With the United Republic of Cameroon operating in full force, Ahidjo's goal was not to govern, honestly, the people of Cameroon; instead, he worked harder at subjugating them. First of all, to completely neutralize the state of West Cameroon, the seat of the West Cameroon government was transferred to Yaounde and the prime minister's lodge and the Parliamentarian Flats in Buea left to begin the process of decay.

The Yoke damn, which when managed by Mr. E. A. Mbiwan as head of The West Cameroon Power Corporation (Powercam), supplied cheap, efficient, and sufficient electrical power to West Cameroonians, was quietly dismantled. The citizens of West Cameroon were then expected to depend on Edea with its irregular and much more expensive power supply. One cannot help wondering how strategic such a decision was in terms of national security since disabling Edea meant virtually the entire former West Cameroon would be in darkness. Maybe that is why it was done after all, as a control mechanism intended for the intimidation and deprivation of the Anglophone population should the need arise.

Victoria's (now Limbe) natural deep-sea port was abandoned for Douala's river port, which requires expensive annual dredging to keep it barely functional. The effect of this was the death of Victoria, West Cameroon's economic stronghold, as today's picture of this once bustling town can authenticate. There was to be no more the beautiful sight of lighters drifting purposefully to and from ships berthed within reach of the wharf, with canoes surrounding them as private men and women vied with each other for small-scale business transactions with sailors. Even the hooting of the ship's horn as it alerted the country of its impending departure was to become history. The numerous shops — Printania, R&W Kings, John Holt, Philips, Amens, Glamour, Alliance, to name a few — found all over Victoria then, choked by the dismantling of the Victoria wharf, died naturally or were futilely reincarnated in Douala. Even with the oil, today's Limbe is nothing compared to Limbe of the 60s and early 70s when the town went by the historic name of Victoria, alias Va. What kind of a leader will destroy one part of his country just so another might thrive in its schemes? Nevertheless, that was Ahidjo's tactic and it worked in spite of the thousands of lives destroyed as their livelihood was taken away from them for no reason other than that they happened to be English-speaking Cameroonians.

The West Cameroon banking system was another victim. A banking system that was thriving was handed over to irresponsible and unqualified French-speaking Cameroonians who before long left Cameroon Bank gasping for economic breath. Other potentially corrupt Anglophone bankers, who had been deterred from financial malpractices because of the system of accountability that existed and the zero-tolerance of the legal system in West Cameroon, quickly let go all restraint and also started stealing from the bank. Cameroon Bank was to die without ever recovering, leaving English-speaking Cameroonians wondering what was happening to their beautiful country and its once smooth-functioning government services.

West Cameroon's police force, made up of disciplined men and women who were thoroughly trained — the pioneers in Ikeja, Nigeria, and the later breed in Mutengene, Southern Cameroons and West Cameroon respectively — was not left out. First, their uniforms were changed as they were issued uniforms that looked like those of whatever force it was that was in La République du Cameroun. It has been repeatedly pointed out that La République du Cameroun did not have a police force as such. And this seems to be true, mindful of the degree of adulteration that followed within the ranks of the West Cameroon police force when Yaounde took over control. In the West Cameroon police force, for example, a police inspector had approximately fifty constables under his charge, which made him a high-ranking officer. When control of this respected force was taken over by Francophone administrators who had no experience managing a police force, as evident even today, they churned out inspectors in their thousands, and before long there were almost as many as three police inspectors in charge of two constables or some ratio that ridiculous. In fact, it is not news today to see more inspectors at a roadside checkpoint than there are constables, leaving one wondering if the constables are in charge of the inspectors instead of the other way round. West Cameroonians knew this was a different kind of police force when candidates were recruited based on their qualifications only and without any background checks. Their fear was confirmed when they started seeing so-called "Inspecteur de Police" (Police Inspector) out on traffic control, a thing that could never happen in the West Cameroon police force.

Ahidjo's nightmare, however, was the dreaded West Cameroon Police Mobile Wing (WCPMW) unit then trained at Jakiri, in the North-West Province, by the late Bobe Ngom Jua who was prime minister at the time. Ahidjo could find some peace only after he had successfully dismantled this elite paramilitary group that displayed discipline yet to be encountered, much less paralleled, on Cameroonian soil ever since this force was disbanded. Everything else in uniform in Cameroon today is a travesty of what the WCPMW was. What goes by that name today, notoriously referred to by its French acronym GMI (Groupement Mobile d'Intervention), is an expensive joke comparatively speaking — a bunch of rag-tag, mostly undisciplined drunks and thugs passing for law officers, their only mission to harass citizens and squeeze out bribes from them as the citizens go about their daily duties trying to survive in a country already under a socio-economic chokehold by its pilfering leadership.

Even the educational system of West Cameroon was targeted, and although it is yet to be significantly deformed, thanks to Anglophones' determination to the contrary, significant dents have been made towards its adulteration. Consider the lowering of standards in what used to be The Cameroon College of Arts Science and Technology (CCAST) Bambili. Until the mid seventies, CCAST Bambili was a distinguished high school with a programme and tradition that set it apart from secondary schools and even lycées—its equivalent—in Francophone zones. Students went to class for just three or four intensive hours a day and were virtually on their own to study as they deemed fit for the rest of the day. The uniform was another unique feature of the school. The students had sky-blue shirts and brown pairs of trousers for boys and skirts for girls as a daily wear, and a navy-blue suit for occasions. All of this conveyed to a student who had just left secondary school that he or she was now in a new environment and at a different level. The student immediately sensed the reward for his or her hard work at the Ordinary level (secondary school). With the Francophonization of the institution, CCAST students saw their unique and cherished uniforms abandoned for some less dignifying wear. Next, the campus had a first cycle introduced, a decision which stole the pride, feeling of maturity, and sense of accomplishment that was immediately experienced by students upon arriving their Bambili campus. As if that was not unfortunate enough, the students' privacy and sense of maturity was rudely interrupted and taken away from them by the introduction of so-called "surveillant[e]s", disciplines masters and mistresses whose duty it was to monitor and regulate the activities of CCAST students who had been authorities—mature individuals—in their own right. This was the end of CCAST as it was known before its "Francophonization", which transformed this elite school by downgrading its status to that of any other secondary school or lycée around the country. CCAST was CCAST, and not a secondary school, nor was it comparable to any Francophone lycée.

The international General Certificate of Education Examination (GCE), that was written by Cameroonian students of English background, set and graded by the University of London, was also almost stripped of its integrity and dignity as it was transformed into a local venture like its Francophone versions which are characterized by irregularities. In the case of the GCE, however, Anglophones have struggled to maintain standards, even if not at the same level where they once were, as they keep fighting to prevent corrupt practices from invading this revered examination. The educational system of Anglophone-Cameroon seems to be one of the few surviving legacies of Anglophone-Cameroon colonial experience, besides the use of the English language by Anglophone-Cameroonians. Bongfen Chem-Langhëë's summation of the neutralization of Anglophones is also revealing:

> As soon as the Federal Constitution came into force in October 1961, the federation began moving rapidly towards a unitary system. In 1962, the pound sterling was squeezed out of West Cameroon and the East Cameroon *Communauté Financiére Africaine* (CFA) franc adopted for the whole country. Similarly, in 1964, the Imperial system of weights and measures was abandoned in favour of the metric system. By 1965, some of the residual powers which the West Cameroon government had arrogated to itself had been taken over by the federal government. At the same time the economic policies adopted between 1961 and 1966 gravely undermined the economy of West Cameroon to a point where pre-1959 conditions have not yet been restored (Ardener 1967:309, 314-35). This

has made the West Cameroon State more and more financially dependent on federal subsidies. By 1966, an unsuccessful attempt had been made to harmonize the legal systems of the federated states. In the same year, all the political parties in the Republic united to form the CNU. Three years later, all the trade unions in the country came together to form a single federation attached to the single party, forswearing their former international ties.

As indicated above, by 1972, Ahidjo took the next major step towards the neutralization of West Cameroon. In an impromptu referendum, he claimed Cameroonians had voted to become a united republic and no longer a federation. Initially the change seemed only nominal, but before long Ahidjo's plan began unfolding. The French language was introduced into all schools, and made a "compulsory subject"[6] which English-speaking students had to earn a pass grade in before they could proceed in their education. Notionally, English was also introduced into Francophone schools, but a second glance revealed the fact that it had no more importance than Spanish or German which the students had the choices of learning. Until today, the only other exo-glossic language that English-speaking Cameroonian children can learn is French. The choice of Spanish, German, and the rest, is tastier morsel suitable for Francophone palates only.

Beyond Anglophone children in schools, Anglophone parents were force-fed the French language through many different programmes that were introduced into this part of the country. First, there was "French by Radio" in the late 1960s, a programme which had French lessons broadcast over the lone radio station then in the West Cameroon, Radio Buea. Our parents were then coaxed into more French lessons upon returning from work at 3:30pm, as it used to be in those days. After their meals and a brief rest, they went for more French lessons which were organized and taught in most of the surrounding elementary school buildings like the Roman Catholic Mission (RCM) School Buea town. To those who had a little foresight, the writing was on the wall: Ahidjo was determined to re-colonize West Cameroonians by killing their culture and transforming them into second-generation Francophones, as they would have acquired French and the attendant culture not from France herself, but from a former French colony.

As a further strategy towards the realization of this scheme, conscious of the fact that French-speaking Cameroonians are the majority, Ahidjo started trying to create a kind of cultural human punch by moving government workers all over the country. He sent French-speaking Cameroonians into parts of English-speaking Cameroon and gave them highly influential positions, but the English-speaking Cameroonians he moved into French-speaking territories served as deputies at the very best. In this way, the English-speaking Cameroonian was again forced to learn French if he expected to earn his privileges as a civil servant — promotions, annual furlough, etc., — which unfortunately had deteriorated into personal favours distributed according to the fancy of the boss. The obvious and most influential way of catching the boss' fancy was to speak, or show signs of making the effort of speaking, to him in his preferred language — French. In this light, the Anglophone deputy in a French-speaking zone realized he had to learn French if he were to make his administrative life worthwhile. Ahidjo was thus positive the majority, with time, would swallow up the minority and before long English-speaking Cameroonians would simply cease to exist.

How the annexation of West Cameroon was to benefit Ahidjo, one cannot stop wondering. Yet this move is typical of the waste of time and resources that characteristically yield forth that certain mental disorder which seems always to possess politicians, in Africa especially, leading them to destroy the stability and socio-economic wellbeing of their nations? Why would a leader, while jealously guarding his, think it is all right to deprive his compatriots of their own identity simply because the former is president of the nation and belongs to the majority group? How hard is it to respect a people's culture when even a parent knows that in order for there to be peace at home, he/she must respect his/her children for whom they are, even with their frequent characteristic blunders as they grow up? How much more then, should one respect a people and their history, their essence? To believe otherwise is certainly stupid, yet how true is this suicidal trend when it comes to African leaders, in general, and Cameroonian politicians in particular.

Alas, Ahidjo was not to make it to his self-accorded illusory Promised Land—a Cameroon where the minority English-speaking Cameroonian would have ceased to exist—as he abruptly and mysteriously resigned from the presidency in 1982. He died shortly after that, suffering from some form of paranoia, it has been rumoured, for he repeatedly declared that he wanted *his* Cameroon, which he had been outwitted into handing over to a certain Paul Biya, whom he had groomed, returned. Resigning was an uncharacteristic move by a dictator like Ahidjo, who, it is said, had been intentionally misled by his French doctors into believing that he was ill and dying. In the words of Ntemfac Ofege,

> The French President Francois (sic) Mitterrand who had a score to settle with Ahmadou Ahidjo over the death by firing squad of Ernest Ouandie, Wambo Le Courant and the rest of the Cameroonian Socialists somehow conned Ahidjo to resign because of 'health reasons'.

This, again, was imperialism at work in Africa. From the imperialists, Ahidjo had learned that just as he was manipulated into office at the dawn of La République du Cameroun's independence, he could also manipulate into power whomever he wanted to become his successor; and so enter Paul Biya, the handpicked successor to Ahmadou Ahidjo.

By the time Ahidjo relinquished power to Paul Biya, Cameroon was a thriving nation, and there were not that many south of the Sahara. With an annual growth rate of about 6-7 per cent between 1970 and 1985, the Cameroonian economy was one of Africa's success stories (Konings and Nyamnjoh, *Negotiating* 6). There was, in addition, security, accountability, wealth, and stability, all characteristics Paul Biya does not seem to have been aware of even while serving under his mentor, Ahidjo, otherwise he ought not to be comfortable seeing Cameroon where she is today and still doing all to cling to power. The charismatic but reedy-voiced successor quickly won the hearts of Cameroonians with his good looks and a few slogans he was bandying around— "Rigor and Moralization" was most popular. Considering the sorry state of

Cameroon today, one must wonder if he knew what those words meant or if they were conjured for him by some over-paid aide. Yes, Cameroonians loved Paul Biya, if for no other reason than that he was good-looking and that Cameroonians were simply tired of Ahidjo being at the helm of affairs for decades. Cameroonians, frustrated by the lack of change in their leadership, even if it held socio-economic prosperity and stability, wanted change. It is Shakespeare who said not all that glitters is gold. Cameroonians neglected this wisdom and took the leap, welcoming, and traditionally baptizing and blessing the superficially charismatic Paul Biya wherever he visited within the national territory as they prayed for his wellbeing and a long tenure as president. Only time was to make them aware of the consequences of their premature enthusiasm.

With his most popular slogan, "Rigor and Moralization", along with stories that he was once a seminarian circulating, Cameroonians dreamt of so much positive change under Biya—Cameroon's Moses they thought. They visualized days when they would no longer need to leave all their affairs and travel to the capital city of Yaounde just to get a passport to travel out of the country; they envisaged religion gaining its place back in the school curriculum so society would be accorded a profound moral base; Cameroonians imagined genuine freedom from Ahidjo's secret service which made it hard for a husband to trust even his own wife. Yes, with Biya stepping into office, Cameroonians dreamt big.

After Biya put into place some of his mentor's plans like the institution of a TV station, his popularity soared as the majority of Cameroonians, who had never owned TV sets, shunned the black and white TV and went straight for huge colour sets. Then the Agricultural Shows Ahidjo had put in place as a way of encouraging food self-sufficiency—the green revolution—were still being well organized, and so Biya's popularity kept soaring as he used this opportunity to visit different parts of the country. The Agricultural Show first brought him to Bamenda in 1984. In 1985, he was again in Bamenda for the Cameroon National Union Party Congress. It was at this Congress that Biya was to show he was no longer going to be Ahidjo's puppet as he paved his own way by changing the name of the sole political party from the Cameroon National Union (CNU) to the Cameroon People's Democratic Movement (CPDM). By this stride, Biya simply told Ahidjo to get lost. In spite of his audacity, the truth is that Biya's regime stayed afloat only for the very brief while that he was able to continue implementing Ahidjo's already existing plans for the country.

Ahidjo always had five-year development plans for Cameroon and had the habit of informing Cameroonians about what he did for the month in his monthly almanac called "The Month in Cameroon". It was the practice that this documentary, which came in paper form also, served as prelude to all movie theatre sessions in the country, so Cameroonians could see for themselves what the president was doing for the nation: different projects being executed, the guests he received, and the trips he paid overseas, are a few examples. The documentary earned the moniker "supporting" in movie theatres around Anglophone Cameroon, and "actualité" in Francophone Cameroon.

However, that was Ahidjo, for as soon as Biya dared to forge his own political path, disaster struck: there was an attempted coup. Ahidjo, according to rumours, master-minded the coup in an effort to regain Cameroon, which he had come to consider his personal property.⁷ The coup led to the death of many northerners loyal to Ahidjo, and a total overhaul of the elite force responsible for presidential security—"The Republican Guard"— which ranks were dominated by men from Ahidjo's northern roots. They were replaced by people from Biya's own area of origin, and sprinkled with a handful of Anglophones who had nothing to lose with Ahidjo's exit from office—a clear display of tribalism at the very onset of Biya's reign, even though it can be argued to have been provoked by the coup. The failed coup was the last straw; Biya lost every little bit of restraint and control he had. He suddenly alerted Cameroonians of the need for them to expect difficult times, and as if he conjured such times with a magic wand, Cameroon started on a downward socio-economic spiral. The lack of accountability, the looting of government coffers by servants of the state in high positions and otherwise, all led to capital flight. The rushing of ill-gotten wealth overseas into foreign banks, coupled with a most spineless leadership led to the collapse of an economic stronghold Ahidjo had established. Tata Mentan confirms with equal forthrightness:

> ... the institutionalization of 'kleptocracy' (government by thieves), as part of President Paul Biya's strategy for survival, especially after the failed 1984 coup, crippled the economy. During the first five years of Biya's rule, some 600 billion CFA francs were stashed away in foreign banks. Local banks were ruined by the 'Big Men' of the regime who had been granted loans, which they were 'hopelessly incapable of repaying.' ("Political Economy" 112)

It was shocking, but typical of Biya's style: the president went on national television and questioned citizens' protestations against capital flight because he claimed there was no proof, only for him to turn around within a week or two and confirm capital flight. Simply put, Cameroon crashed, but most painful is the fact that Biya, realizing he had failed woefully as head of state, would not leave when in the 1992 presidential elections the citizens gave him the opportunity to do that; instead, he resorted to all kinds of methods to cling to power—fraud, divide and rule, patronization, and torture. The result is that today Cameroonians no longer know what belongs to Cameroon as a nation, with all the foreigners, especially from France, owning and managing Cameroonian institutions although there are qualified Cameroonians to own these businesses or fill these positions. This is the situation because everything Ahidjo had guarded jealously—the resources and pride of the people—has been mortgaged, if not sold outright to some foreign nation or wealth-seeking firms which now legally exploit the citizens. This is more painful as Cameroonians witness their wealth leaving their shores on a daily basis without receiving any financial remuneration or seeing any overall economic compensation for these things. A closer look at the institutions of Cameroon—the executive, the judiciary, and the legislature especially—will further reveal the tragic nature and impact of Paul Biya's bad governance, this exemplar typical of today's Africa.

Chapter Three
Government and the Status Quo in Cameroon

With independence in 1961, the Federal Republic of Cameroon, made up of two states—West and East Cameroon—was born. In this unique situation, the federal structure and manner of operation clashed with itself because of the dual colonial backgrounds involved—English and French. The colonial powers had, in many ways, greatly transformed the colonies into extensions of their home countries in an effort to control the locals successfully. Whereas in Southern Cameroons (West Cameroon), for example, which had been colonized by the British, one was innocent until proven guilty by the state, in La République (East Cameroon), one, like in France, was guilty until one proved oneself innocent. The conflict between both systems was already too obvious when it is considered that both sections expressed themselves in different administrative languages, the one in English and the other in French. In the same vein, while the country was a federation, both sections of the Federal Republic of Cameroon—the West and the East—had their separate Houses of Assembly, and then there was the Federal House of Assembly.[1] Accordingly, each section had a prime minister, and there was to be a vice president who was to come from West Cameroon if the president came from East Cameroon, and vice versa. In any case, of what consequence is a prime minister when the president is constitutionally the one who wields power?[2] At the time, the president, who was resident in Yaounde, came from East Cameroon (former La République du Cameroun). This, of course, gave La République du Cameroun the upper hand in matters of national interest because of the powers in the hands of the Francophone president.

With the United Republic of Cameroon, a new administrative contraption of a state into which Ahidjo manipulated West Cameroonians, came a number of changes also instituted by Ahidjo. He banished the position of vice president. There was now to be a president, a speaker of the National Assembly, and only one prime minister. Ahidjo's role as political juggler comes to the fore when it is apprehended that although in terms of protocol the speaker of the National Assembly, an Anglophone at the time (Solomon Tandeng Muna), came before the prime minister, yet the prime minister was the constitutional successor in case of any eventuality and the president was suddenly indisposed. Given that the prime minister was a Francophone, the calculated effort to ensure that an Anglophone does not become president is recognized. Once more, the new administrative order, "The United Republic", was bound to work against the former West Cameroon. Today, the Francophone president is the leader of the country, and he appoints his Anglophone prime minister who, of course, is said to be the head of government. This head of government, however, takes his instructions from the president who is also the one who appoints the cabinet with which the prime minister and head of government is supposed to work; there is no better way of defining a figurehead. In the same manner, the president who is all-powerful, the parliament being only a rubber stamp, can arbitrarily replace the prime minister, the brouhaha about democracy and multi-party politics notwithstanding.

THE EXECUTIVE

The President

At the head of the government of Cameroon today, as in most other African nations, is the president, and this time around, Paul Biya happens to be that president, having been handpicked as an heir by the former president, Ahmadou Ahidjo. Usually a president swears to protect the constitution of the land he is serving, and it is only normal that the welfare of the citizens, symbolized by the nation, should be his prime concern. The president is supposed to love his country and citizens to the point of being ready to give up his life for them; after all, he is the supreme magistrate and commander in chief of the armed forces of his country. This supreme duty of the president is not what concerns most African leaders, who, along with their ministers, a scarce exception notwithstanding, are shameless kleptocrats.

In hindsight, and now being able to pit two presidents, the one against the other, one is likely to conclude that Ahidjo was not only a better president, but also a true patriot, his despotic methods notwithstanding. This is the spirit, despite certain beliefs, that leads one to think further that one would rather flourish under a benevolent despot than be free, starving, and insecure under a reckless quisling of an autocrat purposelessly bleating democracy. There are many Cameroonians who seem to think this way—preferring Ahidjo's benevolent despotism to Biya's lip-service democracy. Mwalimu George Ngwane has also observed this tendency, for he writes: "... Cameroonians sometimes look back with nostalgia at the Ahmadou Ahidjo authoritarian years of one party rule, when they enjoyed economic prosperity" (21). Ahidjo stopped at nothing to maintain peace, stability, and economic prosperity in Cameroon. Biya on the other hand, has hardly done anything in 26 years for the benefit of the nation as a whole, other than strategize on how to maintain his grip on power. He started by wasting resources as he did everything he could to wipe out traces of Ahidjo as his predecessor, the most ridiculous strategy being the discarding of expensive banknotes simply because they had Ahidjo's image on them. He introduced new notes with his own picture instead. One could not help wondering what he had achieved as president that warranted his photo on Cameroon's currency or is it just a matter of becoming president that qualifies one's image to be printed on the nation's money? As if that was not enough wastage, Biya embarked on wiping out the much admired and equally disciplined Republican Guard that was responsible for presidential security during Ahidjo's days. In one swoop, he eliminated most of the officers who were from Ahidjo's Northern Province and introduced officers from his ethnic group. Biya also eliminated the name "Republican Guard" before changing their beautiful uniform and wasting money on some funny looking outfit reminiscent of English horse-riders or members of Adolph Hitler's Third Reich. Then the Israelis were shipped in to train the new guards and monitor Biya's security; in other words, to guarantee the fact that he stays in power for as long as he wills it.

Biya became an all-powerful dictator as he manipulated the system in whichever direction his whim ordained. For example, he reshuffled his cabinet so frequently, and for whatever reason he could come up with, so much so that it is said he appointed and dismissed some ministers without having ever met them. That Biya can schedule and cancel elections on the whim is another example of the power he wields. Again, in 1992, in retaliation to uprisings sparked by the belief that he had stolen John Fru Ndi's presidential election victory, Biya, without consulting any state bodies but his ethnic cronies, imposed a state of emergency on the North West Province of the country, Fru Ndi's province of origin. Biya has become a god, worshipped by those gambolling about him for public offices. Positions that in the past were given on merit had deteriorated into gifts for servitude to his whim. One cannot help thinking with admiration of the Ahidjo era when ministers and ministries were so stable one could hardly differentiate the one from the other. Those, comparatively speaking, were the days of constancy, when ministers and their ministries were so committed and permanent they were printed out in books and studied in Civics courses all over the nation. Ask any schoolchild of the late sixties and seventies and he or she will give the names of the Minister of Armed Forces, Saudou Daoudu; the Minister of Transport, Christian Bongwa; the Minister of Justice, Simon Achidi Achu; the Minister of Youths and Sports, Felix Tonye Mbog; just to cite a few examples. Ahidjo's was the epoch when there was accountability; the time when a police officer, for example, accounted for all the bullets that had been issued him or face the consequences. Even if this was just to ensure that sympathizers did not supply bullets to UPC rebels, it made policemen more responsible and alert than most of these travesties in uniform along the streets today. It was even said that Ahidjo's system of accountability was such that nobody was free; so stringent was it that a minister summoned by the president, it was rumoured, gave his family his will before responding to the call. The individual sent for, heaved a huge sigh of relief upon re-emerging from the presidency having only been reprimanded. This was the case because nobody was too well positioned to be free of Ahidjo's heavy hand should the need have arisen. As Albert Mukong, Cameroon's foremost political prisoner revealed, even the overlords of the regime found themselves detained in Cameroon's infamous political prison—Tchollire:

> It was about time, too, that another prisoner arrived at the camp. I think it was already in August 1976 when this one came... he was a big shot from Yaoundé. He was a *Commissaire Divisionel Principal (sic)* of Police, either the Director of Police Judiciare or Deputy Director of *Renseignements Généraux* (General Information). And you know these are the real overlords in this country. He could not understand what was happening to him and those around, too, looked embarrassed at his coming. Who then was secure in the regime? (*Prisoner Without a Crime* 104)

Mukong was later to teach a lesson to those with power from this security baron's imprisonment as the latter made a fuss about how long he had been detained. Mukong pointed out that before he left Tchollire, the *Commissaire* was already getting worried because of how long he had been held. Mukong then added: "When they gave orders and people were detained for long periods they did not notice the harm they did. They had power and used it without thinking of the consequences (104). Biya served under Ahidjo, yet one can only wonder why he has none of his mentor's qualities or tactics besides being a purposeless dictator determined, like Hastings Kamuzu Banda of Malawian infamy, to be president for life.

The picture of accountability under Biya is so bad that police officers use government bullets to joke around with, like kids and toys, without being afraid of anything or anyone questioning their behaviour and the misuse of ammunitions purchased with the taxpayer's money. The nonchalance seems to come from the top of the administrative ladder. Like a child, Mr. Biya has sometimes been very excited about his powerful position that he considered it normal, instead of embarrassing, to display his power on national television. He once, on national television, told Eric Chinje, then Editor in Chief of Cameroon Radio Television (CRTV) how he could easily end Chinje's career by simply shaking his head. The thorough editor's smile, in return, was loaded with disgust; little wonder before long the talented and equally qualified Eric Chinje dumped CRTV in search of pursuits elsewhere that offered more rewards while also respecting him as a person. Mr. President had forgotten that such blatant abuse of power can only take place within totally corrupt nations like the one he is heading. One cannot help wondering if the problem is Biya or the Cameroonian nation that can swallow such garbage. Accordingly, Tim Harford, in a damning paper on Cameroon, observes how tempting it is for one visiting Cameroon to explain away the country's poverty by presuming that Cameroonians are idiots, but he points out emphatically that "Cameroonians are no smarter or dumber than the rest of us" (6). The truth is that the seeming lethargy on the part of Cameroonians is not the side effect of one political dose but of many. Only one of these political doses—holding a gun to his head or that of a relation bloodied by a nocturnal gestapo for example—would dry the fountain of Harford's rancorous inspiration were he to be a resident in Cameroon.

Such rhetoric, therefore, only confirms some Westerners' inability to comprehend, of course, due to lack of experience, the predicament and attendant plight of oppressed peoples, especially those in Africa. These conceited Westerners are on the periphery of these peoples' scrape while claiming to understand it as they hurl insults at peoples who cannot be left to do things their way because of a meddling West that first had to "civilize" Africans, and now must continue teaching them how to stay "civilized". How many times have Africans tried changing the tide of events in their countries only for foreign legions to show up and forcefully maintain the status quo in the name of some stupid accord signed with toddling African regimes around the theoretical end of colonialism. Another frequently used excuse for imperialist soldiers intervening and maintaining Western backed puppet regimes in power is in the name of protecting their nationals who had been doing God alone knows what in the "jungles of Africa".

When Biya made gestures towards multiparty democracy, one can only wonder if he knew what he was courting because before long he was able to see the danger to which he had exposed his presidency. The result of his reluctant move towards multiparty democracy is that, once more, true to his child-like blabbering, he became the only president who taunts and insults his own people in public. It was clear that Biya listens to rumours when in the mid-nineties, on national television, he goaded the people of Douala, "Me voici donc à Douala" (Here am I in Douala after all), as if to say, "You said I could not dare step in Douala, but *here am I in Douala after all*". He is the same president who, again, declared treasonably on national television, during a national function, to Cameroonians who were on a nation-wide strike—the Ghost towns of the early nineties—that "Quand Yaounde respire le Cameroun vit" (As long as all is well in Yaounde, Cameroon is fine).³ One could hardly believe that this was from a person sworn to govern his fatherland responsibly. Most tragic of all was the fact that there were Cameroonians who clapped after the president gaffed thus. But this is the Biya era, and with such blunders repeated over and over, the president himself, without realizing it, declared Cameroon a wasteland without laws and the necessary institutions of state, and at the very least a veritable national circus. Instead of democracy, the whole venture turned out more like a ploy, a state distraction. Whereas opposition party leaders were going about wrangling with each other in the name of democracy, Mr. Biya, like before, ditched everything of national interest in preference for his personal palace at Mvomeka'a and his private investments overseas. Cameroon, like a ship without a captain, was left to run aground in the hands of presidential substitutes—ministers—who in all had degenerated into socio-economic pirates as they ambushed and pilfered from once established institutions of state while transforming the nation into a laughing stock on the international arena. In their hands, Cameroon kept distinguishing itself by assuming different ratings from year to year as one of the most corrupt nations on earth. For two years continuously, Transparency International (a global civil society organization leading the fight against corruption in the world) ranked Cameroon the most corrupt country in the world. If it is any relief, the situation improved by the year 2002 as Cameroon then was relegated to the thirteenth from the bottom in this organization's ranking. This is Paul Biya's betrayal, par excellence, of a people that loved and respected him as their leader, a leader who promised them "rigor and moralization". Even then, the most startling of all is the fact that such appalling administrative leaders and members of government refuse to leave after their blunders so that some other true patriots may try to salvage the collapsing state bastion and make something out of it. True to type, Biya is still clinging to power even after over twenty-six years of mismanagement, while all his hopeless citizens can do is wait for nature to take its course. Even then, the god Biya is said to have told Cameroonians again, recently, when it was rumoured that he had died overseas, that he had twenty more years to go. One can only wonder why he decided to settle for twenty more years only, instead of simply settling for earthly eternity.

The nation is Biya's private property after all, as there is no accountability since there is equally no effective system in place to question what this super head of state does. His concern after having placed the nation under siege is, along with his club members, to remain in power forever, but he forgets one thing to which all must bow—time. That great force, it will heal or else destroy all in due course. In all, Bate Besong's words best sum up Biya's years of buffoonery in the name of governance at the helm of the Cameroonian nation:

There has been a serious dereliction of responsibility on the part of his leadership. He has privatized the state and handed it over to his Essingan kinsmen and the Khalifas of the North. This has led to a manifestation of a most perverted form of governance that flourishes under conditions of social injustice, economic inequality and political opportunism. The fettered past has taken its toll on a Presidency that is afraid to face the facts. He has transformed himself into a Presidential Deity — courtesy of the puppet-masters at the Quaid' Orsay (sic). Mr. Biya imagines, like Appolo of Delphi (sic), that Cameroon history can turn at his beckoning.

We see an absolute Monarch in the mould of a Hastings Kamuzu Banda or a Mobutu Seseseko (sic) who is terribly reluctant to lose power. The fact of the matter, however, is that his New Deal regime has been, for a long time, a nation only on paper.

He has, therefore, neither shown determination nor resoluteness in the pursuit of the goals of national unity. Besides ignoring the call for dialogue on true federalism, Mr. Biya is also running a country full of contradictions.

His exclusionary style of leadership, for instance, has led to the corrupt ogredoms of the Ondong. Ndong's and the Cinderella rags to riches Synergie Chantal Biya's albatross of squander mania. We have now arrived at an effete bourgeoisie that revels, in 23 years of a road to nowhere, in an uninhibited display of filthy wealth, while the mass of the people wallow in destitution and are stupefied by ignorance and disease.

It is in this light again, that Jean-Germain Gros is out of line for lashing out at Cameroonians whom, he purports, are blaming Biya for doing exactly what Ahidjo did. In Gros' own words: "Biya cannot be blamed for having run the Cameroon economy into the ground because of his statist policies when Ahidjo is lauded for the same" ("Cameroon in Synopsis"12-13). Gros goes on to point out that there is a "disconnect and an inconsistency here that can only be explained by the type of convenient collective amnesia that people engage in when they want to discredit living opponents and rehabilitate dead ones" (13). To argue thus is to trivialize as merely sentimental the potent basis on which Cameroonians hinge their judgment of these two leaders. If Ahidjo's government was, and Biya's is statist such that the effects on the economy, but more so on the population's standard of living are different, it is indicative that somehow Ahidjo managed to do something differently from the way Biya is doing it. After all, it is not news that with the same ingredients different cooks can emerge with different tasting broths. I lived in Cameroon under Ahidjo, and under Paul Biya; Cameroonians are not being amnesiac about the Ahidjo regime, for in many ways, it has emerged a better evil when pitted against Biya's. There was peace and stability, even if there was fear; there was security even if it was primarily intended to make Ahidjo feel safe; there was prosperity and national and personal pride in Cameroonians. These are flavours of Ahidjo's statism that Biya's has flushed out instead, transforming the people into a beggarly, pilfering, divided, and unpatriotic lot in the main. About both presidents and their methods, Victor T. Le Vine agrees with me when he points out:

> In sum, the Ahidjo-Biya regime pattern is less a "hegemonic project" than it has been a political strategy to hold and maintain power not so much for a class, but for an elite whose membership has varied *en gros* (wholesale) with the single change of president, *en detail* (retail) positionally as the president and his closest associates change policy lines, seek to bring new talent into the fold, reward the faithful, punish the 'disloyal' or grossly incompetent or excessively greedy, or clean house after a crisis or debacle like the April 1984 coup attempt. Always, the aim is to preserve, and if possible, to enhance the power of the regime and/or its head. *Ahidjo succeeded quite well in this strategy during the almost twenty years he remained in power. Biya, now in power for almost as long, has tried to emulate his predecessor (at least since 1984), but for reasons I do not rehearse here nearly wrecked the whole system so carefully crafted by Ahidjo — and may still do so if he keeps increasing opposition to him and his policies.* ("Ahmadou Ahidjo Revisited" 48, emphasis mine)

No, Cameroonians would benefit nothing rehabilitating a deceased leader's memory in the face of the incumbent were he successful, even if only in maintaining the state of affairs he inherited. The reverse is true: because Biya has failed them, mindful of all his promises after he took over office, Cameroonians are, therefore, forced to remember better days under *Grand Camarade* — Ahmadou Ahidjo. Lyombe Eko is saying the same thing when he writes about this backward glance although with particular reference to Anglophone Cameroonians and their pickle in Cameroon: "Nostalgia is an emotional longing for conditions of a bye-gone era….Nostalgia arises mostly out of dissatisfaction with the present and uncertainty about the future. Individuals or groups who find themselves in situations of political ambiguity and flux usually call upon previous experiences or knowledge for direction and solution". The "disconnect" Gros identifies then lies not in the Cameroonian people's inability to remember Ahidjo's statist policies in the face of Biya's, but in how both leaders practiced statism. At best, world economic trends might have favoured Ahidjo's era with positive returns in the sale of oil and cash crops which made it possible for government to subsidize economic and social ventures in Cameroon without stressing. However, beyond just favourable economic trends, Biya's government, on the contrary, raised capital flight and the plundering of state coffers by government agents beyond an unfortunate sporadic practice into the norm and even a goal to strive for, instead of the criminal act it was under Ahidjo's regime.

That Biya lacked the spine to halt these activities by his associates and protégés led to the complete collapse of the nation's economic health as virtually everyone started stealing from the state, realizing how easy it was to get away with it under Biya. Even those who could not lay hands on cash stole whatever they could find. A friend once joked that the situation got so bad that cleaners stole detergents meant for their jobs. With virtually everybody stealing, nobody could check the other as responsible citizens became deviants instead. But as Albert Mukong had pointed out, nobody was too powerful for Ahidjo to deal with when necessary (104). Biya later tried "putting some bite into his bark", but it was too little too late: the ship of state was past the point of no return in the course of destruction. No, Cameroonians are not amnesiac as Gros is suggesting; they remember very well the trends of both regimes, which is why they cry for the days of Ahidjo. As Gros himself confirms elsewhere in his article:

> Until the mid-1980s, Cameroon was recognized by many as one of the few 'economic successes' in Africa. Blessed with adequate natural resources and a competent bureaucracy, Cameroon consistently achieved respectable levels of growth (over 5 percent) and a positive trade balance. Indeed, it is still one of a handful of countries in Africa to be self-sufficient in food production. Ahmadou Ahidjo followed a policy of economic development which emphasized agriculture, foreign investment, albeit with majority shares held by the state, and relatively prudent spending of oil revenues to avoid inflation. ("Cameroon in Synopsis" 13)

It is not news that Biya's regime has not come anywhere close to any of these achievements. His has been a consumerist citadel that has only succeeded in emptying the barn which Ahidjo had stocked to overflowing for the nation, and now he is dismantling the barn and selling it in parts.

The Ministers

Supposedly to help the president in his executive function as head of state is the job of his ministers, but this is hardly what ministers do in Cameroon. As observed earlier, the ministers of Cameroon under Paul Biya, but for very few who are particularly close to him, are mere pawns who are appointed and dismissed by the president at will. The result is that one sees a group of state officials without souls of their own as they are answerable to the all powerful president who appoints them, instead of the citizenry whose public servants they are supposed to be. Accordingly, one cannot help wondering why it is that they even bother to make so much ado about their appointments, given that they have no clue as to how long they are going to be demi-gods in the worthless political pantheon of a government without a sense of direction.

The greatest joke about this position is the degree of celebration that takes place when these citizens are called to serve the state, or better still the president, since it is to him that they are answerable. After all, appointments are ascriptive, the criteria being different types of loyalties—friends, kin, tribe's people, and even political pawns in the Francophone/Anglophone, and recently North-West/South-West, tug of war, meant to be disposed of as soon as use has been made of them. Tribesmen and women from the appointee and soon-to-be-rich minister's village scramble together their meagre resources as individuals and sometimes as members of traditional groups and show up at the new minister's suddenly upgraded residence to fête his appointment as prince of the New Deal government. The new minister begins savouring the flavour of power and impending wealth, as people sucking up to him begin addressing him "Mr. Minister", or "Monsieur le Ministre", with stupid fawning smiles on their faces.

Others begin declaring bizarre consanguineous and otherwise relationships that they have with the new minister.

The new minister, smiling in confusion, as behind his mind the fear looms large about the uncertainty of the length of his tenure of distinction, endeavours to recognize the different groups and individuals who have come from so far to leave their impressions on him. After all, he will soon be reshuffling his ministry in the natural next step of getting in new and reliable officials from his own village. It is now their time to "chop", and so envelopes full of money are distributed to the visiting groups and individuals who leave satisfied to have a minister from their village.

It has become an established fact in Cameroon, like in most African countries, that being appointed into the government is tantamount to being given the opportunity to fill one's pocket with state-owned wealth and also the opportunity to develop one's part of the country if the appointee has any sense of loyalty to his people. One would think this is the responsibility of the government; yes, in other parts of the world, but not in Africa, and especially not in Cameroon. The government in Cameroon is there to manipulate the citizenry into a state of confusion and destitution reinforced by the policy of divide and rule so as to maintain itself in office. This is a strategy effectively used by the Biya regime against the North-West and South-West provinces of Cameroon so as to maintain these two powerful provinces in a state of conflict at all times, albeit subtly, while their wealth is being squandered by Francophone Cameroonians who are now in charge of virtually all the money producing organizations in Cameroon. This is as painful as it is frustrating when it is realized that the ordinary Cameroonian, that is the person without any political affiliations, generally speaking, has no problem with the other whether the one is Anglophone and the other Francophone. Even musicians do all to sing in both languages in recognition of Cameroon's dual colonial heritage. However, politicians, with their schemes, have continued nursing and exploiting these otherwise natural and imperialist initiated divides, causing English-speaking Cameroonians to continually question what they are doing in a political union that has transformed them into second class citizens and victims in their own country, even as their wealth, their bodies, and all that they stand for are being abused, raped, and disregarded. Fr. Clemens Ndze laments in the same vein:

> A keen observer traversing what history knows as West (Cameroon) or Southern Cameroon is struck by the contrast between the former and the present state of the geographical extent. The housing situation has improved in many places, people have many more means of transportation, divisional headquarters, police and gendarmerie posts of various magnitudes are countless. But the roads linking various formerly active centres of commerce and communications are deplorable. Historical monuments like the Bamenda fort, relics of those days in Mamfe, Buea and Limbe, which used to inspire awe and admiration have nothing but vagueness to show. One would have to be a mental eunuch not to become emotionally involved in this part of the Cameroon's affairs…. The person who is bubbling over with love and enthusiasm for this part of Cameroon, and yet pass over the country, its

roads and streets and witness all the wrong and suffering, the shame and degradation wrought, through negligence or whatever, upon the people, aye wrought by Cameroonians upon Cameroonians, without burning to end it, is, in my estimation, a fraud and a liar in his heart.

Accordingly, there is the simmering unrest in the background simply because Francophone-Cameroon — the Francophone politician better still — does not want to recognize and give to Anglophone-Cameroon that which is her due. Hence Augustine Ambe's distressing representation of the Anglophone's predicament in Cameroon today: "There is a well-designed and engineered economic, social and cultural genocide going on in the Southern Cameroons" (7). Tata Simon Ngenge's summation of the problem is equally revealing: "... the roots of the 'Anglophone problem' in Cameroon are fundamentally institutional and economic, having to do with how state power is exercised in a fractured polity and how the same (i.e., state power) is used to benefit one group at the detriment of the other" (61). This is a major problem; in fact, a socio-political volcano waiting to erupt should the United Nations (UN) fail to give it the hearing it deserves, as somewhere down the line then, Anglophones have to redeem themselves. Even then, why is it so hard for Cameroonians to dialogue and come up with a union that works? European nations, in their separate identities as nations, are still able to forge an economic union that is pushing Europe forward, but not so within a single nation — Cameroon — because selfish and misguided individuals are sacrificing the welfare of their nation for their personal gains by letting foreign nations without Cameroon at heart dictate the pace of events in Cameroon to their alien socio-economic gratification. Whatever the case, the truth remains that Anglophones have done all to approach their problem with La République in a most civil manner. Jean-Germain Gros corroborates this claim when he points out:

> In their struggle to alter the current structure of the Cameroon (unitary) state, Anglophones have used legal arguments to bolster their case. They have taken their cause to international bodies, such as the United Nations, the Commonwealth, the Organization of African Unity and the World Court. They have not blown up bridges, electrical power plants and the like. ("Cameroon in Synopsis" 27)

Cameroonians are yet to realize that government officials, ministers especially, are supposed to be public servants who are neutral in serving the nation instead of functioning as biased tribalistic mouthpieces in government who do all to have things and development sent to their villages of origin or nowhere else. Meanwhile, interestingly, they do all they can to load their newly created foreign bank accounts since they know for certain that the president might decide at anytime that their days of glory are over. Those who stay in office for a little longer are those who trade in their pride and dignity for shameless bootlicking as they praise the president anywhere, anytime, and for absolutely no reason other than that he is president and he appointed them. These sycophants disgrace their education and families as they go around like party thugs threatening all those who are against the president and his regime in exchange for a few more months in office; to them, this is democracy.

Again, ministers in Cameroon are rarely in their offices, and even when they are there, it is impossible to meet with them, especially if one is a Cameroonian. For weeks, citizens line up to see Mr. Minister to no avail. To be able to meet with the minister is a right that has been transformed into a thing of class and a thriving business as well. One has to be rich or well placed within the already corrupt administrative set-up before one can secure a slot to meet with the minister who is forever in meetings which never serve a purpose other than as avenues for stealing allowances from the government. These are outstation allowances, entertainment allowances, and all the rest that Ahidjo put in place with good reasons, but which, like all else, ways and means have been found to abuse these otherwise rewarding incentives. This may sound unfair, yet scrap the allowances and see how many ministers will want to attend their now darling conferences and meetings in different parts of the country, if not for the fact that it gives them the opportunity to parade around again as "big men", and that they love the fawning attention they get from the desperate masses made up of individuals who hope the minister may single them out for a possible favour. How ridiculous it is to realize that it is far easier for a foreign white person to meet with a Cameroonian minister than it is for a Cameroonian with far more awesome credentials and plans for his country. True, even the administration in Cameroon is still suffering from the colonial mentality that forces the gatekeepers in the ministries into submissiveness in front of a white person since at once the latter is considered some "big" expert sent in to "cooperate" with the regime.[4]

Before long, a minister who was appointed only a few weeks ago begins erecting mansions all over the country to the dismay of his subordinates. Interestingly, nobody seems to want to question such sudden wealth, nor is there a state unit to which the minister has to render account. Contracts for the state are issued based on how much kickback the minister can receive from the contractors who compete in corrupting him or her as a sure means toward securing the contract. But, of course, these contractors will make their money back as soon as they can win the contract. It all begins with exaggerating the cost it will take to realize whatever project has to be carried out for the government. And since there is no worthy government auditor to report to, barely months after the incomplete project was started, it is only normal for the contractors to flee the nation, and this is only if they do not have godparents in government. If they do, then there is nothing to fear because nobody can question them and so they go about their affairs arrogantly as if duping the citizenry through the government is some commendable feat. Of course, the president himself is not aware of what is going on as he is never there, or might even be an accomplice in that it is his in-law or some other bogus relation who has just swindled Cameroonians of their money. Remember the scandalous collapse of *Société Camerounaise de Banque* (SCB)? The dismissed bank manager, Messi Messi Robert, in defence of his now tarnished banking integrity claimed Cameroon's late first lady, Jeane-Irene Biya, transformed the bank into her personal business from which she, her relatives, and clients, could "borrow" any amount even without a collateral, and ended up not paying back.

Within the different ministries, messengers in offices have accorded themselves strange titles ranging from *planton*, a messenger with unspecified duties within the system, to *Chef du Bureau*, a kind of a supervisor within a particular office accommodating about four mostly unqualified workers since it is likely they did not get their job on merit but as a favour. The *Chef du Bureau* is a kind of headman who shows up for work late and, more often than not, dressed in castoff suits. His salary alone cannot afford these suits, but with all the bribes he receives from desperate citizens milling around to see that their documents move from one stage to another in the unending maze of dossier migration characteristic of all the ministries, he can afford his used suits along with a certain air of importance. In a day, as a result of this malpractice, some clerks and office messengers return home with bribe to the tune of their monthly salaries and above. Unfortunately, this money, honest people's hard-earned money that has been forced out of them, is hardly used for anything worthwhile other than drinking and the maintenance of illicit relationships. The minister is always busy, and so it is more of a relief for one to believe he knows nothing of what is going on under him. One has, however, learned that sometimes some ministers know but could not care less as this bloats their otherwise shrunken self-esteem.

Another example of the spiralling effect of ministers' ineptitude within their ministries occurred in Bamenda. [5] Once, a situation was witnessed where about ten Cameroonians waited for over two hours for a judge to sign some forms for them which, when he ultimately condescended to do his job, spent only about five minutes to sign all ten forms. How can anyone treat others this way and go home to his family satisfied that he had served his country well for the day? Why is it all right to see people sitting in front of one's office, obviously in need of help, yet the occupant of the office will walk past as if he has not seen anyone? Do we, however, remember how French commandants treated canton chiefs installed by the French colonialists? They were usually kept waiting for hours before they could be given instructions on how to function. This is an approach which has just diffused all over, even into English-speaking Cameroon. And remember, this is "big man" and so he can do whatever he wants. After all, the people can do nothing to him since his appointments come from the president and the people he is supposed to be serving have no say in it. He will keep his position as long as he goes out to campaign for the president each time there is one of those travesties of a presidential election approaching.

Women in offices, influenced by their noble and gentle roles as the mothers of society, used to be better in the way they related to people, but that is all history as women, our mothers, sisters, and dear wives now, without any tinge of guilt, accept and even demand bribes from people. This is another reason why Cameroon's plight might require Herculean efforts to redeem the situation. By allowing our womenfolk to get thus morally bankrupt, generations to come have by this neglect been derailed, as women in Africa are the custodians of family pride and dignity, being the very first and natural teachers of their offspring, of our communities. Alas, these women have been forced to abandon these invaluable roles under most of the current regimes in Africa, as they now must also fend and forage for ways to survive in our economic wilderness characterized by economic droughts ushered in by inept leadership driven only by an obsession for personal wealth and power, even as they transform the citizens they lead into wretched derelicts. It is to avoid this denigration of the women-folk that responsible men in traditional Africa did all to ensure that their wives were well cared for, even if they themselves went with the barest minimum. This was the case because a wife's appearance, in those days, was a major statement on the family of which she was a member. But not so nowadays when women have become something else because of having to join the rat race amidst all kinds of corrupt practices.

Centralization, with its idiosyncrasies characteristic to the continent of Africa, is a major contributor to this status quo. In the case of Cameroon, for example, everything related to government services can only be concluded in the capital city of Yaounde. Ask for a passport and one may have to travel from one's remote part of the country to the capital city of Yaounde. Sometimes this need to go to Yaounde is because of government strategy of centralization, and at other times it is because a corrupt provincial police chief refuses to produce a passport booklet because he decides that booklets have been exhausted; in which case he needs to be bribed for him to produce the booklets. Otherwise, the question remains, are these senior police officers so stupid that they cannot tell when the number of booklets in their keeping begins dropping so as to ask for more? Certainly not; this is where the concept of demand and supply that he studied as an Advanced Level student serves the police chief best. He can arbitrarily raise the cost of a passport booklet simply by hoarding copies and letting people know there are no booklets left. He then presents the choice of taking the expensive trip to Yaounde where another equally corrupt police official will start the process of exploitation all over again, or of giving him money for the trip so he can bring back the booklet. When a citizen is thus cornered, he considers the transport fare to the capital city of Yaounde, a significant part of his monthly salary; the risks it entails travelling on roads along which a sizeable number of the drivers are drunk or tipsy and reckless; the need to stay in a hotel, feed himself, and then face the unfriendly French-speaking policeman, and it adds up to be way cheaper for him to pay his corrupt local police chief the amount he is asking for the passport.[6] To be fair to the local immigration chiefs, the booklets do get exhausted sometimes, but then, as already indicated above, who is in charge of these passports, and why does the individual or group of individuals have to wait for passport booklets in a sovereign nation to get finished? But this, comparatively speaking, is a stupid question after all, for what are passport booklets when salaries sometimes go unpaid for months in Cameroon without the government accounting for this administrative calamity.

At another level, consider the case of a newly employed person trying to get his first salary from the government of his country—Cameroon. First, there is no effective procedure in place to facilitate this deserved service. Better still there was once a procedure, but because of the presence of a regime that cares less which way the state is going, the system has been corrupted so much so that the word "system" no longer applies. For anyone not used to bribery and corruption, he/she could as well just migrate, go to school or start a business somewhere else, and begin earning a living afresh.

First of all, Cameroon, it seems, is one of the few countries in the world where a worker is employed just to show up for work. For the employee to willingly do the work involved in the job description, he has to be bribed by members of the public he was supposed to be serving; this is especially the case with government workers or public servants as they are misleadingly referred to sometimes. And so a starving citizen who has been working for about thirty-six months without a salary shows up at an office block with a maze of corridors and rooms without any directions indicated, and everyone is just walking past him as if he is supposed to know where he is and who he is there to meet. Although Francophones too suffer this fate, the Anglophone's predicament is worse because, from a linguistic standpoint, he may not be able to express himself fluently in French, which is the only language Francophone workers in a supposedly bilingual country's capital city, are willing to be addressed in. Then there is also the problem of distance as most Anglophones not resident in Yaounde have to travel for hours to get to Yaounde before rushing to the different offices where the linguistic gorgon awaits them, along with a usually unaccommodating Francophone compatriot who is supposed to serve them. What trauma! And so completely at a loss, especially since the majority French-speaking civil servants working in government offices refuse to attempt a conversation in English, the English-speaking Cameroonian is at once lost in this bizarre world if he is one of those rebels who had refused having anything to do with the French language while in school. The result is that the concerned just returns to his provincial town completely frustrated, and wondering about the days of which he heard from his English-speaking parents when one got one's first salary by the end of the month, in so far as one was employed before the 16th of that month.

    Back in the province, the fledgling in Cameroon's bureaucracy, typical of Africa south of the Sahara, learns from others what he has to do on his next trip to "chase" dossiers so he can begin earning his deserved salary. One cannot help wondering what the powers that be in such countries as Cameroon think the concerned has been living on for the three years he has been working for the government without a salary. What is he expected to manage his own family with, since he poses in front of them on a daily basis as a worker and supposedly a bread-winner? This is the height of inefficiency on the part of any government and it costs the government more to be this inefficient. First of all, the unfortunate civil servant is always away from his job since he has to travel to Yaounde to "chase his dossiers". Before long, he shows up but will not work since he has not been paid, yet these days during which he is away from his job, or on which he refuses to work, are part of the hours the state will have to pay the worker for whenever that will be.

    Having graduated from his classes on corruption management since his poverty has forced him to learn to be corrupt by requiring bribes at the local level for his services as a civil servant, the hungry government employee dares into Yaounde again. This time he has enough bribe-money on him, has bought enough foodstuffs for his host family in Yaounde, and is equipped with the name of at least half a dozen contacts in the ministry he is planning on invading. His host in Yaounde is the one to lead him to the contacts in the ministry.

    In the ministry, after a number of humiliating reproaches and confusing procedures, our worker from the province, along with his host, finally meets his contact, only to learn from him that his documents are nowhere to be found. But this is why the concerned took private classes on dealing with any ministry in the capital city before daring to go back to Yaounde for the second time. He had compiled another set of documents which he quickly snatches out of his briefcase and hands over to his host. The host then hands the documents to the contact in the ministry who is standing by them looking very reluctant and jittery as if he has much better things to be doing. He is, in actual fact, thinking of the large sums of money — bribe — he could have been making rescuing other desperate Cameroonians in a ministry in their own capital city by rendering them services, which duty is the raison d'être for his employment. Without further delay, juicy sums of money in envelopes exchange hands, and then the contact in the ministry is suddenly all smiles, attentive, and, out of the blue, a willing and devoted civil servant. He then promises to do his best to see that the documents go through. By now, hours have gone by and it is lunchtime, and the starving and yet-to-be-paid employee finds himself having to take the worker at the ministry and his host out for lunch. He provides them wine also, a habit Francophone-Cameroonians got from the French — drinking *vin* with the main meal of the day — and then they part in a more amicable manner with the contact anxiously urging the unpaid employee to rest assured that all will be well. He should return by the end of the month to sign other documents and then receive his first salary and his arrears.

The unpaid worker returns to his provincial town with a feeling of victory as he waits for the end of the month. By this time, however, he is already in debt, so much so that when ultimately he gets his salary for all the years that he has not been paid, it is virtually nothing compared to how much he is in debt. Even then, the provincial treasurer who has to pay him the lump sum is himself corrupt, and so he demands a certain percentage of a man's salary as if it is money won in a lottery, before he can pay him. Failure to comply could lead to a completely new saga as the treasurer can declare that there is no physical cash in the treasury even though he continues paying others. This is the zenith of corruption, of anarchy, and there is a minister in charge of the Ministry of Finance, a prime minister who is head of government, and a president who is head of state.

It must be remembered that a Ministry is that unit of any country that is supposed to guide the nation from a particular perspective — finance, communication, education etc. — yet in the case of many African countries, it is here that corrupt practices are invented and nourished to bizarre levels of notoriety. In the case of Cameroon, Tata Simon Ngenge has observed lamentably:

> Because of the awkward bureaucratic structures established under the pretext of national unity, those charged with the task of processing dossiers preferred to wait until those affected left the extreme ends of the republic to chase them in Yaoundé. Of course, the physical presence of civil servants with problems in Yaoundé also facilitated bribery, which in fact became a *sine qua non* for moving dossiers forwards. Even the national daily *Cameroon Tribune*, no muckraking newspaper, viewed with regret that 'going to Yaoundé for this purpose you must be armed with 'cash' to tip at every table if the dossier is to be processed. (72)

The whole process is frustrating, belittling, and offending, as one finds oneself in the face of uneducated and equally unqualified office clerks and messengers, begging and waiting in line desperately for a normal office procedure to be performed, even after one has bribed, so one can get one's money which is one's right. To Cameroonians, there is nothing wrong with this, and so this macabre routine has remained in place for ever; some dignifying exercise in administration.

The picture begins to be clear, that in Cameroon, like in most African countries, nothing except the wellbeing of the president is what is important to incumbent regimes. It was the same during colonialism: the natives were of no consequence other than to facilitate the realization of the goals of colonialist authorities, even if it meant the lives of entire native communities. The handpicked successors to these colonialist authorities learned well, and so today citizens under postcolonial governments are in the same predicament: they are exploited, embarrassed, and even humiliated by those in power for personal gains.

How strange it is, that it is to these governments that most so-called civilized Western nations and monetary organizations enjoy claiming they have loaned or donated money for the purpose of development and the betterment of the citizenry. Accordingly, one is left to think that it is either that these Western governments and monetary organizations are themselves as corrupt, if not more, when dealing with these "poor underdeveloped nations", or else they are themselves stupid. The latter is certainly not the case, given the minds behind the functioning of these nations and organizations. One realizes, therefore, that these organizations and nations know exactly what they are doing when they transform these poor countries into indebted nations by loaning money to irresponsible heads of states who turn around and steal the money and cart it back to Western banks without the money helping the so-called poor backward masses it was supposed to help in the first place. But then, these beggarly nations are by now already indebted for generations to come to these generous and equally philanthropic first world countries and monetary organizations who loaned money to their corrupt leaders—pretty smart. And the interest on these "worthless" loans keeps multiplying, yet selfish African presidents either deny seeing these implications or just do not care since it is in their personal interest. Here, mainly, lies the blame Africa might have deserved, in the sense that these leaders failed to use the money for the good of their citizens. After all, if nothing else, they themselves would have died by the time their nations begin chafing in an effort to repay their debts or beg for the debts to be cancelled. Meanwhile, these light-fingered presidents' private families would still have money to cater for their needs for generations to come. But even as one tries to blame these leaders for their irresponsible financial habits, Patrick Bond points out in an equally revealing manner: "No one can deny the orientation of so many African state elites towards parasitical, consumptive, unproductive activities"(95). thereby redirecting the blame onto imperialist machinations on the continent.

How can one help not damning these African so-called heads of states for failing to turn the tide of Africa's misery, but just then it comes to light that there is another constraint on the money given them; the money is theirs on condition that they spend it as instructed by the donor organization or nation. When aid does not come with instructions on how to spend it, it is transformed into a kind of political instrument intended to win client states from Africa, allies as such, whose support can be used, when needed, to influence decisions within the UN. The cycle of chaos and exploitation begins all over as the donor or lender-recommended investment pattern reveals the money is indeed not necessarily meant to help the poor suffering peoples, but to win favours and plough back huge interests into the hands of the supposed donor. By the time the loan is cancelled, if it is ultimately, more than the loan amount has already been received in terms of interests, favours, raw materials and the like, and so the cycle of poverty and dependence persists in one part of the world, at the expense of which another part of the world continues to flourish. These desperate African leaders can only be blamed then for transforming themselves into beggarly leaders who are consequently deprived of the right to determine how to invest this money in the best interest of their nations; but then, it is said a beggar has no choice. Of what use then, is a loan that will be spent differently from how it is best needed to benefit the borrower? This, however, is only another side of the story.

All said and done, most African countries are led by presidents who are selfish kleptocrats without any love for their peoples and nations, else why would a president leave his needy people and operate a hospital in a Western country instead? Why would a president refuse building mansions in his homeland but spend millions of dollars acquiring real estate in foreign countries which he ultimately might never use? Why would a president not shop in his own country but spend millions shopping in other countries? These presidents are true examples who justify the saying, "power corrupts", and equally true is the fact that they do not learn from their nor from others' mistakes, else Mr. Biya will certainly remember to question himself late at night as to what Ahidjo did with his own stolen wealth and, better still, Mobutu Sesse Sekou of then Zaire, who could not even go and die in one of his mansions in Europe. Were his real estate property in Zaire, at least his children would have inherited it or even the Zairian government if it decided to seize it after all, but trapped by a legal order, Mobutu's mansion in Switzerland, for example, lies there existentially comatose as it can neither be used nor auctioned given its advance state of neglect. Of this property, Michela Wrong writes:

> ... Les Miguettes, the converted farmhouse he bought on Savigny's outskirts, was entirely hidden from public view by a thick screen of firs...
> The five-hectare, thirty-room piece of real estate, valued, it is said, at $5 million, is easy to locate. On a country road where the Swiss flag flaps proudly over carefully clipped hedges, it is the only property that reeks of neglect. Beyond the wrought-iron railing running the length of the grounds, a neat lawn has grown wild. There are cobwebs on the large metal gates, left carelessly ajar despite an 'Entrée Interdite' sign. An intercom flickers into life just long enough for a suspicious Congolese voice—belonging to one of two homesick sentinels—to inform the curious this is strictly private property. (294)

The ephemeral nature of worldly resources seems to escape these

African paper giants forever as one after the other they keep repeating the same blunder. Alas, their citizens have to pay the price. Yes, most African presidents have transformed themselves from servants to their nations to bloody lords that everyone in the country now works for, instead of everyone working for the prosperity of the nation. So Africans, Cameroonians in particular, are now expected to be asking what they can do for their president and not for the nation; in fact, the nation is no man's property, people seem to think, and so it can rot. It is not unusual, therefore, to hear a Cameroonian rough-handling government property or neglecting his duties at his place of work, arguing, when queried by another with a sense of public consciousness, that the property does not belong to his father nor does his work. Who will not want to be president in such a lackadaisical nation when even the president's blunders are praised and those who dare to point it out are jailed and tortured while also being despised by some suffering compatriots for their audacity? Cameroonians must, somehow, be taught by a patriotic leadership to understand that government property is in fact every individual citizen's property as it is bought with the tax money they pay. Yet this will take a while to set in since most Cameroonians are yet to see government-owned property and institutions now being exploited by the president and his aides as actually belonging to the citizenry. And so the average citizen resigns himself to his supposed fate, that benefiting from the nation's resources is meant for a select few. Only when the people are made the beneficiaries of their tax money will they be able to understand that government property is their property and responsibility. Until then, see Cameroonians rejoicing when a president uses government money for national projects as if it is his personal wealth that he has just squandered on an undeserving nation. What is the big deal about using government money to build a road for the citizens? Yet see misled Cameroonians dancing and sweating in the sun to celebrate the occasional rightful use of their money as a sporadic national project is finally completed years behind schedule.

African heads of states and those in their governments must stop seeing the countries they are supposed to be serving while in office as their private property, banana plantations of some sort, and the citizens as labourers therein. It is this mentality that leads them into mismanaging these resource-rich countries, grinding them into a permanent state of poverty. African heads of states must, therefore, be made answerable to the people, and those militaries that protect corrupt leaders must understand that there is more than enough for everyone if only these countries could be well managed. If this were the case, then soldiers ought not to support a corrupt leader simply because he pays them more than they deserve, while the rest of the nation is wallowing in poverty and structural decay.

If this realization can register, then African heads of states will ease out of office with grace instead of clinging to power until they begin using diapers once again, or until their prostrates force them out of office. If this realization strikes home, then African heads of state will relinquish power with a sense of fulfilment, realizing they have done their best even if their best were a tragic recipe for mismanagement. They will not have to cling to power for fear of what some young radical successor will want to do to them because of the country's wealth they have stolen and stashed in foreign banks. African presidents must remember their culture—elders do not lie to their children. If only these elders would think like, and be guided by the wisdom of our African forefathers, then they would stop stealing and instead make the wellbeing of their compatriots their priority. True, the status quo in Africa indicates a leadership made up of elders who have forgotten their ways; they have stopped bothering about who they are, where they are from, and where they are headed. It is a new day, but unfortunately, it is one that denies Africans the opportunity of being Africans, hence the current state of entropy with leaders stealing from their own coffers and transforming their nations into wastelands.

The Legislature

Cameroon's legislature was initially made up of one house, but it was changed to two and a Senate also added to the National Assembly in 1996 with the emergence of a reviewed constitution. The National Assembly, which meets thrice a year in March, June, and November, and is made up of 180 members, is representative of the people of Cameroon as a whole. Its duties consist, among others, of the enacting of laws that should protect the citizens in society, of laws regulating the activities of political parties, existing trade unions, and even the functioning of the school system.

Although this arm of the government is supposed to be responsible for the creation and promulgation of the laws of the land, it must be remembered that in most African countries, this is only in theory as the president is usually a despot whose word is law. As a result, the legislature, more often than not, is only a rubberstamp and most of the members do not mind this status in so far as they get paid for work they are supposed to be doing. Money is the issue here and not how well they represent the citizenry.

These representatives from the different parts of the nation are the only ones who do some work in order to become parliamentarians, because they have to be able to earn the votes of those in their constituencies, by whatever means, in order to be able to represent them in parliament. However, how effective they are as an arm of government is anybody's guess. First of all, because most of them are people with little political exposure, just being a parliamentarian to many is in itself an honour so great that they could not bother about change; they are now "big men and women" too. They now have power, money, and a car with a pass that is above the law as police officers on the roads can no longer stop their vehicles, or else they are immediately let off as soon as the National Assembly logo on the car's dashboard is spotted.

Then there are those parliamentarians that the president will soon learn to hate because they got into the parliament with the will to serve their people. But there is the rude awakening for these parliamentarians down the line when they realize that they are intended, even during these days with all the talk about democracy, or more ridiculously still, multi-party politics, to serve as rubberstamps and nothing else. Theoretically, they are expected, while in session, to look at things the president wants to institute, and to debate them so they can be passed into law. But this is not what they really do; all the noise making in the name of debate is only a show. Debate or no debate, the president's wishes are subsequently put into place. Completely disillusioned and disoriented by their discovery, some of these good-willed parliamentarians relapse into hand-clappers like the vast majority of their compatriots in parliament. They learn just to be contented enjoying whatever pacifiers the president sends them—financial packages and occasional parties. On the other hand, some of these patriotic parliamentarians, the diehards, continue to struggle in the hope of changing things, only to realize before long that their lives are being quietly threatened, or they are being bribed to look the other way as the nation plunges further and further into squalor and disarray.

Multi-party politics is alien to Africa's culture, and so the practice within the continent comes nowhere close to what multi-party democracy is said to be, since even in the West where the practice is advanced, it is still not without snags. In Africa, Cameroon in particular, the claim of the practice of multi-party democracy is an unfortunate distraction as government is not for the people nor is it by the people. This is because of the fluid and heterogeneous nature of society, which makes it easy and almost natural for people to belong to camps and thereby hold personal loyalties. The outcome is patrimonialism as a system of governance, which amounts to an interplay of patrons and their camps. To these camps they must make available those services, now considered favours, which ought to be normal services rendered by a true democratic government to the entire nation. In this event, no party will accept to be the unsuccessful and so form the opposition, which according to Africa's political trend, would be deprived of power and the means to those favours for their camp. This is quite a problem as an effective opposition is a necessary condition for democracy; yet in Africa, government is for the president and by the president. However, whenever an African dictator wishes to coax in foreign aid that often does not benefit his country since it goes into his personal accounts and those of his close friends, he makes a show of benevolence towards his people by preaching democracy.

It is not that these presidents fool the West; as already established, they just play into the West's trap of getting them further dependent on them. And so Western regimes and financial institutions make much noise about such nations changing towards democracy. As a reward, they send in money that they know the president will steal, and ultimately it is his country that is indebted; remember that dirty cycle described above, it has just started again. Once more, an African nation cannot repay her debts and so her resources are mortgaged and generations of Africa's children, even those yet to be born, are thus enslaved without having to cross the Atlantic. This time they labour from home and their reward is harvested overseas. How convenient!

Furthermore, because multi-party democracy is not African, members of different political parties are yet to understand that their different political parties are there mainly to keep the other in check when they themselves are not in power. They instead deteriorate into rivalling interest groups and sometimes deadly enemies just for belonging to opposing political parties. Accordingly, the country is left to rot while politicians, with their thugs in tow, wage war against each other, bringing about unnecessary deaths, as bitterness is further engraved on the consciences of these nations. How then can democracy along Western lines function when the basics have not been understood and are not likely to be adhered to even if understood, given the peoples' culture, their differences, and the rivalries implanted between them by colonialist tactics? Yes, the colonial government did not go out to institute effective administrative practices as all they did was attempt to operate within the colonies with minimal expenses. Chabal and Daloz confirm this when they observe:

> The colonial period was unquestionably a time of great change. Nevertheless, the extent of the transformation is often misconstrued. Indeed, since the bureaucratic and political structures put in place were primarily designed to maintain order at the lowest possible cost and to ensure the profitable exploitation of the colonies, they were from the beginning distinct from their metropolitan models.
>
> It is now clear, for example, that at the local level, French district officers (or other assorted *rois de la brousse*) paid little heed to procedure and administered their areas of responsibility with a large degree of discretion. Isolated in the countryside and with ineffectual administrative support, theirs was a lonely task. Unsurprisingly, they tended to discharge their duties in a personalized, arbitrary and 'unofficial' manner which ill contributed to the development of modern bureaucratic order. The British practice of indirect rule, for its part, consisted in administering the colonial territory through established traditional authorities and by means of existing political institutions. Here too, therefore, it is questionable whether colonial administration did much to lay the foundations for a properly emancipated state. (12)

They conclude later:

> The historiography of the colonial period in Africa thus paint a picture of a colonial civil service which sought to devise pragmatic ways of adapting the imperial directives to the administration of its subjects rather than a method of inculcating new political and governmental habits. (12)

Yet this alien political system is now being made a *sine qua non* for Western recognition and the most valuable bait for Western assistance, which assistance as already established, is more often than not a Greek gift. Frederic C. Schaffer has observed: "Democracy, after all, is a concept that encompasses both purpose and institution. It is used to refer to both political ideas and a set of institutions designed to realize these ideals" (5). Accordingly, Africa's democracy so far, vis à vis imposed Western expectations, is only a travesty, for it is without the necessary institutions, such as the independence of various arms of the government, which can then facilitate transparent multiparty activities and effective laws to guarantee standards and effectively transparent electoral practices overall.

There is the need, therefore, for Africans to delve into their traditional forms of governance and emerge with a system, or systems even, which will work for their people instead of going around alienating themselves and antagonizing their communities in the name of multi-party democracy which, while a largely successful system of governance in some cultures, does not seem feasible on the continent of Africa as it is today. Yes, Cameroonian communities had their own system of governance even if they were different from what the colonialists brought. Even though he erroneously describes grassland traditional leaders as "often autocratic", mindful of the fact that these traditional leaders found themselves within an established system guided by the elders and could not arbitrarily introduce policies as such, Le Vine confirms existing political forms in Africa while also showing, inadvertently, how the colonialists started destroying these systems by their interference:

> In the Southern Cameroons, the British found a bewildering array of tribal groups, clans, chiefdoms, and other traditional political arrangements. In the extreme south, around Victoria, Tiko, and Buea, the Germans had already created a number of local chieftaincies to rule the principal tribes. Further north, in the Bamenda section, the large grassland and highland areas were under the rule of traditional chiefs (fon), the natural and often autocratic rulers of a number of Tikar, Bali, and Widekum tribal groups. Throughout the territory, numerous village and clan groupings maintained their forms of political organizations. Some had (and still have) explicit authority structures, complete with chiefs, "kings" (of German accolade) or fons. Others had diffused authority systems in which a tribal council, a council of elders, or an informal assembly of family heads constituted the only visible "government." Still others had intermediate forms in which leadership might be assigned to various persons depending upon position in the kinship structure and upon the occasion – such as the conduct of a war or the adjustment of a difference with a neighboring village (*The Cameroons* 198).

Until Africa can revisit these traditional administrative systems and begin benefiting from them, our politicians will continue looking funny with dazed looks in Western suits as some grapple with this whole concept of arguing heatedly with each other while still claiming to be friends and compatriots bent on serving the same chief, fon, oba, or president. Accordingly, most African parliamentarians, given the conflicting trends of their heterogeneous societies, just meet to wine, dine, and then, in most cases, approve of the president's plans.

The Judiciary

Besides the presence of people in any society, that which gives the group any worthwhile value is its judiciary — a system of law and order rendered effective by a police force and a deserving legal system concretized by the courts of the land, be they traditional or otherwise. Where there is no such system in place, which is functional, there is bound to be a breakdown in law and order. Such judiciary systems are not new in Africa as traditional societies had very effective ways of maintaining order and deciding cases even before the arrival of the colonialists with their own legal systems. And so, like their systems of government choked down the throats of their former colonies, colonialists' legal systems are also now in place, the early colonial administrators having dismissed or rendered ineffective established traditional legal practices they met. The result is that like with everything else that the colonialist imposed on the peoples of Africa, Africans are still struggling to make sense of this colonial legal system that has only resulted in corruption and distrust amongst the people. The reason is simple — colonialism alienated the colonized from themselves to a great extent, and so the struggle to re-identify themselves remains an overwhelming task mindful of the vice-like grip colonial values still have on these former colonies. Accordingly, the imposition and perpetuation of Western values as the standard of measure, which was typical of the colonial encounter, the neo-colonial experience, and even today's so-called globalisation, "…not only dispossessed Africans of their own culture, it infantilised and dis-empowered them by forcing them to learn afresh, under the guidance of condescending and overbearing Western overlords, new ways of seeing, doing and being" (Nyamnjoh "Globalisation" 9). Africa's plight today, in this light, is a reaction to the impact of intrusive cultures whose values of individualism in terms of rights and property subvert traditional African ideals of the communal nature of existence. The outcomes are societies tormented by intriguing multifarious ambiguities and conflicts arising from the complexities of the forced coexistence of disparate values. Small wonder then, Walter Rodney posited strongly "…that African development is possible only on the basis of a radical break with the international capitalist system, which has been the principal agency of underdevelopment of Africa over the last five centuries" (7).

Yes, after the traditions of the former colonies, there are penal codes out there in these African countries, yet it would seem to me they are there as a residual effect of colonialism only. Nevertheless, these systems were heavily "modified" in view of what obtains in the countries of the colonialists since, of course, whatever was introduced in the colonies was intended for the colonized and not the citizens of the colonizing nations who happened to be in the colonies at the time.

In African countries, Cameroon being a distinguished example, the law has little or no meaning except when the culprit is an ordinary citizen since the rich, powerful, and well-placed are above the law. True, the laws have been manipulated in many bastions of democracy on earth when the culprit is a "royal" name in that culture, but in Cameroon, like in most of Africa, this is the norm instead of the exception. Anyone with money and connections can damn the legal system and still walk the streets a free person whereas the average person would curse the day he was born for a simple traffic violation.

Cameroon's legal system, it is regrettable to say, mindful of the many learned, talented, and distinguished members of society who have been left no choice other than to serve such a system, is a sham. It has all the ingredients to be amongst the best in the world if only corrupt government officials would let the judiciary operate independently, yet this cannot be, at least as of now, not with a head of state who owns rather than serves the constitution of the nation. Yes, to this thingummy, the constitution has deteriorated to his personal will, which he modifies whenever, depending on the passing fancy of the moment: to divide his citizens further so as to maintain himself in power, and on another occasion, as a way of giving underserved advantage to one section of the country. When the constitution is tough to bend, he rules by decrees, fake rules coined to put in place his private plan in the name of serving the nation. With these all too frequent decrees, the legal system is thrown off its axis as criminals in high positions find themselves freed of horrible crimes, while political rivals are denied the right to run for public offices such as the presidency. Of such scandalous patterns, Ntemfac Ofege, a brilliant freelancer, himself a former journalist of the national radio television syndicate who fell afoul of the powers that be because he could not look the other way and keep mute, as is the practice, while corruption and mismanagement rule, writes:

> Cameroon's Ministry of *Territorial Administration* holds the record for election fraud. MINATD (sic) rigs elections on behalf of the incumbent. MINAT, which decides whose name gets on the voters register, who gets a voting card, who gets to actually vote and where; who counts and tallies the vote and who gets what score. Usually election results are prepared by MINAT two years before elections. Only in Cameroon and only under Mr. Biya would a sitting president get up on the morning of general elections to tell the world that the process cannot go forward. Then, while denouncing those who denounce such gross incompetence as 'enemies of the nation,' the president and his acolytes would then proceed to rig the same elections.... ("Corruption...A State of the Art")

But how could anyone or any institution in Cameroon challenge these decrees, when those managing the different institutions and theoretical arms of the government, the judiciary included, were hand-picked and put there by Mr. President? What folly would it amount to then, for them to attempt to bite the finger that feeds them? And so the president runs wild with his dreams for the nation, which are nightmares to the rest of the citizenry, especially the poor hardworking masses. In fact, corrupt practices in high places listed by Ofege in *Postwatch* read like a litany of hellish achievements deserving of some Luciferian award. And that which is incomprehensible is the fact that no person or institution with the means to do so could effectively challenge such abuse of power.

The chaos in Cameroon's legal system, in spite of a structure which looks well organized — the Supreme court at the head followed by the Judicial Bench, the Administrative Bench, and the Audit Bench, then the Courts of Appeal, and the Court of Impeachment — stems from the fact that nobody knows exactly what legal system is the official one in the country. There is the traditional, the English, and the French legal systems that are all co-existing; the last two being vestiges of the colonial era while the traditional is now partially side-lined due to neglect ushered in by colonial administrators. The chaotic status quo is exacerbated by the fact that Cameroon's government is romancing the idea of bilingualism without being exactly sure of how its version of bilingualism works or should work, and how it should affect the interpretation of the laws of the land.

The colonial roots of both sections of Cameroon, their ongoing influences in the legal domain, as the English legal system is practiced on the one hand and something of the French on the other, with the traditional surviving in between, along with the thriving bribery and corruption axis around which these structures revolve, amount to turmoil. Is a citizen guilty until he proves himself innocent after the French, or is the citizen innocent until proven guilty by the state according to the English system? The choice has boiled down to where the accused is being tried. Yet how unfair this is when English-speaking Cameroonians in detention, political prisoners especially, are transferred to jails in French-speaking jurisdictions with the ridiculous system of being guilty until the accused proves himself or herself innocent. The result is that whereas Francophones are used to being abused by the police, the younger generation of Anglophones are only beginning to think it is normal since the overwhelming Francophone population is bringing to bear on Anglophones practices that were foreign and illegal to these peoples. But older Anglophones who know of better days before this troubling union with La République just cannot swallow this bitter pill.

Whereas a police officer trained in this ongoing sham of a nation, which came into existence after the coup which ousted the Federal Republic of Cameroon, thinks it is alright for him to beat up a compliant citizen in the process of making an arrest, simply because according to his training the citizen is guilty until he proves himself innocent, the English-speaking Cameroonian would file charges against such a police officer during the Southern and West Cameroon days (a time when English-speaking Cameroonians were administered separately after the English judiciary system). In fact, such a thing did not happen since policemen trained before the days of the union with French-speaking Cameroonians would not think of behaving like that. Today, however, policemen beat up, violate, and even kill citizens based on suspicion only, and nothing happens. In fact, such policemen are immediately transferred away from the setting of their crimes to different towns, to save them from mob justice that is now the norm, the people having lost faith in the government. After observing arbitrarily that "... nationalist Anglophone writers have exaggerated how much Francophones have benefited from the Ahidjo-Biya dyad", Jean-Germain Gros, goes on to observe again that "...Anglophone nationalists have idealized West Cameroon experience under colonial rule, when in fact the region was far from pristine". Gros' argument for his latter observation is possibly based on how nonchalantly, if not treacherously, the British treated the territory. Whatever the case, Gros fails to realize that Anglophones' idealization of the West Cameroon experience under colonial rule is based on a comparative approach, mindful of what the predicament is today under Francophone-dominated, Gaullist-oriented administrative structures. In other words, the region could have been far from pristine, yet it was better than Cameroon today; this is the point Anglophone nationalists are making.

Another illustration of the chaotic legal system in Cameroon lies in the fact that the government can sometimes not account for those awaiting trial. To be in that state of limbo in Cameroon called "awaiting trial" is worse than just being thrown into prison. Awaiting trial is a phase in the Cameroonian legal system whereby an accused who has been in police custody beyond a certain number of days, even as charges are still being prepared against him, is transferred to prison premises to make room in police cells. More often than not, the number of days spent in police cells could depend on the whim of the superintendent of police in charge, and this in turn depends on how he has been conciliated with bribes by the relatives of the accused. It must be pointed out that while the accused is still with the police, the right amount of money exchanging hands could secure his release; the nature of the crime is rarely of any consequence, unless it has drawn too much publicity. In such cases even, it is only a matter of time and this same result can be achieved. Should efforts to secure his release fail, for whatever reason, the accused is transferred to another detention unit within prison walls now called "awaiting trial" where he will wait, until who knows when, for his trial. One can only remember those good days when as soon as one was charged, one appeared in court the very next day; but this is no longer the case in Cameroon. There are stories of people who have been in detention, awaiting trial, for months without charges, and again for months after charges are filed against them, without facing a judge. There are also trials that span years for no genuine legal reason other than that those concerned are waiting for bribe, which is slow in coming. Nobody cares about the person in detention except members of his family who must then do all to bribe the powers that be and secure their son's or daughter's release. *The Rape of Michelle*, a play by the Cameroonian playwright, Bole Butake, amounts to an absolute illustration of this quagmire. Rufina and her daughter, Michelle, rival each other at their business spot for the attention of their male clients. Because Michelle's sexual advances are not requited, she frames a male victim, Mikindong, and he is locked up by the police. Just because she has the money, Rufina, corrupts the Commissioner of police to do her bidding. According to a policeman, Rufina is determined to see Mikindong serve a good term in prison. It is not a question of justice, but who has the financial prowess to determine the course of "justice". With such legal malaise, armed robbers arrested by the public and handed over to the police have, within a couple of weeks, even days, been seen back on the streets going about like other law abiding citizens as they get ready for other raids.

Contrarily, in the English-speaking part of the country, and before this union with La République du Cameroun, prisoners were locked up, had uniforms to identify them as such, and were never seen in public without a warder as they marched in a file to and from their destination. The prisons were called "Production Prisons" because the prisoners worked and produced for themselves and the system. The surplus was sold and money made for their upkeep which was, and still should be, a state responsibility. Today, in contrast, convicts are seen all over town and are easily mistaken for ordinary citizens struggling to make ends meet instead of the sometimes-dangerous criminals that some are. The purpose of a prison sentence then, as a way of punishing while rehabilitating an offender, is no longer there. Prisoners, generally speaking, have the same privileges as law-abiding citizens, the only difference being that they must be back for lock-up. They leave by morning into town where they do odd jobs, make money for themselves, buy their food and other needs, and report at the jailhouse by evening almost like adults at some boarding school. As a result of such conditions, criminals no longer fear going to jail. In fact, some have become so arrogant that they threaten citizens who turn them in to the police with "You will see when I get out". They are so sure they will get out, and sometimes without even having faced a judge despite crimes as serious as burglary and murder.

The result is frustration on the part of the public. This has led to the emergence of vigilante groups in most towns and the resurgence of jungle law overall. When somebody steals, for example, there is no longer any point waiting for the police because people know nothing will be done to the thief. The consequence is that now the offender is simply beaten up, and, in the extreme, burnt to death by the public. This is the ultimate demonstration of lack of trust for the legal system in place — the public has now taken the laws into its hands. And there is a president supposed to be the head of such a country. The truth is simple: under Paul Biya, Cameroon has degenerated into a crime citadel even as Biya surrounds himself with thousands of soldiers and police officers for his safety against imaginary enemies.

All said and done, one cannot help wondering why Cameroon cannot boast of an effective legal system, the brains and well-intentioned practitioners within the system notwithstanding. There are great lawyers and judges who just cannot stand the system and would love to see justice being truly blind, but these are in the minority. The result is that their efforts at setting things right just do not even cause a ripple in the ominously deep waters of corruption that have drowned the nation and its institutions. But then, one remembers, the judiciary, like the rest of the nation, is under a chokehold by the corrupt leadership, and without their independence as an arm of the government, the judiciary will continue barking without being able to bite effectively.

The government in Cameroon, therefore, is responsible for the lamentable state of affairs in the country; a government that instead of serving has transformed its citizens into victims, most of whom have degenerated into globetrotting exiles.

Chapter Four
The Cameroonian People: An Abused Blessing.

If Cameroon has only one gift, and this is far from the case, then it has to be the heterogeneous nature of the people and the equally diverse cultural values, hence the country's tourism slogan "Africa in miniature" Patricia K. Kummer confirms this picture of Cameroon when she observes:

> Masked dancers, some on stilts, whirl about at village festivals. Wooden flutes and xylophones made from gourds fill the air with music. A small audience gathers around a storyteller who recites an ancient tale. Men in long white robes enter a mosque to pray. Families in Western dress attend Catholic or Protestant services. Men or women with special skills perform traditional healing rituals. People from all of Cameroon's ethnic groups take part in these activities. The sounds of their many African languages plus French and English, are heard as Cameroonians go about their daily life. Pygmies still hunt and grow crops in the southern rain forest. Fulani herd cattle in the north. Many Cameroonians work in the oil and shipping industries. These are just a few examples of the variety of life in Cameroon. Indeed, 'Cameroon is Africa in miniature.' (9)

After a rich colonial experience which brought them in contact with several Western nations, Cameroonians still use English and French today as their official administrative languages. There are, however, about 250 other officially recorded local languages before pidgin which is the lingua franca in Anglophone Cameroon. It is worthwhile noting that these languages come with cultures so different in certain cases. This is bound to be a blessing anywhere if effectively exploited, but not in Cameroon where the outcome has been bitterness as established and fledgling politicians alike exploit the concept of divide and rule they inherited from the colonialists as a way of keeping themselves in power while Cameroonians who ought to be one and strong continue to slander and backstab each other as a way of surviving in politics.

Cameroon's problem is a complicated mesh, depending on the angle from which one is approaching, with some of the most significant perspectives being the colonial heritage outlook—Anglophone/Francophone, the ethnic standpoint like the Bassa and the Bamileke, and the political viewpoint like that of the Union des Populations du Cameroun (UPC) party members who were massacred by Ahidjo, with the help of the French, at the dawn of his regime.

The Colonial Albatross: The Anglophone/Francophone Dichotomy

Cameroon's greatest rift, even as the government continues playing ostrich to the problem, is between the English and the French-speaking Cameroonian, a consequence of the conflicting colonial background of both groups. Germany was the colonial power that initially controlled the people of Cameroon as one, but with their defeat after WWI, Cameroon was split between Britain and France in compensation for their contribution towards the defeat of Germany by the allied forces. One can only conclude that the reward for hundreds of thousands of Africa's sons who fought in this war was that they now belonged to a civilized nation. As already established, tearing Cameroonians apart and handing them over to nations with different cultures only alienated these peoples from themselves. After independence for which they had again to fight and die, they were forced back together since the choices they were given were not looked upon in terms of how they favoured the Africans, but how they would affect the colonialist nations that had been in charge of these different peoples. Accordingly, the cultural differences inflicted on these peoples during their decades apart, the one [mis]managed by the English and the other by the French, has led to constant wrangling in Cameroon today as "water" and "oil" are now being forced to mix.

This inability of the French and English-speaking Cameroonian to coexist successfully has given birth to what is today called the Anglophone problem. It is the Anglophone-problem because it is the Anglophones who find themselves struggling to adjust culturally and otherwise in order for their political marriage with French-speaking Cameroonians to work. This is the case because the Francophones are in the majority and own the government, hence the fact that every policy in Cameroon today is designed with their satisfaction as the guiding principle. Interestingly, however, some Francophones, and other saboteurs masquerading as Anglophones, have questioned the existence of an Anglophone problem in Cameroon, with many others positing high-sounding fallacies against the Anglophones' struggle to liberate themselves from Francophone domination; a foremost display of ignorance or bad faith on their part, to say the least. One cannot help wondering if such illusionary thinking is an unconscious manifestation of the phobia of losing the socio-economically invaluable Southern Cameroons territory and the attendant consequences it will have on La République du Cameroun, or if this is just a sincere display of ignorance characteristic of a generation starved of the history of their nation. In the book *Gaullist Africa: Cameroon Under Ahmadu Ahidjo*, the writers, who are not Anglophone Cameroonians, were able to understand that the Anglophone has a problem in Cameroon, for they point out, with regards to the structural presentation of their text, that in the final chapter of Part II, J. F. Bayart focuses on "analysing the ways in which the constitutional autonomy of Anglophone West Cameroon was progressively undermined by the central government" (Joseph xi). This is certainly indicative of a problem, yet some Cameroonians refuse to see that there is a problem. Of course, it must be remembered that the plight of the oppressed is openly acknowledged only by the oppressed and not by the oppressor. If these detractors fall in any category that thinks its members are likely to be lost should the Anglophone secede, then their fear is unfounded as Anglophones had always been very accommodating until the misleading strategy of divide and rule was transformed into a government weapon against Anglophones. In fact, Southern Cameroons had her borders open to fleeing UPC partisans when they were being hunted down by Ahidjo and his French aides even before the Federation of East and West Cameroon came into existence. Of this, W.B. Morgan and J.C. Pugh have written:

In 1955 the leaders of the ultra-nationalist French Cameroons party, the

Union des Populations du Cameroun, fled to Kumba in the British Cameroons and their policy of re-unification found support also from J. N. Foncha, who created his own party, the Kamerun National Democratic Party. (709)

To those arguing against the Anglophone cause, it must be emphasized that there is an Anglophone problem in Cameroon today, and Anglophones can prove this anywhere, anytime. The least anyone can do is read a true history of Cameroon, which is, no doubt, relegated to the background in the Francophone curriculum in preference to French history which continues to assure them that they are French citizens, even as Francophone Africans are being hunted down in France for resident documents (Douala). Anglophones, therefore, must beware of a new tactic that is subtle yet potentially effective in threatening and complicating their cause. It is those Francophone saboteurs around today masquerading as Anglophones. These Francophones have learned English and are now writing as if they are Anglophones; they send out literature attempting to misrepresent, distort, and complicate the Anglophone problem and struggle by urging Anglophones not to tear apart our "beloved" country. Accordingly, Anglophones must scrutinize the roots of those writing in English yet contradicting the Anglophone struggle. Find out who they are, who their parents are, if possible, and the ethnic group to which they belong. Then only can Anglophones differentiate between Francophone saboteurs and Anglophone traitors.

Common sense indicates that nobody likes to be oppressed, at least not forever. For example, that Anglophone students were able to determine in the 1980s that their cherished educational system was almost being destroyed in the so-called harmonization effort, is indicative of the fact that even the very young know right from wrong. In this regard, only an Anglophone traitor will speak against the liberation — whatever guise this will take — of his or her people. As Anglophones, we want our colonial heritage to be respected and protected the way the Francophone-dominated governments respect and protect their Francophone heritage. The government's unhealthy disposition towards this problem so far indicates that this can only be the case in a two state Federation as it was before Ahidjo's manipulation of the federation into a United Republic in a fake referendum reminiscent of African elections and their characteristically ridiculous results that are ever in favour of the incumbent, even when he is as unpopular as hell. It is either this return to the two state federation, or as a last resort to which Anglophones have been pushed by the Francophone regime's recalcitrance, we follow Adamu Ndam Njoya's advice while he was a minister of state, and seek our sovereignty elsewhere. The union with La République du Cameroun has already cost Anglophones a lot in every way, for which reason secession had never been an option to the majority as we thought we had put in too much to bail out now. This, however, is no longer the case today — with many now favouring secession — as the government continues refusing to acknowledge and deal with the Anglophone problem and so accord the Anglophone minority a true sense of patrimony.

Consider what the Anglophone goes through when it comes to communicating with his Francophone counterpart in the ministries and figure out if this does not constitute a problem. The theoretical concept of bilingualism seems to have propelled itself naturally into a comfort zone, as both languages are bandied about anywhere anytime, but with Francophones thinking it is only natural for Anglophones to switch into French each time there is an encounter between both groups, the venue notwithstanding. Even though Cameroon is truly bilingual, administratively, and multilingual naturally, the government is only pretending to be encouraging bilingualism because, but for the no-nonsense Anglophone population, it is a fact the English language would have been wiped out and the Anglophones transformed into second generation Francophones. After all, that was, and may still be the plan, and all that is lacking is an effective way of putting it in place without a war erupting. How often have there been rumours about plans to merge the North-West and Western provinces on the one hand, and the South-West and the Littoral provinces on the other, a step that according to the conspirators, hopefully, will completely neutralize the Anglophone population as they will begin internalizing Francophone values. But that is, very likely, the trigger that would transform Cameroon into one more war zone in Africa as it would intensify the desire and expedite Anglophone-Cameroon's secession from La République du Cameroun.

As far back as the 1960s attempts at changing the federal structure of West Cameroon had been reported, but such threats met with swift reactions from the Anglophone leadership. Such was the case when *The Mirror*, a Kumba newspaper reported similar threats on 1 October 1966. The then Prime Minister, Augustine Ngom Jua, immediately reiterated the federal nature of the union between Southern Cameroons and La République before warning that any attempts to alter the federal structure would jeopardize the union. But Ahidjo was a Machiavellian, and so his goal, and not the manner of achieving it, was what mattered. Cameroon today, is almost entirely where Jua and the rest feared we were headed. It is particularly awe-inspiring when one remembers that most of the founding fathers of Africa's "modern" states as revealed by their Cameroonian counterparts, did not pretend to the high-sounding diplomas today's generations brandish. They were mostly "Grades I & II" teachers as they were called, yet they were wise, foresighted, and true patriots who stood for what they were honestly convinced was right for their people. How much unlike the numerous pretenders to academic thrones, with high-sounding diplomas, capering around today, yet all they seem to have learned and earned distinctions in, is on how to betray themselves, their people, and their fatherland for a few worthless temporary positions from which they degenerate further into thieves pilfering from state coffers. Hence the near hopelessness of Cameroon's socio-political impasse.

As a result of the confusing structure of Cameroon's bilingualism, the overwhelming Francophone population in government, for example, tends to treat Anglophones as second-class citizens. This is obvious even from the fact that although the government prints its documents in both English and French, a careful look will reveal that stupid idea of putting the French version in bold print and/or upper case keys, while the print of the English version is faint and/or in lower case keys. Equally revealing is the fact that, with regards to government documents, the French version is considered authentic and the English version just a translation. Only the government can explain why this is the case, as if the Anglophones pay less tax or are less Cameroonian than their Francophone counterparts. Some moronic bureaucrat must have thought it an effective way of Francophones imposing themselves on Anglophones and introduced it to the government. Since the government is one without a head, and certainly without a well-intentioned think-tank, this insulting practice was given place within the system, and it has thrived since then.

Even with this pretence towards being a bilingual nation, the truth comes to light when an English-speaking Cameroonian finds himself in Yaounde "chasing dossiers" as Cameroonians themselves describe the tedious and equally corrupt means of escorting and expediting one's documents through its otherwise normal stages and channels to the office of the one who is supposed to approve and legalize them by signing. An Anglophone daring enough to address a Francophone official in English is either snubbed, or else the latter becomes insanely angry and berates the Anglophone for talking to him in English, one of the so-called official languages of the country. And so the Anglophone who cared less about French must rehearse his French before going to Yaounde to "chase dossiers", or else employ a private translator and escort for his accursed encounter with government officials in the head offices of the capital city of Cameroon. How unfair! Yet when Francophones come into the heart of English-speaking Cameroon, they still speak to English-speaking Cameroonians in French, and some English-speaking Cameroonians struggle to reply to them in French. This is the problem with bilingualism in Cameroon today: nobody knows for certain what it is describing and how it is practiced.

Accordingly, it would appear bilingualism in Cameroon means the English-speaking person has the responsibility of learning French since it might come in handy when he meets with the first-class Francophone citizen wherever their paths cross. One would have thought only the semi-literate and/or illegally employed in the ministries would behave like this, but no, even some educated Francophones seem to think it an insult to be addressed in English by an Anglophone. The greatest joke, however, is when an Anglophone who has been in Yaounde forever pretends to be Francophone and goes on torturing his Anglophone compatriot by speaking to him in French all the time until, thanks to God, his identity is mysteriously exposed by some stupid error on his or her part. Recently though, the Francophone Cameroonian has realized that English is not an Anglophone language but a world language and one that is very alive, and so they are scurrying to learn English so as to interact with the world, but in this little nation called Cameroon, some still think French is the only way to go. This has in any cases worked in favour of the English-speaking Cameroonian. The vast majority who are interested can harvest both ways—as Francophones, and as Anglophones—until they are betrayed by their names Whatever the case, the form of bilingualism in Cameroon today is to the detriment of the Anglophone. The only redeeming feature comes when one enters the international arena. Most international job openings in Cameroon require a thorough knowledge of both English and French. Until recently, only Anglophones could exhibit this ability, hence they had most international jobs given them. The result is that intelligent Francophones were then energized and so decided to begin learning English not because Cameroon is bilingual, bust so as to be able to get some of the international jobs that went to Anglophones whom the biased system had obliged to become bilingual.

Because the French-speaking are the majority, they think it gives them the right to lord it over their English-speaking compatriots. This illusion is further fertilized by the presence and ongoing role of the French, supposedly the former colonial administering authority of La République du Cameroun, in Cameroon. On the other hand, the English, misled into considering Southern Cameroons more of a liability than an asset, dropped their former protectorate without any second thoughts. This happened as soon as the opportunity presented itself during the clamouring for independence by African nations; an anti-colonial drive at the time that also infected Southern Cameroons, a UN trust territory then under British administration. Even though the British will today claim they did what they had to do, the truth remains that had they, for once, taken a lesson from the French and clung to Cameroon like the French are still doing today, it would have benefited Her Majesty's kingdom a lot more along with the English-speaking Cameroonian. After all, that is why the English tried building the British Empire in the first place — to sponge on the colonies. And so with France behind the French-speaking half of Cameroon, the tendency has been for this part of the country to try to impose herself and her French-inherited culture on the English-speaking Cameroonian. This clash of cultures has led to internal strife before, and today things are no better. Ask any English-speaking Cameroonian presently above forty-five in age and the story will be the same — English-speaking Cameroon was better off, except in infrastructure, before joining French-speaking Cameroon. This stems from the colonial policies of both the French and English.

The French considered their colonies France overseas, and so invested in developing the colonies with an understanding that French citizens themselves were going to settle in these colonies; they did and are still there today in the thousands. With this colonial policy, it is not surprising that until recently, some French-speaking Africans still considered France home. What a farce! The English, on the other hand, did nothing to develop their part of Cameroon, then administered from Lagos, Nigeria, and later from Enugu. They were in the colonies only for what they could get, and so any penny they had to spend on the colony was dependent on how it facilitated their carting away of resources from there. The roads and railways in then Southern Cameroons were constructed for this purpose — the carting of resources to the coast for exportation. It is for this reason that after the English left Cameroon, there was nothing in existence to show they had been present there, nothing but for a few winding tracks passing for roads, whereas German infrastructure is still surviving in Cameroon today, even with the neglect it has suffered at the hands of the Francophone regimes in power.

The Francophone/Anglophone divide in Cameroon is palpable, and perpetrated by that feeling of Francophone superiority complex that characterises daily life in Cameroon. This thought is also evident from the fact that an English-speaking Cameroonian has never held any strategic position of power in the country, not to talk of becoming president, although Cameroon has had only two presidents; at best, Anglophone officials are always sterile deputies. The tide seems to be changing though as both sections, especially the Francophones, are beginning to realize that they must work together for the common good. This, unfortunately, is at the level of the common person only and not the policy makers. Although Mr. Biya clung to power after the 1992 elections, it is the consensus that John Fru Ndi beat him hands down in spite of the irregularities, according to international observers, that marred the electoral process. The meaning here is that even Francophones wanted Biya out; they wanted a good and patriotic leader and could not care less the package he came in — Anglophone or Francophone. But there are powers beyond Cameroon that are scared about this possibility and have been working hard to maintain a Francophone led government in place, even if it is not helping with the growth of the nation.

Still, in keeping with the Francophone administrators' determination to remain always in control, it is common knowledge that there are ministries that English-speaking Cameroonians have never been given the opportunity to head, not because they are incapable, but because it will amount to handing over too much power to Anglophones. This, it is believed, can ultimately lead to an equilibration of the intended power disequilibrium in favour of Francophones. Examples of these ministries are Armed Forces, Finance, Foreign Affairs, National Education, Territorial Administration, and Public Service. In these ministries and others, English-speaking Cameroonians can only be Secretaries of State and nothing more. Even the office of vice president was tactfully avoided by Ahidjo since it had to be an Anglophone, and this meant power to the dreaded lot in case something happened to the incumbent French-speaking president. Accordingly, when in 1975 Ahidjo realized he would eventually be giving up the office of president, he created the position of prime minister to which office he appointed the then servile Paul Biya. It is not surprising then that in 1978, only three years after creating the position of prime minister and appointing a Francophone to it, he made the prime minister successor to the president in case of any eventuality. The plan was completed in 1982 when Ahidjo resigned from the presidency and Paul Biya became president.

What really is this scheming and manoeuvring all about, if indeed it is true that Anglophones should feel as a part of the Cameroon nation today? Instead of our leaders managing our country for the good of the citizens, they are afraid of one section of the country being in power and so create problems where there ought to be none. Why do Francophones in authority think it is all right for Anglophones to stomach what the Francophones will not stomach were the situation reversed? It is this connivance against Anglophones, for whatever reason, that has led to thoughts of secession. Were Anglophones made to feel they belong, it would certainly be insane for them to begin thinking otherwise. Francophones in power who are nurturing this unhealthy climate must remember that neither French nor English is an African language and so ought not to be a *sine qua non* for acceding to power in any African country let alone Cameroon. Indians, in 2004, were ready to have their late son's Italian wife, Sonia Gandhi, in her capacity as head of the Congress Party, to take over the managing of their nation, but Cameroonians cannot seem to tolerate another Cameroonian running as president simply because he speaks a different colonial nation's language from theirs? How unfortunate! Accordingly, if Cameroon must remain peaceful in the hope of beginning to thrive economically and otherwise, then we must all begin thinking as one people in spite of our linguistic differences even at the local level—Bafut, Bakweri, Bali, Bamileke, Banyangi, Bassa, Douala, Ewondo, Foumban, Kom, Mankon, Hausa and the rest. And this is quite possible, for I believe it is not normal, in fact it would appear pathologically problematic, a certain kind of mental illness even, for a human being to hate another simply because he looks different and/or speaks a different language. Why is it so hard to realize that this quality of being different is in fact one of the greatest gifts of life? What a boring world would it be were everything to be identical, yet humankind cannot seem to work together, especially in Africa, as they go around hungering faultily for a deranging dystopia characterised by the lack of variety.

Despite this Anglophone-Francophone divide, the truth is that it is only being fuelled by selfish politicians as both groups have come to appreciate each other. The ordinary French-speaking Cameroonian has come to accept that as a people we can, and have to try and stand together in order to ward off foreign manipulation, which has only left Cameroonians poorer, albeit in the midst of plenty. Again, listen to Cameroonian musicians, for example, and this fact becomes obvious as they all now acknowledge the Anglophone and Francophone culture of the country in their songs by singing in both languages and sometimes more even. Yet Cameroonians must remain wary of their conniving politicians who still seize the slightest opportunity to maintain themselves in power by stoking this possible-to-put-out flame—the Anglophone-Francophone divide.

The North West/South West Complex

At a lower but strategically significant level, there is another kind of divide amongst Cameroonians, and this is the most baseless, if not absurd, of all. This is the case because the divide is between the English-speaking peoples of Cameroon whom, in spite of the various ethnic groups present within the population, colonial activities had lumped together under the English. Until today, these peoples still use the English language as their main medium of communication. True to type, however, they were nominally separated by politicians, for political and selfish reasons, into two separate provinces—the North-West and the South-West. This way, the politicians, Francophones in the main, believed it would be easier to manipulate and swallow them up.

In terms of their local cultures, the Anglophones are different peoples, yet so are many communities in Cameroon even within a 20 mile range, generally speaking. Within this range, one is likely to meet a different language and different ways, yet these peoples were all bundled up into administrative units by the colonialists and so have tried staying that way else, even at the international level, there would be need to restructure some of the arbitrary boundaries installed by the colonialists. The point is that cultural differences between the North-Westerner and South-Westerner ought not to make them different peoples because of their unifying colonial heritage. Like the French-speaking Cameroonians who consider themselves one because of their colonial history and heritage, being Beti, Douala, Bassa, or Ewondo notwithstanding, so too must English-speaking Cameroonians be one because of their colonial history and heritage whether they are Bafaw, Bakweri, Banyangi, Mankon, Bafut, or Bali.

Yet this is almost always not the case, and this division caused by impetuous politicians is still being exploited by some government officials to their selfish ends. The result is that West Cameroonians seem to have forgotten that the concept of a North-Westerner and a South-Westerner is recent.

The truth, however, is that these used to be one people, despite their ethnic diversity, such that the Nkambe Division of the Southern Cameroons days was, at the time of the unification crisis, an Endeley stronghold as it stood for Southern Cameroons remaining as a part of Nigeria. Again, it must not be forgotten that parts of Mamfe Division and Bamenda Divisions were once considered part of the grassfields until recently. Discussing the unification issue, Le Vine observes:

> The only other Endeley stronghold that remained firm for Nigeria was Nkambe Division, on the northern fringe of the grassfields, long dominated by the strong personality of the CPNC's Rev. Samuel Andoh-Seh. In the grassfields (Bamenda and Mamfe Divisions, but in particular the former) it was the effective mobilization of existing party support that produced almost overwhelming support for the unification alternative. (*The Cameroons* 212)

Interestingly, therefore, these peoples were so much one people as a British trust territory. However, Francophone politicians trying to destroy Anglophone unity, according to the hidden agenda, have been experimenting with different strategies. As indicated above, they ultimately emerged with the decision to separate West Cameroon into the North-West and the South-West Provinces. Today, with the help of some selfish and myopic Anglophone politicians and community leaders, Francophone dominated regimes have almost completely achieved their intention of pitting these provinces against each other. Piet Konings and Francis B. Nyamnjoh are right then to conclude that Ahidjo's decision to make official "…the ethno-regional boundaries between coastal forest and Grassfields areas by dividing the erstwhile Federated State of West Cameroon into two provinces, the South West and the North West Provinces…" (*Negotiating* 16) after the establishment of the unitary state in 1972 was so as to reduce any danger of a united Anglophone front. This strategy played into the hands of selfish Anglophone leaders who, because of conceit and belly-politics failed to see the danger of dividing the former West Cameroon. Some even went on to make more ridiculously disturbing suggestions lately. One such political adventurer, it is rumoured, was recently advocating a further division of the North-West Province into two new provinces just so that he could be appointed governor of one such new states. At this ridiculous pace, true of selfish and bigoted African politicians, towns would soon begin passing for provinces just so that power hungry political minions might be made governors.

Another example of politicians falling prey to the Francophone goal of divide, govern, and exterminate, towards Anglophones is the disturbing case of a one-time governor of the South-West Province, Mr. Oben Peter Ashu. A South-Westerner himself, Oben Peter Ashu incited ethnic hatred by calling people from the North-West Province, settled in the South-West Province, "Come No Go", a derogatory local coinage for an immigrant. In other words, the governor of a province was calling Cameroonians "foreigners" simply because they are settled in his native province. Although this earned him the sack from the administration in due course, the government failed to speak up against such corrosive and divisive tactics by politicians. Because Oben Peter Ashu was aware of the fact that the president himself was using the divide and rule approach, he failed to realize that the president was a lot more subtle in his strategy. So, believing he was showing allegiance to the president, the governor "wept more than the owner of the corpse" and got himself into trouble. Oben Peter Ashu's behaviour is more disconcerting when it is recalled that this is an administrator who lost his administrative milk teeth in the Bamenda Grassfields where, while a fledgling administrator — District Officer — he was nurtured by these same North-Westerners. In Bamenda, Oben Peter Ashu was well received and treated with affection, for which reason he even acquired land and built a house in Nkwen. He equally made many good friends, as far as Ndop even, all of whom he later betrayed by his political campaign strategy of calling the North-Westerners in the South-West, "Come No Go". One can only imagine how Oben Peter Ashu would have fared as an administrator in the North-West Province had the people treated him unlike one of them, just as he tried treating them when he got promoted to rank of governor of the South-West Province. Georges Nzongola-Ntalaja also recognizes the devastating effect of such political irresponsibility, for he points out about the ways of such political miscreants:

> Even more devastating than the failure to respect the decisions of democratic assemblies and to honor signed agreements, are the lack of patriotism, the criminal fanning of ethnic hatred, and the willful destruction of the economic and social fabric of the country. (17)

Still along the lines of pitting Anglophones against each other, consider yet another strategy: once upon a time English-speaking Cameroonians of the coastal areas were influenced into believing that other Anglophones, especially those from the hinterlands considered them lazy, yet this is a view that was put forward by the colonialist instead. The Germans first considered "coastal people, and particularly the Bakweri, ... inept and indolent..." (Konings *Labour Resistance* 59) simply because they were more interested in farming cocoa which supplied them regular cash thereby making it unnecessary for them to look for jobs on the plantations. British administrators later corroborated this opinion by referring to the Bakweri in several administrative reports as being 'backward farmers', or 'lazy farmers', or 'not farmers at all' (Konings *Labour Resistance* 39). In the same vein, Coastal people were also nudged into considering themselves superior to the grassfielders of the hinterland because the colonialists first got to them before daring into the hinterland where they met with incredibly fierce resistance. In other words, "civilization" got to them first. This myth, with the equal paucity of its logic, had long been debunked, as common sense dictates that being conquered and exposed to the ways of the victor first is not a mark of superiority, nor did colonialism usher civilization into Africa. Ultimately, in any case, those who came to be colonized by the English found themselves in the same boat and certainly not by choice, yet that was history in the making, and so it is today as all is being done to tear them apart.

Dr. Augustine Enow Bessong, a psychologist currently resident in the U.S., shared similar feelings of disappointment about what is being done to the Anglophone population in Cameroon when he ran into secondary school classmates of his in Minnesota. After screaming out in joy, laughing, hugging and celebrating our days in St. Joseph's College, Sasse, before reviewing the mess Cameroon has degenerated today into because of irresponsible politicians, Bessong lamented: "When we were in Sasse man, we knew ourselves as Sasse students, Cameroonians, and not North-Westerners and/or South-Westerners". Yes, indeed there ought not be any differences between the North-Westerner and the South-Westerner that these people cannot resolve, because not only do they share a common colonial history and heritage—which detractors are now trying to present as superficial—they were once the Federated state of West Cameroon, they inter-marry, and they are settled in each other's geographical territory. To say their ways are different is to claim the ways of the Banyangi are no different from the ways of the Bakweri, which is not true, because different as the ways of these people are, they are still one people of the former Southern Cameroons and later West Cameroon.

The North/South Divide

One is likely to think that besides the Anglophone-Francophone divide, the most important divide in Cameroon is only between the North-Westerner and the South-Westerner, but this is not the case. There is the divide between the north and the south of the country, both territories being of the former East Cameroon.

This divide escalated when Ahmadou Ahidjo was president and did all he could for his Northern compatriots. With their "son" in power, the Northerners wielded so much power and control in the country that they could literally get away with almost anything. Virtually all the contracts given out by the government got to the Northerners, and even the police were scared of having anything to do with them. It is generally said that Ahidjo got his brothers, who had only been herdsmen, out of the bushes where they spent most of their time with their cattle and brought them into the administration of the nation. They were recruited in large numbers into the military and the gendarmerie to help maintain stability in the nation.[1] This, of course, meant maintaining Ahidjo in power. The much dreaded and equally respected Republican Guard, which was in charge of presidential security during Ahidjo's reign, was a northern affair. The majority of the soldiers were Northerners and so were their leaders, and they were directly answerable to the presidency of the republic, that is to Ahidjo himself.

Then there was the notorious gestapo, with the acronym BMM (*Brigades Mixtes Mobiles*), which instilled fear into the heart of virtually every Cameroonian. This was Ahidjo's torture machinery which helped him maintain "control" over the people of Cameroon because of its legendary torture techniques, its basement cells, and the number of people it eliminated for simply daring to oppose Ahidjo. The notorious group was made up of mostly northern soldiers who knew nothing else but subservience to their benefactor, Ahmadou Ahidjo, who was symbolic of northern power. They would kill without thinking about the consequences of their actions, simply because one seemed to be a threat to national security—the stability of Ahidjo's regime. An extract by Abel Eyinga from a report sent him by a comrade who, because of the intervention of his French wife in Paris, was miraculously freed from the BMM when Commissioner Abdoulaye Mouyakan headed it, is especially revealing:

> ... it is particularly of your brother Ebolofou, whom I found in the B.M.M - and some other compatriots I met there - that I wish to tell you about today. I was able to witness the terrible suffering of these men and women during their 'interrogations' at the B.M.M. I cannot go into all the details of how I saw people night and day, for months and months being tortured, hung from the ceilings by their arms or feet ... in the room which the boss of the B.M.M., Mouyakan, christened 'the chapel'...being given electric shocks while two or three soldiers from North Cameroon, especially chosen for their cruelty, beat them with unbelievable ferocity. One could never forget the screams that came from that place. The sight of the quivering human specimens brought out of this room, bodies and what remained of their clothing covered in a stinking mixture of urine, vomit, excrement and blood made me fully realize the deep hatred being sown among Cameroonians. These individuals, not allowed any contact with the exterior, were imprisoned in a barely ventilated cave, incarcerated in numbers up to a hundred: men and women in a room which could barely hold twenty individuals... they were able to dispose of their bodily waste only by using a barrel at the top of a stairway.... These men and women received no medical attention, were badly fed, and could only go to the shower once a week out of which they were kicked after five minutes... They were allowed to leave their cave only to undergo 'interrogations', most often accompanied by torture, or to be carried away at three in the morning without warning and to an unknown destination...it is in such a sinister place that I saw honourable patriots, and even former deputies and ministers, made to undergo the greatest humiliation, the worst physical and moral violence. (215-216)

This arm of the Ahidjo administration made things worse in some sense, although the grudge could never come out in public since it meant certain death or long years of incarceration in remote political prisons. This secret police force exacerbated the situation in the sense that it cultivated in the population a sense of hatred and anger towards the large mostly uneducated northern group that wielded power in the nation simply because Ahidjo was the reigning dictator. With Northerners seeing themselves in control, they lorded it over the South and the rest of the nation for all the years that Ahidjo was president of Cameroon.

With Ahidjo's demise and the entrance of a southerner into the presidency, the rest of the north, virtually, considered it almost a betrayal. But Ahidjo was an astute politician and did not want to pit himself against another northern son who might soon relegate him into the archives of northern memories, so he gave power to a southerner he believed had always been a puppet of his—Paul Biya. But power is capable of so much else, and so it is not surprising that as soon as Biya was in power, he set out to create his own legacy by first of all destroying anything that was reminiscent of Ahidjo. In Bamenda in

1985, although this was after a failed coup d'état intended to remove him from office, Biya eliminated Ahidjo's sole political party, the Cameroon National Union (CNU), by renaming it Cameroon People's Democratic Movement (CPDM). From this point onward, Biya was determined to completely take control of the State of Cameroon, which Ahidjo intended maintaining control over by remaining as the chairperson of the CNU party while Biya ruled as a puppet president. Ahidjo had underestimated the fragile looking civil servant out of whom he had made a statesman, and so once more, the power of power came into light. From the elimination of the Republican Guard, which was mainly peopled by northerners, to the destruction of the highly valued banknotes that were in place during Ahidjo's regime, Biya unwittingly ushered in the socio-cultural and economic bankruptcy of the Cameroonian nation. How Biya could think that Ahidjo's legacy, after he governed Cameroon for over two decades, would be so easily erased and forgotten remains to Cameroonians a mystery that only Biya could fathom. This might have been a possibility anyway, had Biya done any better than Ahidjo as head of state. Today, however, it is common knowledge that there is no comparing between the two regimes, as but for the ruthlessness of dictatorship which led to a lot of killing on Ahidjo's part, Cameroon was a very stable and economically buoyant country under his tenure. Biya, on the other hand, who had everything laid in place for him simply to maintain the flourishing status quo he inherited, reduced the nation to a wasteland and Cameroonians to paupers.

Sensing what he had done, Biya went on to concretize and intensify his divide and rule strategy. He surrounded himself, like many a woeful African head of state, with people from his own Beti ethnic group; a people ridiculed in Cameroon today as "chop broke pots", people who spend and consume without thinking of tomorrow. They party with their investment capital instead of the interest brought in by their business. They had long done with the interest and now they are gorging themselves with the investment capital while the nation of Cameroon bleeds to death; the citizens could rot in hell. After all, is it not Paul Biya who once declared during an address to the people of Yaounde, knowing the events were being televised live, that as far as Yaounde was doing all right then Cameroon was fine? This was Mr. Biya's way of saying that the devastating effects of the ghost towns instituted by John Fru Ndi's Social Democratic Front opposition party in 1992, which had virtually brought the nation to a standstill, were of little consequence because Yaounde, peopled by ethnic groups sympathetic to the regime, did not take part in the strike. According to the president of the nation, therefore, the rest of the nation could rot and it would mean nothing to him in so far as his darling ethnic land was fine. The president did not realize that Yaounde, in so many ways, is at the mercy of the rest of the nation. When he found out, he struggled to improve upon Yaounde's chances of surviving without the rest of Cameroon by carrying out another ridiculous project typical of African heads of states south of the Sahara—he built a huge ultra modern airport in Nsimalene even though the smaller Douala International airport is still underutilized. Like such white elephants in most of Africa, the airport is rotting away in its remote forest location with monkeys grateful for a new Bikutsi party ground provided them by the government of Cameroon, even as towns and cities are without well-maintained roads linking them.

With Ahidjo now supposedly obliterated from the memories of Cameroonians as Mr. Biya had expected, and the former's northern workers and soldiers relegated to the sidelines of Cameroon's corridors of power, the divide between the north and the south seemed to be increasing, as now the northerners, though quiet, have not forgotten their humiliation in the hands of Paul Biya after the resignation of Ahidjo. Things seem quiet, but Cameroonians believe the relationship in former East Cameroon is that of another active volcano which is only temporarily dormant.

Cameroon is therefore a land with diverse peoples equally blessed with rich cultures that could all be assembled into a powerful whole by a true patriot of a leader towards the emergence of a powerful and successful nation. Regrettably, selfish and equally bigoted politicians who pit their peoples against each other while draining the country of its resources for personal gains and those of their political puppeteers overseas have instead turned this recipe for success into an albatross about the neck of the state. And so the world jibes at Cameroon for being poor, and in recent times corrupt, as the citizens struggle to survive in this atmosphere of disorder ushered in by Western puppets at the helm of affairs. If a president or a politician must divide his people in order to stay in office, then the strategy is as treasonable as it is unfortunate, Machiavelli notwithstanding. For a true nation requires a community of people, despite their heterogeneity, that is capable of identifying as a whole by transcending tribal and other sectarian allegiances for the social, political, and cultural survival of the whole which then and only then becomes a nation. Cameroon's challenge at the beginning of independence as painted by Le Vine is still very true today:

> ...as the Cameroun moved into independence, Camerounian nationalism, though it had widespread popular support, had yet to be translated into essentially national aims and solidarity. The biggest obstacle to the realization of this goal lay in Cameroun diversity, which expresses itself in a variety of particularisms: regional, urban, rural, religious, tribal, and economic. Translated into political demands, they raise a babel of conflicting voices in which expressions of unity, however strong, are soon lost. (*The Cameroons* 218)

With dichotomies rife in Cameroon today, and in most African states, the question remains about the essential nationhood of most of these countries. Without being partitioned and forced into artificial states by the colonialists for their own convenience, these African communities would no doubt have evolved naturally into kingdoms, empires, fondoms, chiefdoms, or nations that would have been able to function effectively as expected of such political entities, without the domestic divisions characteristics of African states today, hence imperialism and its effective bastardization of postcolonial Africa. Of civilization, which is what the colonialists claimed to have come to Africa to do, Oswald Spengler had observed:

> [A culture] dies when [its] soul has actualized the full sum of its possibilities.... Every Culture stands in a deeply symbolical, almost in a mystical, relation to the Extended, the space, in which and through

which it strives to actualize itself. The aim once attained—the idea, the entire content of inner possibilities, fulfilled and made externally actual—the Culture suddenly hardens, it mortifies, its blood congeals, its force breaks down, and it becomes Civilization (qtd. in Monga 81)

It becomes obvious then that as a result of the encounter with the West, coupled with the effects on Africa, Monga is correct when he argues that: "This sympathetic but somewhat naïve reading of the 'normal' course of a culture obviously cannot be applied to Africa, whose inhabitants have been forced to suffer other forms of violence". (81) Consequently, Monga is also categorical about Africa's bastardization for he observes firmly "African cultures were not given the time to go through all the phases of prosperity…" spelt out by Spengler, "rather, they collided with the harshness of history, resulting in problems of identity for many of their peoples". (81) This ushered in Africa's bastardization, as "Caught within the upheavals of politics and history, Africans have been obliged to fit themselves into social molds that were conceived by others and to improvise the development of new codes and cultural markers" (Monga 81-82)

Chapter Five
Cameroonian Resources and the Exploitation of the Masses

In terms of natural resources, Cameroon is certainly endowed. The country produces timber, cocoa, coffee, banana, tea, gold, diamond, bauxite, and of course, crude oil and a lot more, but that is as far as it goes for the citizens as they, but for a few accomplices of the president's, know nothing about revenue the country makes from these resources.

Timber, for example, is being voraciously exploited while being barely replenished. From the logs alone, Cameroon earns approximately U.S. $ 120 million annually, but the rain forest, its primary source, is receding at an alarming rate. Patricia K. Kummer captures well this atrocity:

> Across southern Cameroon in the east and inland from the coast in the west, rain forest covers the land. This is the northwestern part of the Congo Basin rain forest that spans five other countries. Since 1980 about 4.8 million acres (1.9 million hectares) of Cameroon's rain forest have been cut down. That leaves about 40.8 million acres (16.5 million ha). At one time, however, Cameroon's rain forest covered about 86.4 million acres (35 million ha). Hardwood trees such as ebony, iroko, obeche, and mahogany grow in Cameroon's rain forest. Because wood products from these trees are very valuable, logging is a big business in Cameroon. (31)

On a daily basis, for decades now, Cameroonians have become accustomed to seeing huge trucks towing equally huge tree trunks to the coast for shipping, yet the citizenry knows nothing as to what company is doing the exploitation, who the buyers are, and for how much they are buying their wood, which of course is then converted into finished products and sold back to them at cut-throat prices. Nfor N. Nfor's comment on this is particularly revealing:

> The destruction and exploitation of Cameroon forests by French companies to Francophone political elites is seen as no crime. France in the temperate zone is an exporter of tropical wood within the European Common Market while Cameroon in the tropics that God had blessed with such a large variety of hardwood does not rank that much. (80-81)

This is true of virtually all the valuable natural resources that Cameroon is producing and exporting overseas. The most notorious case is that of our oil.

Oil is that "black gold" that brought change in status to virtually every nation where it was discovered, whether in the Gulf region or in Africa, except for Cameroon. Nigeria, for example, was able to make her citizens realize that somehow there was a windfall, even if only for a while; at least the citizens experienced the power of oil. Look at the fantastic road networks that appeared in Nigeria, so much so that emerging from the village of Ekok, a border post in the South-West Province of Cameroon, into Mfum, a border post in the Cross

River State of Nigeria, one appeared like a mudfish—all covered in mud after weeks of digging along the economically strategic Kumba-Ekok or Bamenda-Ekok route. A journey of about two hundred and fifty kilometres at the most, is done in about a week by cargo transporting vehicles, and a day or two by passenger vehicles during the rainy season, and for long, tedious and equally dusty hours during the dry season. True, even today, one needs a shower before entering Nigeria in either season when coming from Cameroon. With all her wealth, nothing in terms of financial remuneration from the sale of Cameroon's natural resources, especially oil, is reaching the hardworking masses of Anglophone Cameroon in particular; not even in the form of good roads. Nigeria, on her part, tarred her roads and flourished, at least for a while with great hospitals, excellent universities and distinguished professors healing and training millions of Africans, even if today typical African politicians are almost ruining these institutions. The truth is that one failed to have noticed any such spells, if that is what they were, in the Cameroonian oil landscape besides the yearly salary increments Cameroonians enjoyed under Ahidjo, which is only natural for any thriving economy, oil or no oil.

Why is it that a nation's resources have degenerated into private property to be exploited at the whim and caprices of its so-called president and his clique? Why are Cameroonians not given any accountability as to how their resources are being exploited and traded? A Cameroonian minister of state, Francis Nkwain, once threatened a journalist for asking him a similar question. Of course, the poor man was there to earn his living and knew nothing about these transactions, and so saw the journalist's question as a ruse to get him fired, as that is what would have happened had he attempted answering the question. He was later dropped, in any case, after the president was sure he was of no further use to his divide-and-rule scheme. This abuse of the people is so blatant that even Jean-Germain Gros, who does not seem to think much of Cameroon's problems, especially from the Anglophone perspective, has this to say of Cameroon's oil revenue:

> ... no one, except perhaps the World Bank, the International Monetary Fund (IMF) and the French Government (all outside actors), really knows how much revenue Cameroon earns from oil sales, for the authorities in charge of oil-related transactions answer only to the head of state and oil revenue is *hors budget* (off budget). (*Cameroon in Synopsis* 7)

Again, is anybody bothered that Cameroon, which produces oil, has about the most expensive petrol prices on earth? With many people on monthly salaries of 200,000 frs CFA or slightly more, except in parastatals, how is it possible for a litre of petrol to cost 594 frs CFA? The situation becomes glaringly tragic and frustrating when it is imagined that on such a salary a Cameroonian needs approximately 45,000 frs CFA to fill his car's tank. The meaning here is that with such a salary and the cost of petrol, the individual can only fill his car with petrol four times a month, leaving him with next to nothing for food, any sort of bills or anything else. Yet Cameroon produces oil. Interestingly, every now and then, the government increases the price of petrol, leaving the people completely helpless. What kind of government is this that exploits its own people in every way possible? It would have been a different thing if the money squeezed out of poor hardworking citizens was put into effective use, but show me the effective use when an average job like repairing the broken Mungo bridge could not be finished even after months; when streets are gaping death traps because of unbelievably huge potholes; and when highways remain buried in encroaching bushes that for years have never been trimmed, resulting in frequent accidents caused by blind curves. So where does all this money go?

In most sane societies on earth, the government operates to help its citizens with a better standard of living, but not so in Cameroon. The government in Cameroon squeezes every drop of life-giving financial juice from the citizenry for the benefit of those in power. This is not to say there are no devoted civil servants longing to see a better Cameroon; these are so far apart they are of little or no consequence. Yet everyday new ministers are appointed and new fleets of cars imported for the presidential entourage. The result is that the Cameroonian does not feel like he belongs to his country, as much as the citizens love that once upon a time beautiful homeland. This is because all they get from the government in exchange for their stolen resources are higher taxes and repeated increases in the cost of utilities along with falling standards of living. But of course, the president and other well placed members of government enjoy these facilities—water, electricity, transportation—for free since the government is billed for their expenses. This unfortunate scenario has transformed the bulk of a wonderful population—friendly, hospitable, and generous—into passivists on the one hand or desperados on the other. The outcome is an overall lawless population as the people are all doing something wrong to help them stay alive, or at least give themselves some esteem, of which they have been cheated by a pilfering and anarchistic leadership. This picture will be more lucid when certain core areas of the Cameroonian society are explored.

Education

Like most African countries, Cameroon has a solid educational structure from kindergarten to high school level, but with a rather unfortunate higher educational structure, despite the very distinguished professors who lecture in the system. Cameroon's educational structure is such that there is kindergarten, primary/elementary school, secondary school, high school, and then university. In elementary schools, pupils study at least five subjects every day. In secondary school, the curriculum is more intense as students immediately begin studying ten to thirteen subjects every week. In high school, a student, having decided on whether he or she wants to specialize in the sciences or the arts, studies at most five and at least two subjects, respectively.

The strength of the educational system lies in the fact that the pupils must pass three exams every year in order to move from one class to the next, and at the end of each major phase in the academic ladder, they have to take a national exam which they must pass in order to move on. An elementary school child, for example, must at the end of seven years pass his First School Leaving Certificate Examination and the Common Entrance Examination to get into any worthy secondary school. Some children with a lot more confidence in themselves, attempt these examinations just after six years in elementary school. During the five-year secondary school Programme, the student is again expected to pass three examinations each year and with a pass in English, French, and Math, all else notwithstanding, in order to go to the next class. The student must also pass the General Certificate of Education Examination at the Ordinary Level (GCE O/Level) by the end of these five years so as to move on. Without a pass in at least four papers at the GCE O/Level, a student cannot officially go into high school. Even then, the student must also have what is called a "combination" of subjects that make it possible for him to enter one of the many career series that are structured in high schools.[1] In high school, during which the student must still pass the three examinations administered in the first year in order to get into second year, the student is again expected at the end of the second year in high school, to pass the General Certificate of Education Advanced level (GCE A/Level) examination, without which he or she can never get into a university in Cameroon.

    This system is good because it brings out the best in students, but it is confining. Once a student is past a certain class, there is nowhere up the academic ladder where he can change his mind and pursue a different field. This is because all the basic courses that form the foundation (pre-requisites) to any course or specialty are done with by high school and so a student is doomed to be what he had decided he wanted to be by high school; and many decide without having ever discussed with any kind of counsellor as a guide. The unfortunate thing here is that many Cameroonians get stuck in fields they end up not liking but cannot do anything since they cannot see themselves going back to secondary and high school for the basics. This is where the American system of education has a huge advantage. At the college or university level, a student can still spend a year or two and do his generals which are the basics in any subject area and then move on to earn a degree in a new field of choice. Hence the relative ease with which an American can change careers much later on in life. In like manner, this is why Cameroonians who were arts students back in Cameroon get to the US and can change and become scientists instead—from a student with a degree in English to a pharmacist, or even a medical doctor, something that cannot be conceived of in Cameroon given the present educational setup. The argument in Cameroon would be that the student did not study Anatomy or Biology and Chemistry in high school instead of the concerned just taking his generals right away and then continuing in his new quest. Alas, true to things in Cameroon, the government still peopled by victims of the colonial mentality, does not believe in its own experts and so nobody or group is trusted enough to be given the task of reviewing the educational system to see how it can be modified to better serve the citizens. The deranged leadership would rather spend time and money trying to francophonize Anglophone curricula instead; an exercise which benefits nobody except those stealing the money allocated for the worthless venture.

    In my opinion, private universities aside, the state of Cameroon has only two real universities so far, with the different colleges sprinkled all over the country masquerading as separate autonomous universities. What is the difference between the University of Yaounde I and the University of Yaounde

II? At best, the University of Yaounde II is an extension of the University of Yaounde I with only two faculties on its premises. A good university, even with on-line Programmes nowadays, should have its own campus on which most of the schools and colleges of the university can be found, and which can be visited from time to time by anxious students and faculty alike as they move from lecture to lecture in different faculty auditoriums in search of knowledge. A student in the University of Yaounde I, for example, who is interested in some guest speaker giving a talk on some topic like the legal implications of police behaviour in Cameroon, must ride on that death channel of a road to Soa to benefit from such a talk, instead of waiting for such a guest speaker to visit the law faculty of his own campus. A good university should also have its own university press; above all, it should be governed by a senate on the one hand, and a well organized students' union on the other. This is not the case in Cameroon where, in the past, organized students came up with a students' union only for them to be threatened with dismissal or have an unthinking police force unleashed at them.

Unlike in most successful Anglophone/English systems, where the vice chancellor (VC) is elected by the faculty who know him, in Cameroon the VC, to begin with, is appointed by the president of the nation who knows nothing about the integrity of the professors from which group he is making a pick. In fact, the VC might not even come from the professors on campus; it is not strange for the president to remove some lackey of his political chorus from the ministry and put him at the head of seasoned professors. With such arbitrary practices and the concentration of power in the hands of one man, it will not be surprising tomorrow if the president begins choosing who should get married to whom in Cameroon. Indeed, Cameroon under Paul Biya is a nation resting on its head, with its butt in the air.

The VC's allegiance, as has been the situation in most cases under these circumstances, therefore, is to the president and his government and not the thousands of students and the faculty in the institution of which he is head. The result is an ever-present antagonism between the VC and the student population, unlike in good universities where the VC works with the students for the good of the institution. Because the president handpicks the VC, even the latter's relationship with his colleagues becomes horrible as the all too frequently hollow ones begin spiting their colleagues, some of whom are superior scholars. Consequently, colleagues who are not willing to betray their consciences for politically motivated offices avoid the VC while desperadoes clamour fawningly around him in the hope of receiving favours or at the least being in his good books. His colleagues must now grovel to him for what they are due. For example, a promotion that was long deserved by a colleague within the system was leaked to him by a now late colleague, just before it was made public, as if it was a favour that had been done him, since the late colleague said it was he who had recommended his qualified colleague for something he deserved. The promotion never left the minister's office, himself a former VC, because about this very time, the concerned was accused of discussing politics in his classroom, and the almighty minister was the culprit being discussed. Yes, the lecturer was supposed to use foreign examples to teach Cameroonian students even when more lucid local examples abound. And so instead of our VCs striving toward academic excellence through the maintenance of an effective scholarly atmosphere on campus, they now begin striving towards ministerial positions. And once that is achieved, then these educated men seem to lose their senses and consider themselves little gods. One ordered a colleague around during a graduation ceremony as if he was his orderly instead of his colleague within the university system. He must have considered the younger looking colleague a very stubborn underling who would not execute his orders as, at best, he mistook him for a student officiating during a "university" graduation ceremony, given his age at the time. Ridiculous! The colleague, for example, was ordered to summon the director of his institution, the director himself a better scholar than the professor turned honourable minister, as if the director was a house-help on the honourable minister's private payroll. But that is Cameroon, and this younger colleague must have forgotten that the former VC was now minister and so could not care less about his colleagues in the university.

One thing that is hard to fathom, is how supposedly learned professors became learned without an ounce of humility in them, since somewhere along the undulating academic landscape, as they perused volumes in their march towards erudition, they should have realized the vastness of knowledge compared to the little they were trying to grasp which earned them their titles of scholarship and distinction. Yet most of our scholar-politicians are arrogant, conniving, and treacherous in their dealings, as most indulge in backstabbing each other in their struggle to be appointed to positions of power, so they can go around with ministerial and presidential trains, smiling stupidly like some sedated exemplars of political allegiance, yet oblivious of their role to society. Professor Cornelius Lambi's insinuations documented in a Cameroonian newspaper after the students' strike of November-December 2006 confirm all this. After refusing to resign from his position as vice-chancellor (after a strike that ended with several students dead), since Lambi enabled one to gather that he was being set up for failure by someone within the system, the scholar-administrator comments: "Anybody who organized the strike and called in troops to kill the students so that I should resign would be disappointed. I would leave when the President removes me" (Achobang and Dipoko 6). What revelations about the system in place! How is it that a university is on strike and the vice chancellor is not informed? Who is it who took it upon himself/herself to summon in the idle uniform officers with a notorious reputation for hurting and killing students and members of their own public? The answer, in typical Cameroonian parlance, is blowing in the wind yet indicative of the backstabbing and infighting. Yet to make claims to the throne of learnedness while failing to recognize the values of "serving" instead of "lording" it over others is a sure sign one is a pretender to that throne. True education elevates the spirit, yet it accords humility and the desire to serve as one immediately realizes the ephemeralness and meaninglessness of all if it is not grounded in service to humankind.

To anyone who has tried visiting a VC in a Cameroonian university, the expression "Il est en session" (He is in a meeting), is now a laughable cliché. They are always in meetings but one can never tell with whom and to what end. Is anyone surprised then that the University of Yaounde I, after all the years in existence, does not have a worthwhile alumni association? It would seem the students and ex-students are very angry with, rather than proud of the institution and the powers that be. Mostly unqualified administrative staff members treat both ex-students and current students as filth. Most of these workers were placed where they are by relations of theirs, and so who is a student or former student to demand services from them? How disheartening it is to see students—graduates and undergraduates alike—being psychologically tortured as they rush from one administrative building to another in search of a transcript, or some other commonplace document which is their right, as if they are begging to be paid scholarship money they do not deserve. Of course, scholarships for Cameroonian students as a whole died with the collapse of Ahmadou Ahidjo's government. In this former leader's days, Cameroonians were automatically on scholarship as soon as one qualified to get into the university. It conjures the picture more effectively when put this way— Cameroonians were being paid by Ahidjo to go to school: think of Ecole Normale Supérieure (ENS) students and their scholarships in those days, then think of the Bamenda Nursing School students and their salaries while still in school, and one will agree with me.

To discuss faculty without even a cursory look at how they are recruited will be to leave out another flavour unique, yet typical of higher education in Cameroon. The process, in a nutshell, is a nightmare. Of course, the usual prerequisite—one must have a godparent within the system or some kind of guide or else one must be a very lucky person, and lucky people are far apart in Cameroon without money switching hands. First of all, nobody outside a very tight circle knows when a faculty position is open as by the time it is advertised, it is obvious that one cannot assemble all the documents required and still make the deadline. The requirements are, to say the least, absurd. To begin with, to qualify to teach in a state university in Cameroon, the applicant must have a Ph.D.[2] This is particularly disturbing as there are great candidates without this mysterious Ph.D., yet they cannot teach in universities and similar programmes in dire need of teachers. What is wrong with hiring Masters Degree holders and encouraging them to work towards a Ph.D. if it must be earned? This happens in great institutions around the world, but not Cameroon. One has to have a Ph.D. or forget it, and so great minds are left to rot in remote villages teaching at some ridiculous level just because they do not have a Ph.D. If this were a system with positive intentions, then a Master's degree is good enough for undergraduate programmes at the very least.

Amongst an intimidating list of requirements, the applicant is also expected to submit his doctoral defence report, the private property of the university from which one graduates. Why would a university require this of an applicant after it is obvious the applicant was successful in his programme? The point is simple—everything is being done to make it difficult for applicants to meet the deadline so that favoured candidates with godparents, even if unqualified, will be those with complete application files. In keeping with this rather inhumane system, the viciousness is such that even the person charged with the search committee's effectiveness could easily pull out documents from an applicant's file just before the committee studies them so that the applicant is rejected because, apparently, his file is not complete. Why an educated person would behave in such a rustic manner is beyond me, yet this is the norm with the recruitment process in Cameroon and more shamefully so, because this is within the citadel of learning and supposedly integrity, at least professional integrity if not otherwise.

Despite these vicious practices, in terms of qualification, the faculty members in African universities are amongst the best one could find anywhere at any time. It must be remembered that most of them studied, or better still went through academic boot camp, in Africa before going overseas to earn higher degrees in some Western University where things are overwhelmingly different as they are designed to help the student succeed instead of fail, as is the case back in most of Africa. If the reader wonders what this might mean, the answer is simply that virtually everything is designed to work in favour of the student in most Western universities, unlike in African institutions where programmes are intended to sieve the student population so only the very best can go through. In Western universities, beyond the facilities that students have, even their professors, generally speaking, do all to assist them with their work so they succeed. Here one must acknowledge those great universities in Africa found south of the Sahara, where the work was very rigorous, and one hopes still is, because these institutions wanted to maintain standards, unlike those that are just out to frustrate their students. And there are many such great schools in Africa, and so one hesitates to name even one, lest somebody feels such and such a distinguished university was not mentioned.

What is it then that happens to the majority of these great professors when they return to their countries, that they suddenly forget the effective systems under which they earned their higher degrees in Britain and North America? All of a sudden they become impatient, passive, and even vicious towards their students whom they treat with little respect and sometimes with condescension even, since now the students' lives are in their hands; in the words of a former colleague who often joked and toyed with the concept — "They have the yam and the knife".

Like Africa's politicians who love spending time and the wealth of the continent on Western shores but would not build and develop their countries such that they would enjoy vacationing there, these professors forget all they saw and experienced while studying for their higher degrees overseas. At once, they gloat over the fact that they have their Ph.Ds and could not care less about their students, as all of a sudden they begin imitating the very challenging if not belittling local system of grading that leaves their students at a loss as to their real academic worth. There are, for example, stories about a professor in one of Cameroon's universities who randomly decides students' fates even from the first day in class. This professor, it is said, goes around and, as if joking, declares to certain students, "You, I will meet here next year". How is this possible from a professor who was himself once a student? How is this possible from a professor who is also a parent or about to be one, and who knows what other parents are going through to keep their children in school, given the beggarly salaries Cameroonians now receive? In plain terms, this is just not right and amounts to an insult to one's education were any scholar to behave this way, yet this is commonplace in some institutions of higher learning in Cameroon.

Then there is the professor who enjoys delaying students or holding them back, as they put it. A post-graduate student, for example, has finished his work and is ready to defend his dissertation, and all else is virtually in place, even the foreign examiner is set to come in for the defence, but the said professor who has himself been involved in the training of this student, is just not making any progress as an examiner. He sits on the dissertation, leaving the poor student in a state of limbo as he can neither go on to defend and graduate, nor can he approach this god to find out what is wrong for fear of being victimized, as is already the case without him knowing. In most cases, the student has done nothing wrong. One cannot help wondering then, if this professor is just afraid of the student's potential growth, or why such foolishness on the part of one who is, or is supposed to be, a parent as well as a scholar? In the same vein, it was my greatest shock to discover professors in the Yaounde system not finding anything wrong with a student whose dissertation they claimed to have directed or supervised fail the defence with them present and participating during the exam. How is it such professors do not realize that for their students to earn a fail mark for a dissertation they claimed to have directed is a statement on their own qualifications and abilities? There is absolutely no excuse for this kind of behaviour, and it ought not to be tolerated. The young shall grow, it is said, and there is nothing anyone can do about this other than to fertilize this growth, knowing that as a rule of nature, one is bound to reap the benefits before long.

Alternatively, consider that professor who, instead of working hard enough and publishing a book, transforms his notes into computer printouts, "polycops", which he forces students directly or otherwise to buy. What are these students to do? Take them to court? What courts are we talking about here, when the professor's cousin or friend who is a police officer could easily cause a case-file to disappear forever, and as often as this service is required? Should the file miraculously succeed, after some years, in going through the judiciary police system, then the professor's brother who is a court clerk inherits the policeman's duties. Little wonder cases are theoretically alive in Cameroon for decades. But then, who has heard of a student suing a professor in Cameroon? Such a "mad" student is not yet born, nor is the system that would consider such a student mentally sound. It was once thought that this unprofessional behaviour on the part of professors could be as a result of their ridiculously low salaries and the appalling conditions under which they function mindful of the incredible resources they spent acquiring their diplomas. As a result, they have become bitter towards their students instead, realizing that they themselves, except for a few, could never tell their minds to the head of state, or a vainly bloated colleague now passing for minister or vice chancellor.

Take a school like Ecole Normale Supérieure Annexe (ENS) Bambili, which has been in existence for over forty years, but is yet to have buildings of its own; this is uniquely Cameroonian. Until at moment, 2008, ENS exists only on paper, and, at best, physically in dilapidated buildings which were too old to serve even a high school and so were abandoned by the high school. Yet this is where a university college has been in operation for decades and has trained some of the best brains in the country.

In Bambili, there are no offices but for a block that is compartmentalized to serve as the office of the director of the institution, and the secretariat. There were no toilet facilities even, until the arrival of Professor Moses Fon Asanji as director. He is the same director who gave ENS Bambili a hall, and did all to treat his colleagues as colleagues, instead of a bunch of Ph.Ds and third cycle doctorates of whom he was in charge as is usually the case with heads of similar institutions. One cannot help wondering that in spite of the thousands of students—Anglophones, Francophones, South-Westerners and North-Westerners alike—graduating from ENS year in year out, nobody in the government of Cameroon has been patriotic enough to care that the school has no buildings; that Professors use their cars or shades under trees for offices; that students lack good classrooms, benches, laboratories, and a good research library? Why pretend that such an institution exists if the government did not want to accord the province or the English-speaking population such an institution. It were best to leave the people without such a travesty of an academic institution just as the North-West is today without a state university, instead of giving the people a nightmare like ENS Bambili to look forward to, an institution that was stillborn because of a bad-faith government. To argue thus is not to disregard the incredible sacrifices made by the faculty and staff of that institution to train the thousands of students who have passed through their hands; it is to register one's frustration at the tactics of unpatriotic regimes. After all, compare the campuses of ENS Bambili and the main campus in the French-speaking city of Yaounde and see. No, leaving the extension of an institution in a dilapidated condition is not the meaning of "annex". True to that confusion that is distinctively Cameroonian, Bambili is sometimes called the annex and at other moments the First Cycle. Probably, the government of Cameroon is yet to decide which is which; after all, the school is yet to be in place, and possibly still, never will be.

Another shade of the plight of ENS Bambili students is that they have started paying fees, unlike in Ahidjo's days when they were paid for going to school, and even then many shunned the college because they did not want to be "mere" teachers. Ahidjo must be exhumed or invoked one way or the other so he could pass on the details of his secret of managing Cameroon. And the point here must not be missed: ENS Bambili is not in this state of neglect because Cameroon is one of those poor African countries that cannot build structures for her universities. No! This is a case of deliberate neglect. ENS Bambili is in Bamenda, within the Anglophone region, hence an illustration of Anglophone marginalization in the country. Further still, from another perspective, this amounts to an exaggerated display of a bad sense of prioritization, mindful of the fact that an ultra-modern airport has been built in Nsimalene and left to rot in the jungle—with monkeys partying on the runways—because of how inconvenient its location is to travellers and carriers alike, all because of the dirty, unpatriotic, and immature politics in the country.

The leaders of the country are short-sighted Cyclopes still with the village mentality; they fail to realize that developing Bamenda, Bafoussam, Buea, Ngoundere, Douala, Yaounde, or Limbe, which may not be their village, amounts to developing Cameroon as a whole, which is their nation. These are all towns to and from which all Cameroonians travel and sometimes even reside in to work and earn a living. And so Cameroonians suffer twice—from the colonial and then the tribal divide. In this vein, the French-speaking Cameroonian does not care about ENS Bambili having a campus because that would be developing Anglophone territory, and then a South-Westerner who could turn the tide refuses to do so because that would be developing the North-West part of the country instead of his. The result is a certain mental and infrastructural backwardness that has left a few squandering the wealth of the country while the true patriots are languishing in misery; yes because not only North-Westerners or Anglophones constitute the graduates of this ageing institution that is yet to be accorded a campus with buildings and the respect it deserves.

Even more frustrating is the fact that this college of the University of Yaounde I, ENS Bambili, is made to be managed as if it is the private property of whoever, in recent times, is unfortunate enough to be the director. The director, enter Paul Biya's regime, has absolutely no facilities with which to administer the school but his wit and the respect of his colleagues, which if he is smart enough to earn then his already tough job is manageable, but if he is the arrogant type, then he is on his own, and this could make life really hard. ENS is the only university college, even in Cameroon, without a vehicle, and so the director has to use his private car for both private and official matters. Yet this is in a country where hundreds of motorcycles are bought to be part of an already overcrowded presidential entourage. Once there was a funny looking white Toyota Corolla that, from its looks, one could not help thinking must have been donated to the school after somebody had exploited it as a taxi along the then nightmarish Bamenda-Bambili death trap of a road, but it was given by the government to Bambili. Even if it had been new when that cheap Toyota Corolla was given to Bambili, are those in power waiting for some god to inform them that because it was the lone vehicle serving a university college it had quickly deteriorated into a road hazard after over a decade?

The most frustrating part of having anything to do with ENS Bambili, either as director, faculty, or student, is the fact that their qualifications and positions notwithstanding, they all virtually have to beg from some staff with vain administrative titles on ENS Yaounde campus in order to get that which is due them. It is always ridiculous that each time faculty members from Bambili go to Yaounde for one school activity or the other, they are expected to struggle to meet with some half-baked administrator in a worn-out castoff suit and tie, just to get served for the benefit of ENS Bambili as if it was their private property.[3] In a sane society, it is the responsibility of the director of ENS Yaounde, who is the overall director, to receive his colleagues from the annex. But these professors usually have to fend for themselves when in Yaounde and return without even seeing, let alone meeting with the director in Yaounde. The so-called outstation allowance which is later paid them is nothing without the courtesy expected from a true director playing host to some of Cameroon's best brains.

Interestingly, again, faculty members from Bambili, some with Ph.Ds from internationally acclaimed institutions, are treated as second-grade professors simply because they teach in another college of the university which is unfortunate to be in the province and not the capital. It is said to be a condescension acquired from the French who think if it is not in Paris, then it is hardly worth it. How is one to make these Africans, Cameroonians, in Yaounde understand that Yaounde is Yaounde, a burgeoning city in the heart of Africa and not Paris, even if French is spoken in Yaounde along with red blooded French men and women milling all over the place? As intellectuals, or administrators in an intellectual environment, one would think they have been decolonized and are not still calling France home and aping it in every way. If this is still the case, then it is a shame for those guilty of this mentality. Such individuals must realize today that they are Africans and nothing else all else notwithstanding. They must understand that as regards their relations with France, they are no different from the child in Achebe's *Arrow of God* (3) whose goat it is in so long as he has to see to it that the goat grazes, but the child soon finds out the real owner because he only hears about it but is not part of the decision making body when the goat is to be slaughtered. France could not care less about these self-proclaimed French Africans, *évolués* or not, milling about in their native country, donning recycled suits and considering France home.

See ENS Bambili students in Yaounde looking lost as they struggle on their own to be served by a university system to which they legally belong, and to which they pay tuition, but which loves to reject them. The students tend to want to blame their director in Bambili for neglecting them, not knowing that he is doing all in his powers, to the point of begging even, in order to have his students considered by the powers in Yaounde when it comes to budgeting and the like. This was observed during Professor Asanji's tenure. And when he was queried by a colleague for stooping so low to get what he and his institution deserved, Professor Asanji smiled quietly and wisely as he answered back, "We have to do this if we have to get anything for our students". This was painful and difficult to grasp, not because one is lacking in humility, but because it is simply wrong. Why is it that a true and seasoned professor, a government appointed director of a government institution, must grovel to mostly undeserving administrators, most without the qualifications and merit to be where they are, so he could have a government institution operating? This is a reign when lawlessness is king. It does not matter who one is, what experience one has, or what qualifications one possesses, in so far as one has godparents in the system, one will be made in charge, or else relegated to the garbage heap crowded by usually more worthy Cameroonians, but who unfortunately are without patrons.

In Yaounde itself, which has the main state university campus, an equally old institution, we find academic giants sharing offices, sometimes four in number — full-time professors not part-timers — while superfluous politicians and petty administrators are in large, well furnished, and air conditioned offices. How is it that the vice chancellor never thinks of constructing offices for his colleagues, even when he is later made minister of Higher Education, knowing full well that he might return to campus after just a few months since, of course, his position as minister depends on the whim of the president? The point here is faculty members can hardly do creative work, pursue their research projects, or discuss effectively with their students because of crowded offices and the lack of privacy. Accordingly, both faculty and students are left frustrated, and thus quality is sacrificed by egomania.

Once upon a time, faculty were well paid, but that was when Ahidjo knew the value of maintaining peace in the university environment; that was when being a professor at the University of Yaounde meant respect, although these were also the days when the eccentric scholar Professor Bernard Fonlon called the institution a glorified high school. Today, university professors, and all teachers alike, earn chicken feed, in spite of their years of studies and the responsibility given them to mould the minds of the nation and the leaders of tomorrow. This may be a source of the damning attitude of some, especially towards their students and to a lesser degree their colleagues, but to what end since these are mere victims also and not culprits?

True, the conditions of faculty members in Cameroon are bad, but dear colleagues, do not transfer this frustration on to your students. Stop enjoying the fact that your students are failing after you claim to have done your best—as is expected of all teachers—teaching them. A professor should be worried that something is wrong with his teaching methods if the majority of his students cannot pass the examination he gives them which is supposed to be based on what he has been teaching for the term or semester. Such an outcome is in itself, a pronouncement on the teaching ability of the professor. In a university in a country with a worthwhile sense of purpose, such a professor would lose his or her tenure. After all, university students just do not fail, and certainly not in Africa where the system is such that only the very best and most determined make it to universities. By the time these students succeed in getting a position in any university they already know what they want, and coupled with what they went through, they need no other incentive to work other than to make their degrees and get out.

Again, stop forcing students to buy "polycops" (computer printouts of the professor's notes) as a *sine qua non* for passing your courses. There is nothing wrong with producing them, but it becomes unethical when students are forced to buy them or else fail. University professors should struggle to publish as expected. Granted this is difficult and almost impossible in a country with, at best, two state universities neither of which even has a press. The few surviving privately owned publishing houses that are there can barely survive with the ridiculous taxes heaped on them, and so most can only produce works that are poorly finished, a deterrent towards the publishing venture as a whole. The truth remains that until they can formally publish these books, professors must not emerge with "polycops" which they force students to buy *or else fail*; it is simply disreputable and not the standard professors should strive to set.

True, everything in Cameroon is working against the citizens in all their different professions, but, as educators, professors should do all to come up with better-spirited graduates who are equally well equipped intellectually. Only then can the nation, the oppressed in other words, hope that those who people positions in Cameroon's governments tomorrow would be people with consciences to change this country and bring it back to the jewel it was in the sixties, and even the seventies, yes, under Ahmadou Ahidjo. Professors should give their students what they deserve, especially considering how humble, respectful, and hardworking these students are. Professors must do all to make life easier for their students, else of what use is their own education as professors? Some great minds have often said it is better to give the students what they merit instead of frustrating them. Give them their qualifications, if they have earned them, and one can swear these students deserve them, and then let them go; the opportunities will present themselves before long for these graduates. After all, it is an emotionally healthier taxi driver or *bendskineur* (bike-taxi rider) who goes about toiling along the pot-hole-decorated roads of Cameroon knowing he has his degree but is yet to have the opportunity, as opposed to the embittered dropout who has his unfeeling professors to blame for his plight. By being unnecessarily strict and failing to realize that learning is a process and not an immediate end, many professors have ruined numerous potentially great minds in higher institutions of learning in Cameroon. Yet one wonders why, when there is so much joy in helping these students and seeing how they appreciate it.

Cameroonian professors as a whole must change the country by first changing their own attitudes towards their students. Every professor must ensure that no student goes through his or her hands without thanking God for having encountered such a professor along the streets of his or her academic topography. Consider Professor Tchouamo, Isaac Roger of Dschang University, who, according to students, used his international connections to make scholarships and free books available for some of them but had to stop because others, envious of course, were already trying to make his life miserable. How is this possible when young Cameroonians, many of whom remain thankful to Tchouamo, were the ones benefitting? As academics, professors cannot continue screaming foul against the regime when they themselves are doing the same things — maladministration — even if only in the worthless manner in which they treat their students. Having righted themselves and their dispositions towards their students, professors should turn around and form powerful unions that will get the government to do what is correct, not only for university professors, but for Cameroonians as a whole.

As already stated, the student body in Cameroon, like in the rest of Africa, is one of the best one can find anytime and anywhere on earth, and for obvious reasons: they are willing to learn, so much so that they treat school as the only chance they have in life. African students are humble and have great respect for authority. The conditions they are subjected to are the most gruelling, with a system that is intentionally or otherwise designed to frustrate them. Even if these conditions were simply inherited, as they are, from the colonial days, all the more reason why they should have been restructured, just like the curriculum which required African children to sing about "Baa, baa, black sheep" and wool.

After a most challenging experience in elementary, secondary, and high school where a student will be made to repeat a class for some of the flimsiest reasons possible, why is it so hard for these students to get into universities in Cameroon, especially after meeting the set requirements? The recruiting situation is a lot more challenging, if not impossible, when the student is trying to get into some of those professional schools like the Government Nursing School; the Teachers Training Colleges; The University Centre for Health Sciences (known by its French acronym as CUSS); the military training institution, EMIA; the Post and Telecommunications school; The National School of Administration and Magistracy, (ENAM); and even into the police training colleges in Yaounde and Mutengene. The truth of the matter here is that it is not the best necessarily that get in to these professional schools, but those with the money and the right contacts. What kind of a country is it where in order to become a policeman or magistrate who should uphold the law and justice system, one begins by breaking the law, as one must find someone to bribe. As ashamed as one is about these facts, they amount to the truth, and not to say them is to betray Cameroon twice in a manner worse than those employed by these corrupt persons. Ntemfac Ofege makes the picture more vivid when he writes about these public exams for entrance into professional schools, notoriously known by their French terminology, concours:

> Public service examinations are never meritorious. The official rate for bribes into professional schools in Cameroon is known:
> - CUSS (Medical School) 1.000.000 FCFA;
> - ESSTIC (ASMAC School of Journalism) 500.000FCFA;
> - Ecole Normale Sup (sic. Higher Teachers Training School) – 500.000;
> - Ecole Normale Annexe (Teachers Training Lower Cycle) – 300.000FCFA;
> - Polytech (School of Engineering) – 1.000.000FCFA;
> - EMIA (Military Academy) – 1.000.000 or some months of scholarship);
>
> Others – 200.000-500.00FCFA depending on the cycle. These amounts are paid by those who are not from the Chosen Tribe while those from the right tribe sail in like water under the river; (sic) ("A State of the Art".)

This is the same nonsense—authorities imposing their own cooked up list of candidates into the University of Buea College of Medicine in spite of the university's already published list—that led to the student strike of November-December 2006, which culminated in the death of students. This becomes especially painful and treacherous on the part of the government when it is realized that the deceased are peoples' children for whom they have worked all their lives in an effort to train young men and women who will help them in their old age, the National Social Security Fund (retirement benefits) of the nation having been obliterated by mismanagement. Why is it all right, in any case, for the police always to confront students with live ammunitions? Why is it all right for the police to kill Cameroonian students each time there is a demonstration on campus? Who is the incompetent police superintendent who cannot manage his men and women in uniform? But above all, who is the idiotic university authority who rushes in the police in the first place? Students are intellectuals, at least in the making, and not morons like some of their gun-toting oppressors, and so when they cry foul, something must be wrong. It takes only common sense to know that these students can be reasoned with, instead of ushering in trigger-happy government sponsored terrorists in uniforms to impose calm on campus. But of course, how can those in power dialogue with students when their corrupt ways are so glaring even for the blind to see?

Even then, despite Ofege's pricelist for passage into different institutions in Cameroon, to be recruited into a professional school, having money is one thing, and knowing who to bribe is another thing altogether. There are numerous cases of students who gave their money to the wrong contact, and never got into the institution, nor were they reimbursed. That those without the money and contacts do not stand a chance of getting into a desired professional institution in their own country is disturbing. It is for this reason that many of Cameroon's very best were trained in Nigeria, foremost, and elsewhere subsequently. This has been the trend for a very long time as many refusing to have their minds warped by a corrupt system simply leave the country. Others, unable to come up with anything better, jump into the mess and either fail to graduate so often that they degenerate into "professional students" or else make it, but with their understanding of what education is all about completely distorted. Not to have succeeded in the University of Yaounde is not a discredit to the student per se, as the stifling and truncating hurdles are just too many. For example, it is only normal for textbooks not to be available and that is the student's responsibility as the almighty professor could not bother. Does the University of Yaounde even have a current bookstore? One cannot help wondering because the last building designated a bookshop was only that nominally, nor was there a library worth its name.

Another major setback for the students is the fact that they are at the mercy of the professors' whim and caprices as there is no system in place to check any excesses on anyone's part. The result is that it is not impossible for an instructor to hold a student back in class for reasons that have nothing to do with academics. Numerous stories exist of students being victimized thus, especially male students, simply for sharing the same carnal palate as a professor. For a professor to use his powers against a male student rival is not to lose with grace. Were our students vandals, then a student could also decide to retaliate by having his friends in town beat up such a professor to an inch of his life. Now how fair would that be? It is equally graceless to use one's powers as a professor against a female student simply because she rejects one's amorous advances. There is hardly anything illegal about one dating one's adult student; after all, many successful marriages have emerged from these relationships. It becomes wrong, however, if the professor is in a position to influence the student's academic performance; for this, and many other reasons, a student, especially male, may not move on with his or her studies. Those that are wise, then, do all not to cross paths with the powers that be. These things do happen on any campus in the world, but the reason some African schools stand out is the degree of reckless abandon with which they occur, and nobody seems to think anything is the matter. In institutions elsewhere, sexual harassment is a punishable act.

This is the character typical of the powers in the realms of higher education in Cameroon. The rancorousness in the system is such that one cannot begin to comprehend. It is especially disturbing to realize that this is in the area of academics, supposedly a territory in which the minds that one comes in contact with ought to be minds that know, and so should be virtually free of belittling vices, but this is not the case. The goal to some, especially those with insatiable appetites for political offices, is to frustrate—students or colleagues alike. Small wonder then, studying in some African institution can easily be equated to experiencing an academic boot camp: only the best, or those with certain resources, make it, and this is a shame since every citizen deserves a chance to benefit from his or her country and vice versa. These damning circumstances are most unfair when it is realized that virtually everything necessary for a buoyant academic environment is present, or could easily be made present but for political reasons, amongst which is the lack of goodwill. Accordingly, like a voice in the wilderness, one can only urge these professors to give these deserving students their degrees so they can go out and fend for themselves even beyond Cameroon and Africa, instead of transforming them into prisoners within college walls for whimsical reasons.

Africans taking flight is no longer news. Their flight is a survival technique and not because they do not love their native shores—flee or die.

Others have come up with a system whereby they go out into the world for a whiff of fresh air and sanity before returning to the nightmare into which most African countries have degenerated. Overall, the result today is brain drain, as some of the best have left and are serving other countries while their native countries are languishing in the hands of unpatriotic kleptocrats. Those who have stayed are no longer at their best, as they are only struggling to survive under conditions that could never let them function as they are capable of, or ought to function. And so, undeservedly, Africa continues retreating further into the laughing stock of today's world simply because some citizens want to treat others the way they were treated when colonialists were in control. Why is one not surprised that anybody can stand and say any nonsense or damning thing about Africa and there are no outcries from Africans themselves or anyone else? There are two reasons for this: firstly, African leaders have no pride as, even with all their resources, they have succeeded in painting portraits of themselves and their nations in the tradition of little Oliver Twist. Secondly, many people outside of Africa do not know that much about the continent, and so, already influenced by mythologized deprecating depictions of the continent all through Western history classes, media reports, and stereotyping movies, Westerners in particular think that most of the sloth, even lies and de-contextualized facts they are served about Africa, is true. This has continued because African scholars, after encountering these usually fictionalized and often misleading presentations of the continent, just do not react, or else their reactions are not given the publicity given garbage written about Africa. How sad!

Health

Another area that shows how a people with resources end up exploited and deprived by their own government primarily, is health. Like everything else in Africa, the health facilities have continued to shrink such that today one cannot even tell if anyone cares any longer about the system—its perpetrators and the victims, government officials and the public. One cannot help wondering then why all in Africa must keep rotting away in spite of the quality manpower and all else that the continent has to offer in every area of society, if not because of a system of government, borrowed from imperialists, that alienates instead of uniting the citizens. But then it dawns on one again, that this decay in the area of health is the case because the corrupt leaders can afford to fly to foreign nations for medical check-ups while the wretched of their nations are left to make do with sub-standard medical care. Why must a president, his clients, and members of their families leave their country for medical consultation overseas instead of investing wisely by building and equipping hospitals that would benefit their nations? The answer is simple: most African leaders are not patriots and are unfortunately equipped with a weird sense of self-importance that only has meaning when they see others around them without the facilities they enjoy, albeit criminally in most cases. Of course, but for greed, it would be easy for the World Health Organization and other international institutions making so much ado about helping poor African countries to start by making it impossible for African leaders to get medical treatment anywhere else but in their own countries. If this were the case, then Paul Biya of Cameroon, for example, would have thought of building a hospital in Nsimalene, even if only for his tribe's men and women, instead of an ultramodern airport that has degenerated into liability for Cameroonians. How many Cameroonians fly overseas that we need Nsimalene in addition to an underutilized and now virtually abandoned Douala airport? Chances are the president was planning for the year 2070? But let us go back to health facilities and the conditions at home.

Our doctors, to begin with, are no different from other civil servants. It must be pointed out that these doctors—like other experts—have spent time and money training to become who they are, men and women who understand best the human body and its functions. This is no small task, and for this they must be respected. And so it is, for to say the least, doctors are highly respected in Africa. But then, when one looks at how some doctors are behaving today, one cannot help questioning what their intentions were when they decided medicine was the profession for them. One would think that the will to help suffering people should have been the driving force behind the ability to survive those gruesome years towards becoming a medical doctor. And there is nothing wrong with hoping to be rich, but if this is the only reason, then one begins seeing why some of our doctors seem to be in the wrong profession.

Most of our doctors in the past worked for the government, and they were well paid for their services, which were good and earned them genuine respect from the public. Today the story is different. Even before blaming the doctors, the government, their main employer, is to blame. Doctors in Cameroon, just like the rest of their compatriots with higher degrees who work for the government, earn miserable salaries. Consider a doctor earning about a third of what a high school dropout makes just because the latter is a uniformed officer who, supposedly, is responsible for national security—the safety of the dictator in power.

In the midst of such misplaced priorities, these disillusioned doctors have come up with ways to help themselves also. After all, like the overpaid civil servants in uniforms, these doctors also have families for whom to cater. It is no longer surprising then, to realize that almost every medical doctor in Cameroon nowadays, with or without the experience, is gunning for private practice. Most are still on government payroll, but only show up to cater for patients at the government hospitals where they should be working fulltime, as if they are part-time workers. They then hurry back to their private clinics where they attend with more care to their private patients for higher fees. Patients who can afford this do not complain, but the vast majority who cannot afford it have no choice but to wait *ad infinitum* at the government hospitals for these doctors to show up whenever they feel like showing up. Those doctors without private clinics have established a system whereby at their place of work, where they are employed by the government, they charge their patients an unofficial fee in order to attend to them. This is certainly unfair, given they are being paid by the government, even if they are being underpaid. But one thing Cameroon under Mr. Biya has done is kill the consciences of the citizens, and so everything goes, until interrupted by someone in authority whose interest is not in setting things right, but in earning a bribe for himself after which bribe the practice can proceed until another bribe-seeking official with the necessary powers puts himself in its path.

Another painful practice in the health terrain in Cameroon is the lack of respect most of the doctors show their patients, and this has nothing to do with their poor salaries from the government, because as already established, they have found a way to make up for the slack in their salaries. It is, in plain terms, a certain haughtiness often associated with parvenus who, finding themselves in a position in society where they never dreamt of being, suddenly become arrogant and condescending in disposition. A doctor can be as late as two hours but never considers apologizing to his patients for keeping them waiting. In fact, the patients are expected to be glad that he even showed up after all, as he/she walks past with a god-like mien. Alternatively, consider a doctor being in his office and hearing that there is someone outside trying to meet with him, yet he does not care, and this is not because he is attending to any patients, but just because he is a doctor, a "big man". A mutual friend was once kept waiting by a doctor and former schoolmate outside the doctor's small office in a government hospital until, fed up, the friend walked away disillusioned. It remains a mystery what the doctor thought the friend had come to do, probably beg for a free consultation, or else it was just his way of making his former school mate feel and come to terms with the fact that he is now a medical doctor and since the friend is not, then he is nothing, or at best his footstool.

The impression one gets then is that these doctors do not like, nor do they feel committed to their patients, since the patients are mostly poor uneducated folks, or else they plainly have a superiority complex they are trying to rub off on others by spiting them. How painful it is to watch some of these doctors attend to their patients. Some would treat a patient as if he is so beneath them that they need not bother touching the patient. Their attitude is one of "I am condescending to do you a favour". In short, doctors who are supposed to be nice, approachable, considerate, and full of affection and explanations about their effort at attempting to diagnose and heal, distance themselves from their patients by their haughty attitude. In like manner, they do not make the slightest effort to explain anything to the patients about their condition. This leads to what I call the arbitrary administration of medication to patients. Our patients are just given medications and not expected to say anything, let alone ask questions about their medications. Yet the ideal situation is such that medical personnel should educate their patients on the drugs and overall treatment they are administering to them. They should talk to their patients about the healing process: what the drugs are, and how the drugs would affect them. In this case, patients know what to expect and are not taken by surprise by a drug's side effects and the like. In practice, however, the furthest the vast majority of medical staff go is rush over the dosage and hardly anything else. An inquisitive patient is considered disrespectful, pugnacious, and a show-off who is trying to challenge the medical official; yet, this is not the case. Without this education, how does a patient know when there are unexpected and consequently potentially dangerous side effects so as to rush back to the hospital and so on?

Another perspective is equally revealing of this poor medical staff and patient relationship. When doctors are to go on rounds, for example, how puzzling it is to see nurses rushing relatives from the side of their loved ones as if a dangerous criminal is approaching, instead of the doctor who is trying to heal the patient. What is so private to a husband about his wife's illness such that even though they are in a private room the husband still has to leave before the doctor can look at her chart? One is not talking about any complex procedure here other than looking at the patient's record and monitoring her progress. The very best doctors in terms of attitude manage to ask the patient how she is feeling today and that is it. Some just walk in, grab the patient's chart, look at it, scribble on it and walk away without as much as noticing the patient. And then they leave instructions with the nurses and move on to the next patient as if this is some doctor-nurse affair while the patient is left completely at a loss as to her condition. In awe, the patient dares to ask the nurse later about what the "almighty" doctor has said regarding her illness. In most cases, the nurse's explanation leaves the patient in no better position, and so one meets a patient who can hardly tell what is wrong with her. Again, it must be remembered that these patients are very respectful and equally submissive—good patients, in other words. It is probably because of how poor they are that some of their own sons and daughters who have managed to become doctors treat them like scum; yes, because, as unfortunate as it is, doctors' attitudes towards the rich on the one hand, and the poor on the other hand have been observed and marked differences noted.

Doctors must see Christ in every patient, and if they have nothing to do with God, then they must be human and at least see themselves in these patients, and they would treat them a lot better: with care, concern, respect, and the dignity that they deserve simply because they are human. Padre Pio, (now St. Pio), one of the greatest souls of all times, a "poor" Capuchin friar who died in 1968, had so much love for the poor, sick, and suffering that he ended up building a hospital, thanks to donations from his spiritual children from all over the world, since he did not own even a franc. He called the hospital *Casa Sollevo della Sofferenza* (Home for the Relief of those in Suffering), and this is what he told the doctors upon its inauguration:

> You have the mission of curing the sick, but if you do not take love to the beds of the sick, I believe that medicine is of little use. I have experience of this when my doctor treating me gave me a word of comfort above all else. Love can't work without words that raise the sick spiritually; it is worth more than any other cure.

May our doctors be humble and learn from such words. May they realize that theirs is a noble and sacred job, as they are out there to serve the suffering lot of mankind who may appear worthless in the eyes of man because they are poor, but who are, no doubt about it, God's dear and invaluable children. How sweet it is, when one knows that one has been able to bring joy into another's heart? Let it not all be about money; let there be genuine love and the understanding that it could easily be the doctor in the patient's position, but for the grace of God.

Our nurses are hardly any better. Most seem upon graduation to forget the ethics of their profession. It may sound unfair here, as there are angelic doctors and nurses out there in Cameroon, but not so with the majority at all. In 1988, for example, a couple rushed a choking child to the Bamenda Provincial hospital only for the husband to end up resuscitating their son himself, while a male nurse in the outpatient office did not as much as budge as the husband struggled with his son in his hands while his teary-eyed wife looked on helplessly. The nurse was, in a most unconcerned manner, asking them stupid questions that had little, if not nothing, to do with their child's dangerous condition at the time. If this nurse had been busy on the child while asking those questions as a way of knowing what kind of medical approach to take, it would have been different, but the young man sat in his chair looking at the traumatized couple as if nothing was amiss, even as their child continued gasping from time to time. The couple left for their house without this so-called nurse as much as touching the patient they had brought in, the husband's own private and limited experience with cardio-pulmonary resuscitation having paid off.

At the delivery room, where things ought to be different, at least for the sake of the new life being brought into the world, one encounters a calibre of nurses who carry the uncaring attitude to extreme. This is where women's lives are on the line because of the ever-frequent delivery complications typical of these environments. One would expect that the nurses would be doing all to help the women in labour pangs, but it is not uncommon to hear a midwife insulting or teasing a woman in labour about sex. Even if this is done in jest, as some may argue, such a joke is out of place and certainly tasteless at that particular moment to anyone with common sense. Strictly speaking, such behaviour is criminal, and ought not to be allowed. And then interestingly, unlike in other cultures, the husband is locked outside of the labour room as the wife struggles in there alone in the midst of virtually hostile strangers. Anyone can by now guess the reason why cleaning staff and night-watch men are permitted to parade the labour room but not the husbands of the women having babies. With successful delivery still almost a chance affair instead of the norm, one would expect an understanding medical team to be around; instead, the pangs of labour and delivery are made worse by the disgusting attitude of some of the medical staff.

Again, there is the need to emphasize that although this is the picture of the majority, not all nurses are like this. There are some wonderful men and women who have served, and are still serving in the same Bamenda Provincial Hospital who treat people with so much care it is hard for them to go unnoticed – consider Messrs Peter Nkeng, Thaddeus Tanwanyi, Samuel Takeh, and Alhaji Oumarou Sariki, to name a few. These are exemplary nurses who make one feel like one is human and has value as they attend to one; the smiles on their faces, the respect, and the genuine concern they resonate make one feel already safe and surely on the way to recovering. To these examples and their likes, may God bless them and reward them in like manner, and may they serve as a source of inspiration and role models to some of their rather lukewarm and nonchalant colleagues.

Are our doctors and nurses qualified? They are very much so. What then is the problem, one cannot help asking? Their working conditions are horrible, yet this is no excuse for the attitude these professionals display at all times. Consider the fact that medical personnel, because hospitals are not well equipped with tools and medications, now bring their own medications into the wards and sell them to patients at exorbitant prices—how unethical! Ethics, however, is not a word in the administrative vocabulary of Cameroon under Mr. Biya. Else, how is it that even dosage instructions on medications in Cameroon are more often in French? How is an Anglophone doctor to understand the workings of such medications, their probable complications, generic names, and the rest? This is quite a challenge even if the Anglophone doctor has some working knowledge of French. But of course, the Anglophones are of little or no consequence and so they better learn French or die of drug overdose because of the machinations of an unpatriotic regime. Consider an all-English country like the United States of America and see how a citizen's rights are respected, and at once Cameroon's abuse of her citizens, especially those of Anglophone origin, comes across as truly monstrous.

In the United States, the government respects almost every language that has a reasonable following, even though this is an English-speaking nation. How heart-warming it is that even in small institutions like hospitals, the authorities respect a language like Somali, among many others. An immigrant from Somalia or a citizen in the US who cannot speak English is not lost. Hospitals have translators for them, and even their documents in the hospital are written in all the languages used within the community, even if, as it is, these languages are not official languages—Somali, Hmong, Chinese, and Spanish to name a few. Indeed, one had never heard some of these languages before, but the authorities do all to ensure that these people can navigate their way as soon as they get into the United States. Is anyone surprised then that Americans are so proud of their country, all else notwithstanding? Yes, their government makes them proud to be citizens. Yet in Cameroon, a most significant part of the population, being English speaking, is treated as if it is begging to belong to the nation. Within so-called government buildings and facilities, for example, these citizens are forced to speak a language they do not understand. This is plain madness and outright stupidity under any circumstances. Accordingly, one cannot help wondering what it is that makes a people think they can impose their own ways on others. Mr. Biya's government and subsequent Francophone governments in Cameroon must simply stop being stupid and criminal by acknowledging the existing problem as the beginning of a true effort towards working for peace by giving the Anglophones the respect and place they rightly deserve in Cameroon. Playing ostrich as is characteristic of Yaounde governments, is simply courting trouble, and it is only a matter of time before that infested tumour of a nation ruptures. Piet Konings and Francis B. Nyamnjoh sound an equally warning note:

> It would be a grave error ... to assume that Biya has defeated the Anglophone movements and thus solved the Anglophone problem. His persistent refusal to enter into any negotiations and his divisive and repressive tactics run the risk instead of further radicalizing the Anglophone movements and community. The adoption of armed struggle by the SCYL, the recent proclamation of Southern Cameroons independence by Justice Fred Ebong, and the resurgence of heated discussions of the Anglophone problems on the Internet, furnish a clear proof of such possibility. ("Biya and the Anglophone Problem" 226)

Jing Thomas Ayeah is even more militant in sounding the same warning in his paper on the Bamilekes in Cameroon when he posits:

The writing on the wall could not be any clearer. Rather than blame the Anglophones for checking out, the Bamilekes should spend more time oiling their guns and preparing for trouble. Dark clouds are up, lightning is flashing and thunder rumbling and come what may there is going to be rain. Pius Njawe is already calling on the troops to enter the laager. To southern Cameroonians, the appeal is belated.

The adverse working conditions along with the marginalisation of Anglophones which all lead to brain drain amounts to the exploitation of a people by their inept leadership. So, after all the years in schools, African experts end up not helping their own countries as they must look elsewhere for conditions congruent with what they have been trained to do. Whatever the case, their horrible salaries notwithstanding, doctors and nurses must give their best to their patients, as through that they will find some comfort and that fulfilment, at least, which money cannot purchase. Whatever the case, ways must be derived and used to twist the employer's hand such that better working conditions are provided. In their writings on Cameroon, Krieger and Takougang, Piet Konings, Francis Nyamnjoh, and others have covered so much about rebellious groups given birth to by the recalcitrance of the Biya regime towards the plight of the people such that one would too obviously be duplicating effort trying to cover this aspect of the political buffoonery in Cameroon masquerading as governance. It is probably true there is no nurses' or doctors' union in Cameroon, hence the government's ability to toy with such invaluable employees of theirs while so-called "guardians of the peace", uniformed men and women who spend their time doing nothing but harassing citizens all over the country while drinking themselves into retirement, are earning fabulous salaries for their mostly unskilled labour. What a sense of priority!

Utilities

Before the political manoeuvre which brought West and East Cameroon together as The United Republic of Cameroon in 1972, English-speaking Cameroonians had no problems whatsoever with their utilities. The problems came in with the companies that took over from those that were serving the people before reunification, and conditions have only worsened.

i) Water and Electricity:

Before reunification, whereas local councils and community efforts supplied water to the people, Powercam, the electricity corporation, supplied electricity in West Cameroon and at an incredibly cheap rate; even though somebody might try to make the argument that the Franc CFA was stronger then, than now— a lame argument in my opinion. Water was free, and was supplied through public taps to which there was a twenty-four hour access every day. With electricity, families' monthly bills ranged from about two hundred francs to a thousand and slightly over for homes that consumed heavily. Today, the French-backed government, citing waste, has with tact eliminated public taps, and so people are forced to pay expensive water bills for private consumption. In the case of electricity, the story is worse; the basic household consumption is about a third to half the family's monthly budget. From two hundred to about a thousand francs for monthly bills in the West Cameroon days, electricity today is costing the average Cameroonian from about ten thousand to hundreds of thousands a month. Whatever the case, only a failed economy or an irresponsible government swindling from its citizenry could have brought about such huge changes in prices for whatever commodity.

Water is today supplied by a corporation known as Société National des Eau du Cameroun (SNEC) and electricity by La Société National d'Electricité du Cameroun (SONEL).[4] Both are commonly known by their French acronyms SNEC and SONEL. In a nutshell, their services are plain bad, and their customer-relation a nightmare. To these corporations, the public is desperate to have their services since one is likely to think from their poor public relations that they are serving the public for free instead of the inflated fees and bills they heap on the masses.

First, just getting water and electricity connected to peoples' homes is a huge task, as one has to stand in line for hours sometimes, or else beg and bribe to get SNEC and SONEL technicians to get off their lazy and corrupt butts and go do the work for which they are being paid. One is lucky should one have a friend working for these corporations who will then, as a favour, expedite the services to be rendered. This confusion lies in the fact that the technicians look at their work as if they are doing the clients a favour instead of rendering services that bring in money to the cooporation, from which money they are paid their salaries. This kind of nonsense can go on because nobody cares, as everyone is only struggling to show to people that he is the "big man" around, while the company, like the country itself, is slowly dying because of mismanagement. The only reason companies like SNEC and SONEL are surviving is because of their undeserved monopoly as sole suppliers of water and electricity in Cameroon. If there were competition, SNEC and SONEL, but more so SONEL, would not last a week because of the company's bad services.

First of all, like everything else in Cameroon, these companies toy around with the prices of water and power as they deem necessary, without thinking they owe any explanation for the frequent and usually uncalled-for increases in the cost of the poor and unstable services they provide. In fact, in keeping with their bad services, it is true to state that one is usually surprised, in the case of SONEL, to try a switch and find that indeed there is power. Power outages are now routine, and nobody seems to care about the destructive effects this has on businesses and private property, as every now and then people throw away millions worth of produce and supplies that went bad because power went out on them causing their freezers to thaw with all the contents subsequently going bad. What arrogance on the part of the company, or precisely its public relations department; after all, what can the poor "ignorant" people without a government structure to support them do, mindful of the fact that they have become slaves to these commodities?

That which is incomprehensible is how expensive water and electricity are in Cameroon, yet walk past the home of the provincial delegates of SNEC and SONEL, or any of their workers for that matter, and see how water and power are being abused. Water flows freely in their homes and they can even use it to water crops in their gardens and wash their cars without thinking of the bills they will get, because they do not get any bills. In the case of electricity, very large bulbs with heavy wattages are an established marker of homes occupied by those working for the electricity corporation. If water and power can be cheap to SNEC and SONEL staff, why not to the Cameroonian population as a whole? Are the rest of the people being punished for not being able to work for these corrupt and mismanaged corporations?

In Cameroon, more than anywhere else, the concept of fringe benefits has illegally established itself as policy. Because one works with such a corporation, one is automatically entitled to the services provided by that corporation for free or next to nothing while the other citizen trying to use the same corporation's services pays through the nose. What kind of logic is this? Why should SNEC and SONEL staff pay next to nothing for water and electricity whereas another Cameroonian cannot even afford portable water, nor can he light up a single room in his house, talk not of using an electric iron because of the insane cost of power? How is it that the citizens of the same nation are being served differently thus? This is frustration at its zenith. The end result is that Cameroonians now resort to stealing electricity from the corporation by illegally tapping current from the main lines and by-passing the meter, or else they get an electrician to reset their meters such that they no longer turn at the official speed. It is this or they go without electricity simply because the system fails to take into consideration what the citizens are earning and the different bills they heap on them.

Interestingly, this illegal service of stealing electricity is rendered to the public clandestinely by SONEL staff themselves for a tip, and then later on, when in need of more money, they betray their private client who is then pounced upon by other SONEL technicians who are accomplices of the culprit technician. They unofficially threaten the offender, disconnect his lights completely, and then charge him exorbitantly. Those who can afford it pay right away and are issued fictitious receipts, and then the marauding SONEL technicians go away with the money, which they do not even put to good use. Offenders who cannot afford the fictitious bill find that their case is reported to the SONEL office by the technicians, and they are officially billed for some imaginary consumption to the tune of their one-year salary or more. They are made to go without power until they pay the bill. SONEL's management fails to understand that if their rates are reasonable, then the citizens will all be able to afford their bills and will not go about stealing power and thereby cheating the corporation of billions. This is corruption extraordinaire, and it takes place in Cameroon because the government of that once beautiful and peace-loving country has no sense of purpose. All the leaders do is get dressed up in foreign suits like caricatures, and smile stupidly at cameras as they idle around wasting Cameroonian resources. For anyone who was around when Ahidjo was president, we all know this could not have happened during *Grand Camarade's* tenure.[5]

In the case of water, it is a lot more difficult to steal water, but every once in a while, the people seize the opportunity to fill up their containers when they are lucky and a pipe breaks somewhere for whatever reason. Again, to show how malicious these corporations are, they do everything to force the citizens to get water from them and nowhere else. A good example of this exploitation of the masses comes to light in the ocean town of Limbe. Anyone who grew up in Limbe in the sixties and early seventies knows *Tim-Tim*. *Tim-Tim* was a source of pure water, a man-made fountain pumping clean water from underground directly under the then senior district officer's house, next to the Limbe River from the Centenary Stadium side of the botanical gardens. Here everyone quenched his or her thirst after strolling in the gardens and giving oneself up to the varied fruits that adorned the orchards in those days. But for fear that citizens will not get their water from SNEC because of its expensive rates, SNEC technicians, incredibly, disconnected this landmark in the town of Limbe.

Overseas, *Tim-Tim*, which got its onomatopoeic name from the sound produced by the pump as it pumped fresh water from underground, would have been a tourist attraction, but not so in Cameroon. Today, *Tim-Tim* is a vague memory, missed only by those old enough to have seen and used it, while to the young the term means nothing. This is corruption, exploitation, abuse of power, and the consequences it has on a people and their environment. And the people of Limbe stood by and watched as *Tim-Tim* was being disconnected! When are Cameroonians going to realize that the government ought not to do things the public does not approve of, or better still, that the government is supposed to work with the people and not just heap ridiculous decisions on citizens they are supposed to be serving? In other words, that citizens have the right to say "no" to a government that is about to misuse its powers? How could a landmark like *Tim-Tim* be disconnected? Who was mayor of Limbe when this slur was being smeared on the faces of the people of Limbe?

SNEC and SONEL, like most organizations in Cameroon, are so disorganized that even their method of collecting payments amounts to an insult to their customers. Because of the very unreliable postal system in Cameroon, the electricity and water corporations have employees who go around on bikes distributing people's monthly bills, but they cannot come up with an effective means of collecting the payment. The result is that with people's busy schedules, they show up to pay their bills at the very last moment, and this leads to queues that are sometimes about half a mile long. This happens because of the lack of creativity on the part of senior SONEL and SNEC officials, coupled with the fact that those who should take the initiative and innovate are never present in their offices when needed since an office belongs not to the corporation, but to the individual who has been appointed to that position by some godparent. Accordingly, when that individual is not around every administrative process grinds to a halt at his level. This happens even with the public service, government offices in other words, as for weeks nothing can go on because one person in an established procedural chain is missing. Thousands of citizens, therefore, must waste their time waiting, day after day, only to leave without being served. In this unfortunate process, their own private affairs also come to a halt or collapse totally because of the length of time they spend away trying to catch an absentee civil servant in vain, and so the entire nation is indirectly brought to her knees. One cannot help questioning what assistants or deputies are for, since in fact they do not only exist but abound in Cameroonian offices. It seems to me the reason for this administrative climate is simple: nobody wants to clash with the incumbent when he returns, because rendering services he was supposed to render implies the substitute took the bribe he was supposed to take, and so where is the money? This seems to me to be the case, else why is a staff person indispensable?

In the case of SNEC and SONEL, realizing that hundreds and hundreds of clients are present and anxious to pay their bills, why is it that other make-shift payment stations cannot be opened within the same office? And why not in different parts of the town, even in banks and the post office for example, with other staff who are usually idling around put to collect the money and at the end of the day straighten out their financial records with the official cashier? In this way, customers are treated humanely as they are not left to cook under the sun as they struggle to pay for SNEC and SONEL's poor services. Alas, month after month, and year in year out, the same nightmarish play by these corporations and their customers is acted out with nobody thinking of how to improve upon their services, even though new delegates come and go surrounded by enviable fringe benefits for which other Cameroonians pay greatly in the form of exaggerated bills.

ii) Post and Telecommunications

In Cameroon, a whole ministry is responsible for these services, and in keeping with the traditions of the public service, Post and Telecommunications (P&T) is a disaster. Like the town-crier of old, this is that ministry charged with keeping Cameroonians informed and in touch with each other and the world at large, but it has failed woefully.

There was once a postal system in Cameroon, but not anymore. In the past, not only was mailing reasonably priced, it was effective and reliable. The cost of a stamp for mailing letters used to be thirty francs and sixty francs for local and international mail respectively. Today, local stamps cost hundreds of francs and international mails, thousands. What a leap in cost. This would have been understandable had the services improved or even remained the same. The truth is things are incredibly chaotic, unpredictable, unreliable, and worse off than ever before.

Nobody will believe that the postal system in Cameroon, unlike before, no longer has a time schedule, as is the case in some parts of the world where it can be guaranteed that within the country a letter will get to its destination in three, four, or five days. It is a blind deal in Cameroon, and so one can never tell whether it is the recipient who has delayed in replying to a mail, or if it is the post office that failed to deliver. One is simply grateful that the mail makes it whenever it does, and it is the customer's business to find out. Of course, this is only a formality as there is nothing a customer can do if his mail fails to arrive, registered or not; not these days.

Consider buying stamps, one of the most basic transactions in any post office. First, there is the semblance of some organization in the post office as one can see labels of services being provided above the different locations – "stamps", "telegrams", "money order", and so on, but it is only a semblance. It is a most ineffective method of division of labour as the stamp person might be swarmed while the telegram person is alone, but she cannot help with stamps because she is supposed to be selling only telegrams. In fact, it is a common sight, even at such busy moments for the stamp person, for example, for one to see other female staff contemptuously applying nail polish instead of figuring out ways to attend to customers, and one dares not try to reason with these workers. Many a time, one has wondered if these sales women at the front desks are recruited based on how rude they can be. Interestingly, these post office workers are hoping to be paid at the end of the month. The postmaster who is supposed to walk around from time to time to see how his or her workers are doing is locked up in some posh office in the back, or upstairs making expensive international phone calls at the expense of the Ministry of Post and Telecommunications.

A post office functioning like this is a nightmare when compared to other post offices in the world. Consider the United States of America (US), and let nobody claim it is unfair to compare Cameroon to the US. After all, the US is equally peopled by human beings and has her own problems too, but those in authority do all to identify these problems, acknowledge their existence, have them addressed, and hopefully resolved. What is so far removed from the normal here that Cameroon cannot emulate? Walking into a U.S. post office, generally speaking, is always a pleasure because one knows that one will get served politely and within a reasonable amount of time, even during peak periods like Christmas and other holidays when millions of gift packages are being shipped to destinations all over the nation and beyond.

Beyond the customer-conscious and friendly dispositions of post office workers in the U.S. for example, the workers' devotion to their work is remarkable. Even though it is a government owned operation, the workers work with a certain dedication that is fascinating, whereas their Cameroon counterparts could not care less which way business is going because the post office is not their private property, yet it is the source of their livelihood; what an unfortunate mentality. Again, besides the fact that one's mail is virtually guaranteed to take about three days from one end of the U.S. to the other—coast to coast—in a country way more territorially extensive than Cameroon, in the case of Cameroon, mailing a letter is like gambling; it might get to its destination, which means one wins; it might not, and so one loses. Remarkable!

In addition to certainty of service in U.S. post offices, they offer incredible options for mailing: there are overnight services which get very urgent mails to their destination anywhere in the U.S. within thirteen to twenty hours, and should this fail to take place then one's money is reimbursed and their service at that juncture is free; there is the opportunity to have one's mail certified, insured against damage or loss, and a lot more for a few dollars more at the most. Are these standards that Cameroon cannot emulate? No, these are standards that Cameroon once had, at least West Cameroon, even if not in every detail. Alas today, in keeping with the idea of government jobs not belonging to anyone in particular and so could be performed lackadaisically, coupled with a tradition that has no system of accountability, post offices in Cameroon have, with time, deteriorated into nonsense.

The recent bane of the postal system in Cameroon is stealing. Mails that look like they might contain money, or are from destinations like the U.S. never make it to the addressee. Very often one mails pictures and even has it written on the envelope that the contents are pictures, even then, they never make it to their destination. The supposedly smart thief-of-a-postal-worker thinks one is trying to outsmart him or her by indicating that the mail contains only pictures. How low some men and women working in postal offices in Cameroon have fallen. This was never the case before as mails always made it to their destinations with the contents intact, even those that had cash in them and were not certified. But this is no longer the case with the postal system in Cameroon today. If it had any records, not to say statistics, it would be obvious today that its business has dropped by at least 60-70%. Who wants to deal with a service provider who is this unreliable? It is a shame to see that people trust public bus drivers in Cameroon more than the government postal system. As a result, people now prefer to drop off their mails and even money at bus stations where they register the mails with the worker on duty, and then pay a certain sum. They then contact those to whom they are sending stuff to advise them to go to the particular travel agency in the city where they are, and to pick up their mail or parcel by the estimated time of the particular bus' arrival in that city. It is that simple and it is working well, but not the government postal system.

In the case of telecommunications, the same scenario is unfolding even though there are slight modifications today with the coming of cell phones. At one time in Cameroon, owning a phone at home was a class symbol that was for the rich only. With time, however, many Cameroonians found themselves at some point in life where they needed these services, even without being that rich. However, because of obsolete technology, and there not being enough lines available for everyone to own a phone, the process of having a phone installed in one's home became one of speculation and discretion. As a result, one waited sometimes for months to hear of openings in one's neighbourhood. And one only got wind of this opening because a P&T worker was bribed to serve as one's eyes and ears in the decision-making offices.

It is common knowledge that such openings should be broadcast in whatever way possible so that those in the affected areas could reactivate their applications, but this is not what happens. Those with the information hoard it, and besides those who bribed them, only inform friends or the rich. It must be realized here that the delegate of P&T may not even be aware of this scam, but this is the exception. The rich client, after being informed of openings, then bribes with large sums of money and his phone is installed. If a worker who has direct rights to install such phones had contacted the client, of course he mentioned the delegate's name as having authorized the installation at the rich man's residence, knowing he will receive some kickback for his delegate which money he keeps for himself; the delegate's name was only used to facilitate his selfish goals. How unfair is this since in the case of an innocent delegate, he is being seen as corrupt by the client, whereas the delegate knows nothing about the fact that his office had been used to coax a reasonable size bribe from a client. The corrupt worker would even ask the customer to oil his own lips too, in addition to what he has already taken, since the bigger parcel was, supposedly, for his boss, the delegate. Out of the scene, he puts both bribes into his pocket, not caring about the damage done to his boss's name. This is the way for many corrupt workers, and they are very happy because of these illegal benefits they are making. In the days of West Cameroon, this could earn the culprit long years of imprisonment, but today this is so commonplace the victims even expect it.

Getting a phone into one's home then was a near impossibility even with a huge bribe serving as bait. Most interesting, however, is the fact that getting the phone installed was not even a guarantee of services as thieves started making away with telephone lines that they used in fabricating trinkets and other jewellery that they sold to make money with which to feed their own families. This is a day when the government has turned otherwise responsible citizens into marauders, since they too must survive even as the "official thieves" in government thrive. In the end, depending on the neighbourhood, people started having phones in their homes that they could not use because the connecting lines had been stolen, yet they still had to pay for the equipment in their keeping. It was like this until the arrival of cell phones. Now, nobody cares about landline phones. Ironically, with cell phones all around, people are now being begged, urged, coaxed, and forced to keep phones they had in the past but without services because of technical problems to which no P&T technician was responding. The organization, having lost most, if not all, of its clients to cell phone companies, has learned a bit about competition and customer management; it is a little too late though, as nobody wants to hear about P&T again because of their bad experiences with this government ministry in the past.

Oil

Another area in which the people of Cameroon remain shamefully exploited by the incumbent government has to do with the country's oil. But for the fact that Cameroonians see those huge tanks and the mesh of pipelines in Ngeme, Limbe, the whole idea of Cameroon being an oil producing nation would have been a fairy tale as there is nothing happening to the people economically or otherwise to show that the country produces oil. When Nigeria, for example, struck oil, a lot happened to tell the Nigerian something was going on: great road networks were constructed, and industrialization boomed, leading to urban exodus as, unfortunately, farmers abandoned farming in search of quick money in the cities.

In the case of Cameroon, nothing has ever happened, not even with President Ahidjo's promises at the onset. The town of Limbe itself, where the refinery is, which should have been transformed into a sophisticated city because of the enormous wealth brought in by the oil, has in actual fact been side-lined as a different road has been constructed linking the refinery directly to Mile Two. The oil tankers do not have to go through the township of Limbe again. As if each trip through the town of Limbe was a rude reminder of how the community was being exploited, the tankers now just leave the Sokolo/Ngeme area where the SONARA oil refinery is and skirt the town of Limbe. They then emerge in Mile 2, and off to Douala without as much as a glance at Limbe. This, in many ways, would have been tolerable had Limbe been given the face-lift it deserves, but otherwise, it is another blow to the face of the people of Limbe in particular, and the entire former Southern Cameroons as a whole. Ephraim N. Ngwafor certainly felt the same when he wrote *May Former Victoria Smile Again*, in which he laments the virtual collapse of the once great town of Limbe. Tata Simon Ngenge's presentation of the exploitation of Cameroonians through the manipulation of SONARA by the nation's presidents is graphic:

It has been impossible for most Cameroonians to know exactly the amount of crude oil exploited in any particular year.... However, from foreign sources conservative estimates in 1984 put yearly oil production at 10, 000, 000 tons and that, when converted into barrels at a price of $8.00 per barrel, amounted to $700,000,000 in income per year. (79)

With so much money, not even Limbe, which generates such wealth, has benefited from oil money. According to Ngenge again:

> With the commencement of the exploitation of crude oil, and later the refining of crude oil in SONARA, Limbe became known as OPEC City. The people thought their dream of prosperity had come true. It was hoped that the one-time weekend jamboree town would be rejuvenated. With the tapping of oil, it was also believed that to a large extent unemployment would be reduced and the exodus of job seekers to the industrial and agro-industrial towns in Francophone Cameroon would end. Unfortunately, the location of SONARA in Victoria neither solved the unemployment problem of the area nor has it generated the subsidiary industries that Ahidjo had promised. (80)

The insult is heightened when it is realized that SONARA village, a unique luxurious setting, is not occupied by sons and daughters of Limbe in the main but by Francophones. At large, therefore, Cameroonians are being exploited through SONARA, but the blow is doubly felt by the people of Limbe in particular, and Anglophone Cameroon as a whole. In fact, for anyone who knew Limbe when Limbe was Victoria alias Va, Limbe, today, is comparatively speaking a sorry sight, the oil notwithstanding. Besides small-scale fishing and the smugglers coming in and out of Nigeria with finished industrial goods and electronics to sell, Limbe, with all its incredible potentials, is as good as dead. This is especially painful when it is remembered that it was in Limbe, which was already a sophisticated town in the seventies, where some adults today saw and used their first self-service machine at Press-Book. In the words of Ephraim N. Ngwafor,

> Victoria's strength rested on the advantages flowing from owning a seaport (sic). My family's home at Bota was less than five hundred metres from this port so that I had the opportunity of watching ships come and go. Like most port cities, the local residents profited tremendously from this advantage. Young men were sure of jobs when ships berthed and indeed, there used to be as many as eight ships berthed awaiting the unloading or the loading of cargo....
> Victoria seemed to have everything, in fact, the residents rarely travelled out of the city; instead, visitors kept flocking in from the neighbouring towns of Buea, Tiko, Muyuka, and even Kumba. But why shouldn't the local residents have stayed in Victoria? With names like John Holt, R & W King, C.C.C., I.C.C. and Printania, to name just a few, making up the shopping centres, the people found out that all their needs were being catered for.
> Victoria's site by itself attracted tourists; think of the beaches.

> The Botanical Gardens in which were bred different sorts of trees from all over the world attracted the attention of those who were passionately in love with natural vegetation. Sufficient care was taken of this resort-pavements, (sic) benches and several other amenities were provided. The constant trimming of the grass also made it an appropriate meeting point for lovers and all those in search of a quiet place for a rest. The officials in the Forestry Department did not end there for they later recommended the opening of a Zoo. This dream soon became a reality....
>
> As more and more tourists came in, there became the need to provide sufficient accommodation. That is how and why Miramare Hotel, Atlantic Beach Hotel and Bay Hotel came into being.... So when the Lebanese tycoon popularly called Potokri opened up two cinema theatres, 'Rio' in New Town and 'Rivoli' in Gardens, the population of Victoria was thus introduced to a new recreational activity. There was total excitement. (7-8)

The enigma then looms large: instead of Limbe getting better, the town is barely alive today, thirty plus years after.

In a country that produces oil, Cameroonians can no longer afford to run their cars because of how expensive fuel is, to the point that Cameroonians, like with much else, depended for years on Nigerian fuel for survival. Even though it was smuggled into Cameroon, Nigerian fuel was still affordable, the additional expenses towards smuggling notwithstanding, when compared to Cameroon's. That in itself defines the level of insanity when it comes to the price of fuel in Cameroon. This thriving smuggling business, which provided employment for many jobless and almost frustrated Cameroonians and Nigerians in the nineties, was most tactlessly brought to an end when a Cameroonian war-hungry military officer was given the onus of putting a stop to the illegal importation of Nigerian fuel. It was claimed that he used every means possible to achieve this goal, even to the point of tossing grenades at smugglers in the open sea, instead of dealing with the economic forces of demand and supply within the nation and the supply of Cameroonian fuel.

The situation with fuel in Cameroon today is especially frustrating to Cameroonians in the sense that although they know their nation is an oil producing nation, the citizens do not know what is happening to their oil money. Cameroonians are never given any report as to how anything in the country is [mis]managed, more so with the country's oil money. In his annoyance with the status quo in Cameroon, Tim Harford observes in his derisive article on Cameroon:

> It's all too tempting for the visitor on Cameroon to shrug his shoulders and explain the country's poverty by presuming that Cameroonians are idiots. Cameroonians are no smarter or dumber than the rest of us. Seemingly stupid mistakes are so ubiquitous in Cameroon that incompetence cannot be the whole explanation. There is something more systematic at work.

The truth is that there is nothing systematic at work other than irresponsible leadership breeding chaos. Cameroon is today synonymous with chaos as kleptocracy and the lack of patriotic sentiments have caused corruption to run amok. Disorder is the system in Cameroon under Paul Biya. His is a regime that has taken the nation backwards, but to no era the country has ever witnessed before. Mr. Biya's regime has transformed a once leading African nation into Gehenna, and only an extraordinarily peace-loving people like Cameroonians can take all the garbage they have taken from this regime and still be able to smile and forge on with their private efforts and their determination to survive without going to war. With the cost on human life and property, one cannot help wondering if war is really worth it, yet Biya continues eschewing dialogue while even insulting the peoples' intelligence, thereby leaving the people with very limited choices at constructive efforts towards the rebuilding of Cameroon. How long this will last is best left in the hands of the jokers passing for leaders in Cameroon today as they are mostly self-interested ideologues and bootlickers at best. And so, until every Cameroonian, and not just some provinces, sees it as his or her responsibility to stand up against a corrupt and unpatriotic regime, the status quo will thrive albeit to the detriment of the nation as a whole.

Banks

During colonialism, the colonialists used the banks to siphon money from the colonies to their countries; the situation today has not changed, but this time, it is the corrupt African leaders themselves carting away their nations' wealth and storing it in foreign vaults. Under the Biya regime, until the emergence of privately owned banks, Cameroon's banking sector was a charade. The last real bank was the Cameroon Bank that was suddenly bled to death after the Federal Republic became a United Republic. After Cameroon Bank, one has seen so many banks, even those managed by the French, some initially promising, come and go as Cameroon's once booming banking sector and the nation's economy plummeted to where it is today. The result is that in desperation Cameroonians have formed cooperative unions and other financial institutions like *njangi* houses (tontines) that are managed without government's fraudulent input.[6]

Like with everything Cameroonian, even private organizations like banks fail to train their workers to understand the importance of the customer. Of course, the customers' money makes it possible for the banks to exist and raise their own money from which they pay their workers and carry out other ventures. Yet, an outsider, from the U.S., for example, will be baffled by the goings on in a Cameroonian bank. This is because in U.S. banks, ordinarily, the longest time anyone with basic financial transactions such as withdrawals and deposits spends waiting is around five minutes. Those with transactions that are more complex have somebody attending to them within five minutes of their arrival or else they are made to understand that somebody will be with them very soon. This sounds incredible to one unaccustomed to such business-oriented mentality and strategies, yet this is true. Therefore, as soon as there are several people waiting for a teller, new windows are immediately opened and the customers are served. For this reason, U.S. banks are usually almost without clients hanging around waiting, but not so in Cameroon where even business ventures like banks do not seem to understand the value of time.

In Cameroon, banks amount to something else as one is likely to mistake them for a refugee registration office given the number of desperate-looking people waiting in long lines. Whether one is bringing in money or taking out money, it is of little or no consequence, except during pay periods when those bringing in hard cash are given some value since their money will be used to pay off workers. It must be remembered that people in Cameroon want their salaries in cash. This is the case because workers have lost confidence in both the government and the banking system. After all, how credible can these banks be when they open and shut down almost as quickly as day turns into night and night into day, without some customers ever getting back what they had deposited in them. As a result, people prefer taking out their money as soon as their salaries get to the banks, resulting in shortages during pay periods especially. The result is overcrowding which at once accords bank officials a false sense of temporary importance, which they do all to rub in.

During peak periods, which are pay periods also, the banks are crowded with people anxious to get their money. For this reason, some people get to the banks sometimes hours before they open their doors. When ultimately the doors are opened, the workers are so lackadaisical about their work one would think they are waiting to be trained on how to serve the customers crowding the banks. Before long, angers flare up as people see their time being wasted for no reason, and so they begin thinking of ways to be served before others even if they came in after them. That is the service referred to by Cameroonians as "man-know-man". This is when services are no longer delivered on the basis of first come, first served, but on who knows whom; the long queues notwithstanding. A client who comes in late but knows a teller walks straight up past all those in the queue to talk to the teller who shamelessly accepts his checks and pays him off by the side as if the transaction has nothing to do with the bank, and so those in line ought not to complain. Instead of those in line setting the bank ablaze because of such services, they remain in line lamenting the fact that they do not have their own contacts in the bank. The outcome is the emergence of corrupt practices as desperate clients resort to doing whatever it takes to get their salaries before bank workers intone their notorious refrain: "there is no more cash, so we can't pay until more money comes in". Indeed, mismanagement breeds chaos and subsequently corruption; Cameroonian banks offer adequate proof of this.

With the scene thus set, corrupt tellers begin taking advantage of customers. Bank tellers team up with accomplices outside, who collect pay vouchers from people willing to offer them a percentage of their salary. In an effort not to return empty-handed to a wife who is expecting some food money, desperate husbands fall prey. They promise a percentage of their salaries to the tellers' associates, who then go into the bank with their pay vouchers. When the teller sees his contact, he closes his window, even with hundreds of genuine customers waiting in line, and goes to a nearby meeting spot in another room within the bank where he collects the pay vouchers from his contact. He then calmly returns to his place of work, effects the transactions on these pay vouchers, and then again leaves his window without any explanations or apologies to the customers waiting in line. The corrupt teller goes back and hands over the payment to his contact who then leaves for an agreed upon spot out of the bank where he meets with those workers who gave him their pay vouchers. The contact then subtracts what the impatient workers had promised to pay him before giving them the rest of their money. At the end of the day, the corrupt bank teller meets with his contact and they split the proceeds from their dishonest transactions. Meanwhile, by the end of the day, many bank customers who had been in line for over six hours leave the bank without their salaries because the bank ran out of money, even though others were still being paid clandestinely.

Besides these dirty transactions in banks, the bank workers' attitudes towards their customers, to say the least, ought not to be tolerated because of how insulting and condescending they are. How this can go on in a bank remains a puzzle. The workers in most banks in Cameroon see the customer as a nuisance, someone coming in to beg for money, instead of someone coming in to get his or her money that the bank is benefiting from through investments. They forget that but for the client they would be jobless, or at the very least, without salaries. And so they go about with disdainful sneers and smiles, while pretending to be so busy, doing what nobody knows. Thus, slowly but steadily, they send away customers, and before long they find themselves in the unemployment market wondering how their once powerful bank managed to crash. But if the bank manages to stay afloat by scaling down jobs, then those that lose their jobs find someone in the bank to blame for their being redundant. In the extreme, they go out to look for some vicious means—juju—to teach this imaginary enemy a lesson; and so colleagues die or become permanently sick for no obvious reason since even the hospitals cannot diagnose what is happening to them. In this way, the tragic system in Cameroon is perpetrated, leading to outright chaos and in some cases the death of hardworking citizens from whose services the nation should have benefited.

Sanitation, Transportation, and Attendant Woes

As a child growing up during the Southern Cameroons and later West Cameroon days, the then Native Authority Councils (NA) had sanitation workers whom our parents simply called "Sanintri". Their job, like in most Western countries today, was to go around and inspect homes and their surroundings to ensure they met local council standards. But those were the good old days; the story today is different. Nobody knows what happened to those sanitation workers, and we have seen the effects of their demise on our surroundings.

The streets in Cameroon, generally speaking, are dirty, except in a few cities like Bamenda where Mr. Tadzong Abel Ndeh is doing all to keep the environment clean. Thanks to this man's effort, strategic streets in Bamenda, especially the Commercial Avenue, are swept frequently. Ironically, Mr. Tadzong Abel Ndeh is public enemy number one for trying to keep Bamenda streets clean and organized given the chaotic behaviour of landlords who build like drunkards with houses facing any direction, along with taxi drivers and car owners who park and take off anywhere and in any manner regardless of the safety of other road users. The mentality of the people is that the owner of a car is more important than the pedestrian. Consequently, the idea of priority to pedestrians is nonsense as drivers disregard those on foot, treating them like dirt virtually. It is no wonder even children walking to school are killed every now and then within the township and hardly anything is done by those in authority. In a sane society, the mayor, governor, security officers and the rest would have held a meeting after the first couple of children were killed by reckless drivers, to figure out how to prevent this from happening again. This has never happened in Cameroon; those in authority think it is normal that people must die from time to time in accidents caused by careless and drunk drivers. And so, without having left Cameroon and seen order in other societies, it is hard to see what Mr. Tadzong is trying to do in his native city of Bamenda, albeit being a CPDM member. As a result, instead of this man being praised and honoured for his good work in Bamenda, he is hated for no other reason than that he belongs to the unpopular ruling CPDM party. Bamenda people, please, good players must be recognized even if their teams are unpopular. This is just one more disadvantage of multiparty politics in a tradition that does not understand its workings since belonging to another party in these cultures marks one out as an enemy outright, a sell-out, instead of a person making choices between the mission policies of different political parties. Even on the part of the regime pretending to be instituting democracy, there is hostility towards those supporting the opposition. People are known to have gone without their salaries, lost their duty posts, or simply forced into retirement for belonging to the opposition. What hypocrisy! The result has been Bamenda destroying itself as the people continue burning down their own indigene's investments as a way of showing their frustrating towards the Biya regime. Ultimately, one is forced to question, how, for example, has the burning down of the Bamenda Resort Hotel (BRH) that belonged to Mr. Ncho, a touristic landmark for the North West Province, benefitted anyone?

The public must not mistake the point here. It is not the message here that people should not strike against an unpopular and illegitimate regime, far from that. The point is that it is senseless to rip out one's eyes in an effort to show one's reckless and loveless guardians that one is unhappy with them. The reason is simple: now blinded, it is the disappointed dependent who goes on suffering. Same with Bamenda's situation: we destroyed BRH to make a point to a government that cares less about us; who is the loser? Bamenda, of course! Today, Bamenda is without her darling hotel, yet the Biya regime is there perpetrating one atrocity after another. If need be, striking citizens should target the government and not individuals even if they belong to the unpopular ruling party; it is simply their right to belong to any party of choice. Why should individuals be doing all to make Bamenda grow, having been abandoned by the government, only for Bamenda people to turn around again and destroy major investments in their city as a way of showing a useless regime that they are angry and unsatisfied? Left to the Biya regime, Bamenda could as well seize to exist, so how does destroying a Bamenda man's hotel or another Bamenda man's hospital or school send a message to Biya? Please! March and clash with the moronic instruments of coercion that he uses, if need be, but leave our private investments alone as we struggle to make a sophisticated city out of one that has been denied virtually every government support.

Overall, the sanitation situation in Cameroon is tragic in the sense that the dirt is not by accident or from mere littering; in fact, people intentionally empty their trash in some unfortunate corner of the street, and woe to one if the accursed location happens to be in front of one's house. Here, not only the government is to blame, but also the people. In the past, people had traditional ways of disposing of garbage by dumping it in pits dug in the distance behind their homes. Unfortunately, the use of compost is no longer en vogue, and so because of the nonchalance of the government the streets are now preferred. The least people could have done, when so-called modern councils failed in their trash disposing duties, is revert to the old ways, but no, they preferred the streets and this is what is going on now, even within the capital city, Yaounde. Mountains of refuse decorate main streets in the major cities of Cameroon, and the highest-ranking members of government manoeuvre their expensive cars past these eyesores, yet nothing happens; and there exist urban councils, a Ministry of Town Planning, and another for Territorial Administration that should be concerned about the appearance of the nation's cities. From the looks of the cities, most of these councils and ministries should not be in existence as they have failed in the planning and administering of cities that are now perfect examples of national neglect. In Yaounde, however, the slumbering mayors and ministers are, from time to time, forced into action because of visiting diplomats arriving for one transaction or another, and so the local city officials must, occasionally, give Yaounde a temporary face-lift. Even then, only special streets through which they chauffeur these very important persons are pampered thus. The rest of the city could rot and reek to any level; that, according to the insouciance of the incumbent regime, is the business of the citizens and not the government. Is it not bizarre then to hear of the natives of Yaounde celebrating the fact that the government belongs to them, even as they swim in mud and dust and dine with flies and rodents? Along with the corruption that distinguishes today's Cameroon, Basile Ndjio captures effectively the drama of one such hypocritical operations designed to keep Yaounde temporarily clean until the in-coming distinguished visitors leave:

> The annual Franco-African summit is the kind of event which generally allows the ruling class to display its grandeur and majesty, and to dramatize its importance. Cameroon was chosen to host the event in January 2001 and Yaounde, the capital, had to present its distinguished guests the image of a peaceful and beautiful city. The Cameroonian authorities spared no effort to achieve this objective. One week before the opening ceremony, heavily armed troops were deployed to all key points in the city to prevent opposition supporters ... from 'disrupting public order'. Checkpoints were set up and official identity documents had to be shown by all. Those without the necessary papers had to give cash to appease the officers, and any recalcitrance could lead to being forced to lie down in the mud or to walk on one's knees. As part of a clean-up campaign organized by the authorities, street vendors and petty traders near the Warda and Post roundabouts, whose activities were said to be congesting the streets and dirtying the public space, were chased away by law and order officers: their merchandise was seized, and either destroyed or sold back to them later. Police tanks demolished roadside stalls and booths selling food and drink. Those who protested

were arrested, harshly beaten and taken to the police station. A by-law issued by the Prefect of the Mfoundi Division required the population, particularly those living along the main roads and beside public domains, to paint their houses or shops, and to collect up the household refuse that they usually threw into the street. Whether ruling party or opposition supporters, young men and women, the unemployed and prisoners, were requisitioned, sometimes by force, to clean up public arenas and the routes that the presidential motorcades would pass along. A follow-up committee was sent out onto the streets to check whether the public were complying with these administrative orders or not. For 'the sake of public health, decency and order', the police were given the right to clear the streets of young girls wearing 'tight-fitting pants, short skirts or shirts that left the rest of their body uncovered' and 'irresponsible citizens who transform the *lieu public* [public domain] into a space of pleasure'. Prostitutes, street boys, beggars, lepers and madmen who spend their time on the streets or in public spaces were arrested and removed from the city. These wretched of the earth whose presence supposedly defaced the public domain were to be kept out of sight of the visitors. ("Carrefour de La Joie" 265-266)

What hypocrisy! So the clean state of the city is of no consequence in so far as it is the citizens themselves that are concerned; they can rot in misery, after all, Mr. President has a sanitized island for himself at home, or else he can go overseas if need be and Cameroon will remain afloat, bumping purposelessly on the waves of corruption and filth until her absentee captain returns.

Douala, another major city, is also a disgrace to the nation. One can only wonder what Douala has done to Mr. Biya, or else he has bad memories of the city and so he would rather have Douala self-destruct, as it slowly deteriorates on a daily basis, without his government doing anything to save the nation's economic capital. Tim Harford's words will help emphasize, from a neutral perspective, the picture of Douala today, a city that Cameroonians were proud of before the Biya regime:

> They call Douala the 'armpit of Africa.' Lodged beneath the bulging shoulder of West Africa, this malaria-infested city in southwestern Cameroon is humid, unattractive, and smelly. On a torrid evening in late 2001, I was guided out of the chaotic Douala International Airport by my friend Andrew and his driver, Sam, who would have whisked us immediately to the cooler hillside town of Buea if Douala were at all conducive to being whisked anywhere. It isn't. Douala, a city of 2 million people, has no real roads.
>
> A typical Douala street is 50 yards wide from shack to shack. It's packed with street vendors, slouched beside a tray of peanuts or an impromptu plantain barbecue, and with little clusters of people, standing around a motorbike, drinking beer or palm wine, or cooking on a small fire. Piles of rubble and vast holes mark unfinished construction or demolition work. Along the middle is a strip of potholes that 20 years ago was a road.

There is nothing, not even the human body by God almighty, that does not need maintenance, but Paul Biya's government is yet to have heard of any such word, mindful of how it treats Cameroon, her resources, and infrastructure. Think back of Douala in the seventies, and then visit that hole today, and anyone who was around then would weep in disbelief. Douala was a city anyone could be proud of then, but under President Biya, Cameroon's economic centre has crashed into a tattered garbage heap, accented by life-threatening potholes on every single once upon-a-time beautifully tarred avenue. Along the lines of security, the number of bandits running around in Douala today dwindles in comparison only in the face of the number of rodents that are threatening to take over the city from the humans.

The roads are still those that were there under Ahidjo, and in some cases under the colonialists, and not an effort has been made to maintain them, much less construct new streets. With Douala's population that has increased from "155,000 inhabitants in 1960 to approximately 2000.000 in 2000" (Konings "Bendskin" 49), and much more today, the roads are still the same old ones. The result is that possibly only the traffic jams in Lagos, Nigeria, could threaten the integrity of Douala's traffic jam. But when one takes a closer look, the Lagos situation is understandable given the city's population, which makes their wider roads, even if they are somewhat neglected today, appear small. What is Douala's problem when in terms of population Douala might possibly pass for a neighbourhood in Lagos? And with all that money in Cameroon, why is it so hard for the government with her Ministry of Town Planning to keep on planning Douala by coming up with new streets as the people continue to build and the city to expand?

Has it occurred to the government of Cameroon that only one old and dangerously worn out bridge links the Douala and Bonaberi neighbourhoods, a bridge which by all indications should have been retired by now and at least three new ones constructed in its place? True to the government's unspoken policy—if it is still working then all is well—that death trap is still being used. Thousands of Cameroonians will perish on it some day soon before hurried plans will emerge towards building a new bridge. Projecting into the future and trying to solve a situation before it deteriorates into a problem is not this government's tactic. One cannot help wondering then if some African presidents are not affected by what they see in Western countries where they love to go on private visits to squander our money, or are most of them just plain stupid. If it were Paris, that most love to call home, there would have been at least four bridges linking Douala to Bonaberi, two possibly channelling vehicles in one direction and the other two in the opposite direction. Alternatively, consider the appropriately named "fly-overs" in Lagos, Nigeria, as they literarily rise and descend over residential areas and large bodies of water to facilitate transportation. Why can this not be emulated in Cameroon? The gravity of the situation becomes alarming when it is pointed out that this same old bridge linking Douala and Bonaberi is shared with trains also, as there is a railroad running along the middle of the bridge. This was wonderful in the sixties when there was minimal traffic, but not so today.

Mindful of the number of vehicles on that bridge at any particular time today, to add an overcrowded train to it, and this happens all the time, is as hazardous as it is chaotic. Because of the congestion on this bridge, trains have been forced to stop as crowded vehicles trying to pass other vehicles during the characteristic traffic jams end up caught on the tracks by approaching trains. Travellers beware: one should do all to be in Douala at least five hours before one's departure time else one is doomed to miss one's flight as sometimes it takes about three hours to go across a bridge, which is about a mile long, because of the notorious traffic jams. As Konings corroborates, "Travelling in the city [of Douala] is, therefore, extremely time-consuming and arrival times at work or at home are highly unpredictable;" ("Bendskin" 55) all because of the poorly maintained and obsolete road network of the city.

On this old and dilapidated Wouri bridge, one can only look in bewilderment at the chaotic display, symbolic of the administrative technique of the regime in place and the state of the nation as a whole, as an old and crowded train runs out of steam and whistles in frustration at the sudden disappearance of its tracks overtaken by equally crowded cars and trucks — old and new, cheap and luxurious — honking back in defiance at the metallic reptile puffing threateningly yet impotently at them. Then there are bikes manoeuvring between awkwardly positioned vehicles as the riders try avoiding potholes and angry, cursing pedestrians, all in an attempt to make way where there is no room. As if this is not enough trouble, there are policemen in search of bribes making the situation worse as they stop vehicles right at the entrance and the exit of an already overcrowded bridge. All any right-thinking person can do is question if these uniformed men just do not care, or if it is that they just do not think, because realizing the disastrous implications of their actions requires just plain common sense that even a child has. Most frustrating is the fact that the trapped drivers seem reluctant to reason with the policemen to relocate, or else they are so accustomed to such police malpractices and abuse of power that they no longer recognize the awkward and hazardous implications. Does it call for a college degree to understand that doing the right thing at the wrong place and at the wrong time does not make it worthwhile?

To talk about sanitation, transportation and the attendant woes, and not look at the Douala International Airport in particular would be unforgivable, mindful of its being the international gateway into Cameroon, even as Paul Biya tries to usurp this role with his Nsimalene white elephant of an airport. As young men and women in the 1970s, many Cameroonians spent some of their vacations in Douala, and there remain wonderful memories today, as they enjoyed the city, but those days are gone, those days when a trip to the airport made one stare in awe at the beauty of the people, the infrastructure, and the culture on display. The present Douala International Airport is not big when compared to many in the world, but again the bulk of traffic is one of the factors that help determine the size of an airport. This is why the airport was moved from its old to the present site as many more people started flying overseas, yet by world standards, it is small. In those days, it was fun just sitting there watching the planes land and take off, but not so today. Douala's airport today is a monstrosity as, like the rest of the city, it has been abandoned to its own resources. As a result, the airport is in a state of dereliction. Not only is it dirty and smelly, it is crowded with people who have no business being there other than to make it impossible for officials and passengers to function or even move about. However, the officials seem to love the confusion as it camouflages their thriving fraudulent activities.

The airport has, arguably, not been swept or mopped for the last twenty years or so, in spite of the free water from leaks flowing down walls that were once beautifully designed pieces of art and architecture. It is the kind of chaos at the Douala International Airport, symbolic of the state of the Cameroon nation as a whole, that led one of Cameroon's leading musicians and social critic, Lambo Sanjo Pierre Roger, alias Lapiro de Mbanga, to question about our beloved Cameroon, "Which kana condre this?" (What kind of a nation is this?), in his song *Qui N'est Rien N'a Rien*. It is also obvious that he is addressing Mr. Biya in another song of his, "Na You", when he observes, "Na you spoil this condre, you must fixam o, you go fixam" (You destroyed this nation, you must set things right). Only two things are keeping the Douala airport alive—the will of the uniformed staff to squeeze out money and property from those unfortunate enough to be travelling in and out of Cameroon is foremost. Secondly, most carriers have, for economic reasons, refused re-directing their flights to the new forest-bound airport in Nsimalene, Yaounde. Douala, one of Cameroon's darling cities under Ahmadou Ahidjo has thus been reduced to a shantytown by that neglect characteristic of the Biya epoch.

Indeed, Cameroon is a nation blessed with virtually everything that should bring about progress—natural resources, cash crops, rich manpower, and above all a scant and manageable population comparatively speaking—but the country is rotting away because of mismanagement at the hands of kleptocrats. Even more disgusting is the fact that one president has been in place for almost thirty years and cannot seem to right the wrongs of his regime by bringing back stability, security, and development which were part of an otherwise peaceful and flourishing country when he took over office. Biya's failure has eroded the credibility of the government, especially as it continually contradicts itself in the face of diverse crisis. The situation is sad as the disillusioned citizens forge about their daily routine, in an effort to stay alive, with shocked and dazed looks reminiscent of victims of some cataclysm. But Cameroonians have hardly been victims of any major disaster other than that of bad governance. Theirs is the battle for survival in the face of a thieving and disloyal leadership which could not care less about the pain it is causing honest hard working citizens through the mismanagement of the country's natural resources and its labour force; hence, the idea of Cameroon's resources and the exploitation of the masses.

Chapter Six
Of Uniformed Officers and the State of Anomy

Many uniformed officers of Anglophone origin who came over with the union of La République and the Southern Cameroons, went on retirement having been promoted only once in about thirty years of service, in spite of the awards they received even during the West Cameroon days. Many, certainly, would have been promoted more frequently as they merited, had the forces in Cameroon, in this case the police and the paramilitary mobile wing, continued with the structure left behind by Britain or even West Cameroon. But no, this was not to be, as the overwhelming Francophone population, mindful of the hidden agenda by Francophone regimes — to re-colonize Southern Cameroons — suddenly took over control of everything that belonged to West Cameroon. Because of this administrative coup, virtually everything that stood for the former West Cameroon was abandoned and so condemned to fail, or otherwise flooded and mismanaged into the shelves of history by new Francophone [mis]managers who knew nothing about how these institutions functioned. Even control of the main police force of West Cameroon was taken over by the leadership in Yaounde and subsequently derailed. To the young, this will sound like brouhaha, but those who were privileged to be around and actively involved in the affairs of society when the West Cameroon Police force was functioning and controlled from Buea and the West Cameroon Police College in Mutengene, know and understand the point being made here, and the attendant lament. It is not surprising then, that many retired police men and women of the Southern Cameroons, and later West Cameroon police force days, dissociate themselves from the so-called police force of today in every way possible. These men and women are ashamed of what the police force has become as the high-handed and corrupt money-sniffing mannerisms of policemen and women today has transformed the once noble force from "friends" into "enemies" of the public. Frantz Fanon's words strike home in the case of Cameroon:

> In these poor, under-developed countries, where the rule is that the greatest wealth is surrounded by the greatest poverty, the army and police constitute the pillars of the regime; an army and a police force (another rule which must not be forgotten) which are advised by foreign experts. The strength of the police force and the power of the army are proportionate to the stagnation in which the rest of the nation is sunk. By dint of yearly loans, concessions are snatched up by foreigners; scandals are numerous, ministers grow rich, their wives doll themselves up, the members of parliament feather their nests and there is not a soul down to the simple policeman or the customs officer who does not join in the great procession of corruption. (138)

The Police Force in Cameroon

To begin with, Cameroon, like France, it would appear, is one of few countries on earth with two police forces going under different names. There is the police *per se*, which was inherited from the former West Cameroon, and then there is a second group of men and women called gendarmes who were brought in by the former East Cameroon into the union with West Cameroon. The truth is that both groups function in the same capacity and it is a question of choice, it would appear, on the part of the individual if he chooses to report a case to the police or to the gendarmes. Sometimes, trying to get a clarification as to the roles of these different groups, one is told that the police operate within the townships, and the gendarmes in the suburbs, yet there are so many gendarme *brigades* in the heart of towns and cities. Be that as it may, they are two separate groups, the gendarmes with a French background and the police with an English background, and both are being mismanaged by the overwhelmingly Francophone regime. In this section both groups are referred to as the police, after all, but for the colour of their uniforms, they carry out the same functions in society.

First of all, as earlier pointed out, to get into the police force in Cameroon, one just has to write a competitive public examination, and in all fairness, this examination is only a front. One could know the law to one's fingertips, be as bright as any genius that ever walked the globe, yet the chances of one passing this examination, without well placed godparents, are zero. A candidate must have the right contacts with the right amount of money with which to oil their palms, else he might as well not attempt the exam at all, unless he or she believes in luck, which, in this case, does not exist. Strangely enough for a country without any system of accountability, when it comes to public examinations, account has to be rendered to some bribe-sniffing boss for the very last name on the pass list. It has been witnessed over and over again with all the public examinations into all the schools and services in Cameroon— The College of Medicine (CUSS), The Military Academy (EMIA), International Relations Institute of Cameroon (IRIC) National School of Administration and Magistracy (ENAM), Post and Telecommunications (P&T), The College of Education (ENS), and even the police college, to mention a few[1].

In the past, during the West Cameroon days, officers got in on merit. There was a thorough background check, medical exams, and other set standards that a potential police officer had to meet before being recruited to undergo the rigorous physical training involved. Upon completion, even the candidate felt pride in his or her achievement, but this is not the case today as people get into police schools feeling surprised and ashamed that they could make it as they themselves know they did not merit it. It is not strange to hear of ex-convicts who have made it into the police force and are going around today carrying guns and parading themselves by day as officers of the law only to join marauding bands at dusk.

Equally interesting and bizarre are the reasons many of these men and women give for going into police schools: some just like the uniform and the power it accords them, while others claim they have tried all else and failed, and so they get into the police force as a way of avoiding frustration. Are we surprised, then, at the abuse they mete out to members of the public, or by the fact that clashes between the public, students especially, and the police are usually bloody and with casualties? One would think the students are to blame for most of the policemen and women having failed at other ventures in life before their adventure into the police force. It must be remembered here that the term "abuse" does not exist in Cameroon's legal vocabulary, or else it is there for cosmetic reasons, mindful of what men in uniform do and get away with. This never happened in the Ahidjo era, as any violation of the law by whomsoever, was drastically punished. There was some discipline then, although it was scant when compared to what obtained during the West Cameroon police days. During the Ahidjo era, for example, it was said a policeman was accountable for the number of bullets he was issued; if one got missing, he had to explain or face disciplinary sanctions which ranged from salary cuts to demotions in rank. Some have argued that there was such discipline because Ahidjo was trying to keep his political rivals in check. Whatever the reason, there was accountability and policemen behaved themselves befittingly, all of which is history today. Policemen today kill Cameroonians on the whim, just like game, and nothing happens to them; much less when they are out to quell an uprising. Look at their disgusting record in Douala, where police officers are always killing struggling citizens like the *bendskineurs (bike-riding taximen)* who struggle to eek out a living through hours of hard work on daily basis. It was on 9 July 2003 when Douala erupted because of a clash between *bendskineurs* and the police. A bribe-seeking police man had attacked a recalcitrant *bendskineur* and the victim died later on. True to the arrogance and nonchalance of political leaders in Cameroon, then governor of Littoral Province, Gounoko Haounaye, refused meeting with incensed *bendskineurs* thereby fanning an already burning flame. By the end of the day, police bullets had killed several other Cameroonians. Examples of Cameroonian police waywardness abound as these irresponsible men and women in uniform continue attacking and hurting Cameroonians year in year out. When will they understand that when citizens fight for something it benefits them and their families too?

Even then, the Ahidjo era cannot be compared to the West Cameroon days, when indeed there was law and order for the sake of maintaining a healthy public atmosphere and not for the sole benefit of the dictator in power as is the case nowadays. A policeman could not rough handle a member of the public, as even arrests were made in the most polite manner after a warrant had been served the concerned with utmost respect of his rights as a member of society. One cannot help remembering that during the Southern Cameroons and West Cameroon days policemen carried only truncheons, yet they were able to keep the peace in a much better manner. Compare that to today when the first thing a police officer does which is to begin beating up a responsible and respectable civilian just because he is supposed to arrest the person and the latter asks for a warrant. It is even worse when policemen arbitrarily arrest civilians because they are suspected of some illegal transaction; a transaction that is said to be illegal just because the accused refuses to bribe the policeman. Consider this example at the Veterinary Junction in Bamenda when a so-called police inspector started beating up a young man who had just arrived from out of town carrying an old typewriter which many would not even accept as a gift. The police inspector now playing customs officer, had asked for the receipt for the typewriter—a machine probably older than the police inspector himself. When the young man could not present it, the officer started dragging him out of the taxi in which he was sitting, at the same time slapping and punching the young man repeatedly. Had the young man money to bribe, this scene would not have occurred.

Is this how a police officer should treat a civilian? What would such an officer have done then had he found the young man with an unlicensed gun? Yet abusing citizens seems to be all that the Cameroon Police force of today knows, such that one cannot help wondering if "abuse" is not a course in police schools around the country. Such barbaric mannerisms by so-called keepers of the peace are typical of the corruption that has transformed the police force ever since La République du Cameroun took over training the members. Into these police officers, it would seem the so-called authorities have infused the qualities of the colonial police and military that were fashioned to brutalize and intimidate the locals and so facilitate the easy exploitation of their land and labour. Jacob U. Gordon confirms that:

> To ensure its control over the extraction of resources, the colonial state established an authoritarian bureaucracy that was enforced by its colonial army and police. Working closely with the chiefs, the court messengers, the tax collectors, labour conscriptors, and the colonial courts, these agencies oppressed the African masses. Incidents of rape, extortion, murder, and other forms of abuse perpetrated by them were commonplace during the colonial period. The army's and police's brutal activities on behalf of the colonial state contributed not only to the way they came to perceive themselves in both postcolonial Africa and in contemporary periods (Boahen 1987). Thus, the colonial state was extractive in exploiting African resources and punitive in the way its agencies executed their tasks. (11)

The fact that officers of these uniformed institutions are still trained with colonial goals, albeit by African administrations, is obvious; Gordon's picture painted above is still very relevant today. Else, why is it that the first thing these uniformed men do when called to quell a strike, is rape and kill their own citizens to maintain a corrupt regime in power? And then nothing is done to bring the culprits to order by the state.

Upon graduating from the police training school, the new recruits with their crew cuts can easily be identified, and like the fledglings that they are, they go around in groups as if unsure of themselves. Before long, they become so skilled in corrupt practices that they prefer going about in smaller groups of three to help them better intimidate members of the public and ending up with enough to share amongst themselves. A police force can hardly be more corrupt than it is in Cameroon today. In a nutshell, police officers have just reduced themselves to legalized criminals in uniform. And many would hate one for saying this, but the truth is that most of them are young post-federation children and have not known better. Some of us were fortunate to have lived and experienced life in Cameroon, even though as a children growing up, when a real police force was in place during the Southern Cameroons and West

Cameroon days. These were the days when members of the public would leave whatever they were doing to assist a police man confronted by an outlaw as police officers were loved and considered friends of the public, genuine keepers of the peace, instead of today that they are hated because of the menace they are to society. Police officers in Cameroon must understand that they are servants of the state, by which is meant the public, and so the uniform they wear does not give them the right to go about manhandling Cameroonians. In fact, one would think the police are trained to look at the public as enemies to the state, instead of the taxpayers who pay their mostly undeserved salaries supposedly in exchange for protection and the maintenance of law and order. The truth is that besides whatever law they are taught in police colleges, the programs in police colleges in Cameroon need to be revised and decolonized in the process.

Think of a police force in existence, yet there is no thought on the part of the public of taking a complaint to the police or going to their offices for help with any normal police services without budgeting some money to spend. A stranger seeing the average Cameroonian making plans to visit a police station is likely to ask if he is going shopping. Even if one is lucky to meet those rare police officers with some self-pride who refuse to tarnish their image by demanding bribes from members of the public, these exemplary policemen are bound to need petrol for their private cars which they use in running around for the complainant's case. Police units do not have vehicles but for one that the commissioner himself is using as his private property, so policemen are forced to use their private cars to run police errands. If the said disciplined type of police officer does not have a car, then the complainant has to provide transportation for him, and since the ordinary Cameroonian cannot afford to run a car with the present fuel prices, the complainant has to provide taxi money to the police. What a force, what a government, what a nation!

At the judiciary police, for example, to get even an identity card issued, the applicant is transformed into an idiot as he tries to be as polite as possible in front of the police officer in charge of rendering this basic police service. The police officer works when he feels as to, even with all the people standing and hovering around wasting valuable time waiting for him to do his work. He is in charge here, the Commissioner notwithstanding, and like in the banks, he goes around ignoring these "wretches" waiting to be served. Then when he makes up his mind to condescend and attend to Cameroonians, he is suddenly very angry as if he is working for free. This is especially disturbing when it is remembered that with minimal education and training, these are some of the best-paid civil servants in the country under Mr. Biya.

Sometimes, as the police officer is fingerprinting a citizen for his identity card, the shameless officer, and they are in the majority, asks for beer as if joking, but he is dead serious. A smarter citizen offers without being asked, and then the officer, behaving as if it is nothing, suddenly begins smiling and joking around with the concerned; he is already thinking about his beer, which will be reserved for him in a drinking spot. As if to make a statement on the economic force of demand for these drinking spots in certain areas, they abound around police offices. The officers usually prefer going to those that have other delicacies like roast meat (*soya*) to go along with the beer. An officer with absolutely no shame just tells the person concerned to give him the money since he would not have the time to drink immediately after work. By this means, he squeezes out of the needy civilian more money than what he intended paying for a beer, since now the civilian cannot go around looking for change to give the policeman the exact amount for a beer so he gives him a whole thousand francs FCA instead.

Again, in line with most services in Cameroon, if one has contacts at the police station, then things move along with more ease than for the unfortunate citizen who knows nobody. Those who have been in both situations can tell how saddening it is for the helpless Cameroonian. Therefore, one keeps wondering, why in Cameroon, like in most African countries, must one know somebody in a public office in order to be served? Is this not what those pretending to be working there were employed to do in the first place? But of course, now with a job under a regime without an agenda other than the determination to neutralize the Anglophone population while stealing from the state's coffers, civil servants could not care less about serving citizens whose tax money is paying their salaries.

One must not be left with the feeling by now that this is happening only at the judiciary police; it is happening in every police office—the Judiciary, Public Security, the Immigration, Special Branch, and today's so-called Mobile Wing (GMI). At the immigration unit, for example, there is a set price for a passport booklet and a token fee for the officer who attends to an applicant before his documents can finally get to the superintendent of police (*Commissaire*), for approval. One *Commissaire*, in the mid-eighties would not give a friend a passport for no reason other than that the friend should bribe him, even though the gentleman was an unemployed graduate student.

Time means nothing to most Africans, especially to those in a position of power, and so passports that are ready to be picked up by the owners are locked up by a particular officer anticipating bribe, and then he goes drinking during office hours while Cameroonians are standing by his office in their numbers waiting for this god to return and give them their document. And they better have the bribe ready in exchange for their passports, or else they are asked to continue coming back the next day until they get the point. Yes, many Cameroonians in positions of power have no consciences, nor do they have any sense of pride. Else, how can a man take home such "dirty" money for his family to feed on? And not only men are involved in this mess. Women officers are no different; gone are those days when women were shy, when women were ladies and expected to be treated with some dignity. Everything now is money and they are no longer shy. It is not surprising that Lambo Sanjo Pierre Roger (Lapiro) summed up female morals nowadays in another of his albums, *Pas Argent No Love*, by simply saying "money for hand back for ground" (As soon as you can pay, you can have sex).

Moving out of their offices into the streets, one would think police officers would behave with a little bit more restraint being under public view, but they are the same, if not worse. The most offending thing today in the police force is the lack of respect they have for their uniforms. Police officers, especially those of the Police Mobile Intervention Unit known by its French acronym G.M.I. (Groupement Mobile d'Intervention), are found everywhere in uniform until one begins wondering if some of them have any private wears at all. The reason is simple: being always in uniform multiplies their chances of suddenly pretending they are on official duty. In this way they can quickly improvise and squeeze out some francs or a beer from members of the public. During the West Cameroon police days, it was illegal for a police officer in uniform to be in a drinking spot which was not an officers' mess, unless he was there to serve a warrant or make an arrest. Today, uniformed officers can be seen and heard acting out and shouting profanities at women in drinking places, the officers themselves half- or completely drunk and, without any decorum, biting into chunks of meat or fish roasted in front or by the side of such drinking places. They have just been spending money — bribe — they have forced out of taxi drivers and others on whom they could fix a trumped-up violation.

As if being all day in uniform is not inconveniencing and disturbing, the quality of the uniforms is a disgrace. In Cameroon, the colour of a policeman's uniform is supposed to be a sky-blue coloured shirt over a navy blue pair of trousers, but that is in theory, or else policemen are colour-blind. Anything blue goes for their shirts and same for their trousers. Once a professor at ENS Bambili, Bamenda, was so enraged by this that at one location after Mile three Nkwen, in Bamenda, Cameroon, on our way back from Bambili, he could not help but ignore one of such harlequins parading for a policeman by the road and trying to stop him at one of the make-shift police roadblocks where they make travellers lives a living hell. When the clown later caught up with us in town, now re-enforced by his colleagues, and demanded the driver's license, there was laughter and disbelief when he identified himself, with a ridiculously gestured salute, as an officer with the G.M.I. The driver told him he thought he was a government school kid playing pranks on him because of the strange colour of his uniform. He did not find those words funny, yet our colleague was bent on making a point. He insisted that but for the presence of the other well-dressed officers, he still did not consider him a policeman.

But why is this happening? Is it that Cameroon is so broke that the government cannot supply her officers with identical uniforms? During the West Cameroon police days, policemen were issued everything right down to shoe polish and brush, even a brass shining substance with the trade name *braso* for their buttons and buckles. Their uniforms were tailored in Buea by the police-tailoring unit and this made the uniforms identical no matter where an officer was. Why is it that decades after, a government like Cameroon's cannot ensure that her policemen dress decently? To make matters worse, the mixed colour of policemen's uniforms seem to be the least worry on their minds. There are others with holes in the seat of their trousers even as the so-called officers walk around by day in the streets. Even a private security service in Cameroon will not tolerate this of its officers, yet the police force of a whole nation does not seem to see anything wrong with it.

While this is going on, top ranking officers are impeccably dressed, even though it is obvious from the colour and designs, that they had their uniforms privately tailored also. Why can the police force in Cameroon not contract a Cameroonian tailor to sew uniforms for the police force of that country, or even learn from the West Cameroon Police now virtually extinct, and create its own tailoring unit? The shameful thing here is that it does not seem to bother anybody, not even the delegate for national security whose men and women in uniform these are. In the West Cameroon days, police men and women were recruited according to the skills needed in the force — tailors, drivers, mechanics, barbers, bar tenders, traffic wardens, and then some that were specially trained to man the Criminal Investigating Department. They were otherwise called C.I.Ds. This is not the case today as anyone with the right contacts gets into the police school and emerges without any special job description besides the fact that he can put on a uniform, blow a whistle and harass civilians when ordered to do so or when broke. This is all policemen in Cameroon do today while a few are busy with the documentation departments.

Crime investigation as a police occupation is a travesty. Very rarely are crimes investigated, not to talk of being solved and the public made aware of the results. Arresting gangs of marauding thieves who go about killing citizens is more of an accident these days than a well-orchestrated police activity. The result is the insecurity that reigns in a nation where there is no major catastrophe like a war that could easily lead to a breakdown in law and order. Cameroon is possibly the only country in Africa right now without a war, in which gangs are conscious of how much power they have, such that they arrive at a targeted building and even shout out orders to the petrified inhabitants within. Try calling the Mobile Intervention Unit to see how rapidly they can intervene when a citizen is in need and one is left disillusioned; privately organized vigilante groups do much better in terms of response time.

In these tattered uniforms, these policemen and women crowd the streets by day badgering citizens as they try to go about their business in an effort to survive in a nation that has just gone down the drains in the last twenty-six years since 1982. Cameroonian policemen are best at creating mobile police offices; and do not get me wrong, it is nothing like what any dignified person has in mind. These are usually road blocks that are unceremoniously erected anywhere the police are sure to get a high volume of public transport vehicles plying the roads with passengers trying to get from one destination to another. This was a technique used by Ahmadou Ahidjo during the state of emergency he imposed on Cameroon shortly after our theoretical independence, when hunting down U.P.C. patriots. He implemented a system whereby any Cameroonian travelling from one division to the other had to produce a kind of pass on which was written in French "Laissez Passez", (let go) which had to be shown to gun toting gendarmes at numerous roadblocks. But who are these gendarmes and policemen searching for today when there are no armed "enemies" of the state? But true to Cameroon under Biya, only the bad habits of Ahidjo's regime have survived. And so uniformed officers would mount roadblocks reminiscent of highway robbers, at which makeshift police-post they would stop all vehicles going from town to town asking for identification papers as if searching for a missing person. The truth is they are just trying to squeeze out bribes from passengers for whatever reason they can come up with to make a potential case.

Why must a Cameroonian produce an identity card in his own country almost within every three miles, even when there is no emergency, as he is trying to get to work in the neighbouring city or as he is rushing to catch a business appointment? Having identified the passengers, the disappointed police officer starts looking for other reasons to fault the driver, or the vehicle in the hope of getting a bribe. By the end of an eight-hour shift by the roads like this, policemen make a lot of money to share amongst themselves and then go home satisfied they have been working. This is dreadful to believe, but it is said that the superintendent in charge sends them out like this so they make the money, bring it back and give him his share. In other words, being sent out on *contrôle* as they love to call their roadblock shifts, is a privilege, and so they better make the best out of it if they hope to be out there again, for if the superintendent is not satisfied with the booty at the end of the day, then the affected policemen may never be sent out for *contrôle* again. They are more likely to be sent to go watch a bank in front of which they will be seen in future half asleep in broad daylight with their gun half-slung and dangling almost to the ground. This is a practice that has not only reduced policemen in the esteem of the public, but makes any business transaction in Cameroon a nightmare as a person travelling can never tell when he will get to his destination because of the incredible number of roadblocks on the way — about three is the average in a ten mile distance within urban environments and two on interprovincial roads.

The question one has always asked is how confused the management of the police force in one town could be such that they do not even know they have four to five groups of policemen stationed along the same ten-mile stretch of road. But then it is remembered that sometimes some of these checks are not official, or else the different branches of the police force send out their own treasure hunters independent of the other. It is also not uncommon for a group of policemen in need of money to arbitrarily set up a roadblock for their private benefit; after all, all it requires is something like three uniformed policemen, some whistles and if they are very desperate, a wooden beam with nails protruding from it which they throw across the road in case a fed-up driver tries to ignore them, and they are good to go. A flashlight would come in handy if the attack of their financial craving happens to be nocturnal. Somewhere in the distance, the ubiquitous off-license drinking spot is present, or else they simply carry bottles of beer along, drinking as they interfere in citizens' activities in the name of being on duty. Where will one find a police officer in uniform and on duty drinking while attending to the public if not Cameroon? What a reputation they have succeeded in establishing for a friendly, hospitable people and their once-upon-a-time beautiful country as stupidly, and half-drunk, they try to joke out of their embarrassment when they encounter an international traveller who openly displays his incredulity at their local version of professionalism.

The irony about Cameroon is that even with hundreds of policemen graduating almost annually from the so-called police schools, the crime rate in the country is skyrocketing at a staggering pace. Strange that police officers are everywhere by day, but none can be found after dusk when indeed they should be out maintaining the peace and ensuring that people are safe. Of what use are hundreds of policemen on the streets by day when even Lucifer himself hates to be at work, only for them to run back home after dark, handing the streets over to hoodlums, a product of the recent economic crisis in the country, who can be found in every street corner operating confidently as they are sure the cowardly daytime-police-force has retired for the day? Another lesson from the West Cameroon police days: policemen in uniform were barely seen by day along the streets. They were stationed at strategic locations where they kept the peace. The rest were in civilian attire mingling with the public, only to identify themselves when they had to make an arrest of anyone trying to break the law. It was after dusk that they emerged in full force in terms of their numbers and their equipment, and were on beat along strategic areas of the town or city to keep the peace, with their superintendent going around from time to time to ensure that all was in order. Today there are no beats, nor are there significant numbers out on night shifts other than those at the police station. This shift itself is a mere formality as it is now seemingly official for policemen to go to night shifts equipped to immediately fall asleep instead of being on the alert. What a travesty of a force. Are we surprised then that Cameroonians have lost faith in the police force and are coming up with vigilante groups they call "anti-gangs" which they use to help curb the frightening activities of night gangs, some of whose members, interestingly, have turned out to be law officers themselves? How then can anyone who was around in the sixties until the very early eighties, at the latest, not wonder about what has happened to Cameroon?

The Military

The military in Cameroon, comparatively speaking, is without doubt the most disciplined uniform unit in the country and it probably comes with their training, coupled with the fact that it consists of some of the highest educated Cameroonians. As disciplined as they are, some of the members of the unit still bring shame to this elite group. Once, for example, a friend who had been visiting Yaounde returned and shared his experience with disgust and disillusionment. He had seen a soldier in uniform reeling about in broad daylight, drunk. When he questioned the friend he was with about the possibilities of such a thing in the capital city, he was told the drunk would be immediately arrested by the military police if he were found. But then, where was the military police? And with what impression did our friend leave Yaounde? Had it been a foreigner, what impression would he have left with about the military in Cameroon? That this could happen should be unacceptable, not to talk of giving it the chance to happen until the military police can intervene. Officers in uniform ought to have an Officers' Mess as the only venue where they could drink while in uniform, and this should be in moderation. Otherwise, uniforms should not be disrespected by being taken into drinking scenarios where the uniformed officers insult their uniform, the dignity of their profession, and the state as a whole by getting drunk, wetting their pants and spewing filth at passersby. How are these officers to be respected later on, when they are sober, by members of the public?

The main disenchantment with this group is the fact that it is held that they swore to protect and defend, not attack and hurt Cameroonians. Yet attacking, hurting, torturing, and killing Cameroonians, is exactly what they did in Bamenda, Bafoussam, Kumba, and Douala mainly, and in other parts of the country in 1992 especially, and each time frightened politicians order them out against a citizenry that is fed up with administrative blunders. The political party, The Social Democratic Front (SDF), had just been launched and it turned out to be the darling of the people as, at the time, people saw in its leadership charismatic men and women apparently determined to bring about positive change in Cameroon. So influential was this party that even some of Paul Biya's own tribesmen and women bought its ideas and in the subsequent presidential elections joined the rest of the country to vote Paul Biya out as it is commonly believed by the people. It is said that even in the Presidency of the Republic, SDF won the majority votes, but of course rigging has always been an important tool in the hands of African political leaders as they cling to power; this weapon, once more, came in handy to the Biya regime. Paul Biya did not believe Cameroonians wanted him out of office, or he understood the message but could not care less since what he wants, as an individual, is more important than what roughly 16,000,000 Cameroonians want, and so he did all to stay in power.

Convinced that Chairman John Fru Ndi had won the elections and Biya had manipulated the results, the country exploded, determined that Paul Biya had to go. In virtually every part of the country, except Biya's province of origin, the Centre Province, there were riots as citizens erected barricades and torched whatever they could as a sign of their frustration. These reactions peaked in Bamenda alias Abakwa, Bafoussam, Kumba alias K-Town and Douala. Into these "rebel" cities Biya unleashed Cameroon soldiers with venom. The soldiers were armed as if they were going out to war with another military instead of quelling a rebellion against an unpopular regime believed to have stolen the people's electoral victory. They intimidated, beat, bombed, tortured, maimed, and killed Cameroonian civilians, sometimes by tossing live grenades at them, simply because Biya, who had failed Cameroonians as a leader, did not want to leave office. Yes, when a soldier is called to duty, he has to answer and obey his Commander in Chief, but when that Commander in Chief turns traitor to the nation and asks soldiers paid with the Cameroonian taxpayers' money to go out and hurt Cameroonians, unless a soldier is an idiot, he ought to think twice about his tactics even if he must quell the rebellion.

However, in Bamenda, the story was different. The soldiers were carefully selected Francophone men and women sent to teach those "idiotic Anglophones" a lesson they would never forget—they failed. A patriotic and savvy military would have stood at strategic places trying to protect government property (which was not being destroyed in this case) and there would not have been the bloody encounters that typified their stay in every part of the country where there were protests against the election results. The Cameroonian military did not think twice; instead, they threw themselves at their own people with every light weapon they could find and so transformed a disgruntled patriotic population into an angry, bitter mass. Before long, however, the soldiers felt the government's inadequacy against which the people of Cameroon were fighting: for days, soldiers were abandoned at strategic sites without food, and they had to begin begging for sustenance from the same Bamenda public to which they were to teach a lesson.

The viciousness of the regime can be seen from the fact that they brought soldiers from out of town and pitted them against civilians they did not know personally, and whose language they did not understand, while also playing the Anglophone-Francophone card in their faces. In Bamenda, French-speaking soldiers who could not care less about these English-speaking Bamenda people were brought in under cover of darkness to harass the public into submission so that John Fru Ndi could be arrested and transferred to Yaounde, but Bamenda stood like one people and said "no" to an unrepresentative government. It was a shame to find some of the soldiers themselves more unruly than the rebelling crowd, to the point of throwing stones at whomever they saw. For no reason absolutely, other than that he was young and audacious enough to walk close by, soldiers would pounce on a young man and beat him up before arresting and detaining him. A medical staff almost had his skull cracked open by a stone tossed at him by a thug in uniform. The performance of the soldiers in Bamenda left one with the impression that the Cameroonian military needs serious lessons in mob control (not forgetting that this is not exactly their responsibility), unless indeed, as it was rumoured, they had been sent to teach Bamenda people a lesson they would never forget. Did they succeed in this mission even after all the beatings, humiliations, and tortures that led to the death of many while in government custody? No, the soldiers failed woefully as they found themselves being educated by the Bamenda public as to why they were rebelling, and it made sense to most of the Francophone soldiers whose family members were also suffering from mismanagement ushered in by the Biya regime. For once, the people of Bamenda put to good use the language of their oppressor—French.

The government itself soon realized Bamenda people were educating the soldiers and so began ensuring that soldiers did not spend more than a few days at a particular spot as before long the soldiers started befriending the same Bamenda people to whom they were to teach an unforgettable lesson. Even then, by the time Biya's State of Emergency, which he had imposed on the North-West Province, with the capital in Bamenda, was lifted, his French-speaking soldiers had learnt to respect the people of Bamenda. They could be seen waving goodbyes to the people they now held in such high esteem. They had realized that the people of Bamenda had nothing against soldiers, nor did they have a problem with any other people—Francophone or otherwise—as such. Their problem, like all the other Cameroonian cities that had exploded after the "falsified" election results were broadcast, was with a regime that had hijacked the nation's progress by mismanagement while transforming Cameroonians into rivalling factions instead of a united people.

Bamenda became the scapegoat because not even time could make them forget the rigged results as they continued on rampage days after the state of emergency was called off; and then the Chairman of the only significant opposition party at the time, the SDF, was resident in Bamenda. The government wanted his head, and had in fact sent soldiers to arrest the Chairman of a legal opposition party, but the people of Bamenda said "no!" to Biya's Machiavellian techniques. Even then, here were Cameroonians being made to fight and hurt each other, Anglophones and Francophones, civilians and soldiers, all because of that characteristic selfishness of African leaders who think the office of president is theirs for life, even though they were merely handpicked by a predecessor and given power. The result of such a repressive approach to issues affecting the nation has no midway: it is either outright war or the loss of interest in the affairs of the nation by the exploited and savagely oppressed citizenry. This is especially the case in Cameroon as many of the citizens are yet to rid themselves of the atmosphere of fear, bitterness, and distrust visited upon them by Ahidjo's gestapo that was in place during the former president's reign and inherited by his successor. Joseph Takougang is of the same opinion for he writes:

>...Biya did not dismantle the repressive structures and institutions

bequeathed him by his predecessor (Kofele-Kale, 1987, p 136), and that he had used effectively to enable him to remain in power for over two decades. Both the SEDOC—despite the name change to *Centre National des Etudes* et *des Recherches* (CENER)—with its complex network of spies, and the BMM, were retained as institutions of surveillance and intimidation. ("The Nature of Politics" 79-80)

It is therefore obvious that soldiers, with their special salaries and privileges, are turning a blind eye to the ongoing atrocities being visited on Cameroonians. So what are unarmed civilians without leadership and unity to do in the face of a military loyal to a kleptocracy and an armed force that is trigger-happy in the face of its own citizens? The soldiers kill them every day and not a single inquiry is initiated to find out why the army of a nation would open fire with live bullets on its own citizenry, and who gave the order? It is a difficult task to confront bullets with bare hands, and Cameroonians, especially those of the North-West, the South-West, West and Littoral Provinces have seen the consequences repeatedly, especially as they are determined not to go to war. It is no doubt then that the population has relapsed into a state of apathy as their nation rots, their only hope being to trust in God, as nature will eventually come to their rescue with the demise of another already incontinent dictator.

May Cameroon's military never betray its sacred role of defending the nation and citizenry again in this manner. They could easily have quelled the situation in Bamenda had these soldiers, or even the governor at the time, Bell Luc René, dialogued with the crowd instead of attacking them with tear-gas and grenades.[2] Were dialoguing out of question, then they should simply have let the crowd stage its marches under military surveillance and there would have been no bloody clashes. Alas, these soldiers knew they had the advantage of facing an unarmed crowd and so went on to attack a quiet and orderly crowd marching in protest. Strange enough, they were quick to use grenades and live-bullets against the citizens of Bamenda. Why would a president permit the citizens of his country to be confronted by soldiers using live bullets, even if the citizens want him out of office? This has been the tactic of the Biya regime in Cameroon, a tactic that has tainted the image of what, overall, would be an otherwise respectable military.

A true president who knows what it means to be head of state will one day apologize to the people of Bamenda in particular, and to Cameroonians as a whole, for the lives that were cut short and otherwise derailed by atrocities committed by the Cameroonian military, especially during the 1992 State of Emergency declared in the North-West Province for no other reason than that one Cameroonian thinks he owns the presidency and the entire nation.

The Customs

In virtually every country on earth, the customs department is used as a source of national revenue as it is the role of these uniformed men and women to keep in check goods that enter and leave a nation, while making sure that the relevant tariffs are paid as required by the state. Along with immigration officials and the police, customs officers are the very first line of contact that anyone—citizen or foreigner—has with any country at the ports of entry. Customs officials, therefore, should be on their best behaviour at all times since at work they play host to indigenes and visitors alike, on behalf of the government, the nation. Unfortunately, the customs department of Cameroon is arguably the most embarrassing department in the nation's entire history.

Like every other government job in Cameroon which requires one to pass a public examination before being recruited, the process of becoming a customs official is as corrupt as any other recruiting process in the country, and maybe more so. This is the case because the customs department, overwhelmingly more than the police or military, is a department many Cameroonians are dying to get into because of the amount of money the officers make illegally from bribes; this is no longer a secret. It is not surprising, therefore, that Tchop-Tchop, a Cameroonian comedian of Francophone background, recommends, in one of his episodes, a customs officer as foremost for his daughter's choice of a husband. It is interestingly significant that Tchop-Tchop dismisses love as the basis of marriage and requires only a profession in which the daughter's potential husband should already be established and making surplus wealth through corrupt practices.

Once out of training, a customs officer's dream is to be posted, in order of preference, to a border town, the seaport, or lastly the airport. Any other domestic customs post is considered unfortunate, if not a punishment, as the opportunities of being paid bribes are slim. At border towns, at the seaports, and at the airports, the story of bribery and corruption concerning customs officials is the same.

At the border towns, these officers make more than their monthly salaries in a couple of days from bribes they receive from traders transporting goods across international borders like that of Cameroon and Nigeria. It is one thing to pay what the government expects of these traders, and it is another thing for the customs officer to let go a trader even after he has paid what is due the government. In these dirty deals, the government of Cameroon is losing billions of francs annually to unscrupulous customs officials before going on to spend more money paying their salaries on a monthly basis. The word used in Nigeria for what anyone going across the border has to do is more refined and appealing— travellers have to "settle" the officers. This "settling" of officers is all over the continent of Africa, but Nigerian officials came up with a most adequate word for it.

These border officers, customs, police, and immigration alike, just take money from anyone as an unavoidable primary condition for going across the borders by land. Even without a passport, a person who "settles" the border officials generously will go across the borders with a lot more ease than someone with his documents but without the means to "settle". Without "settling" these officers, a traveller will not get his documents stamped for him to go his way. So picture a traveller distributing his hard-earned money to corrupt officers at a border post simply because they happen to be in uniform and are sent there by their government to collect particular tariffs for the state. These shameless men and women enrich themselves thus at the expense of their countries' reputation. It is a disgrace nobody seems able to do something to stop this unfortunate practice by so-called law officers. Woe betides whoever is a trader or in business of some sort travelling by land across the borders. Along the Nigerian stretch of the border, nobody is free, although some officers with a little pride left, angrily let students go by without "settling". Other officers could not care less whether one is a student or not, especially at the start of their shift. Some are even superstitious as they threaten such a student with bringing them bad luck, as they might not make enough dirty money during their shift since it started with someone who could not give them money.

The seaport in Africa is worse. Here, there is big business because of the sizes of the containers that arrive from all over the world carrying quality and highly-in-demand goods in huge quantities. Because there is absolutely no security at the port in Douala, for example, in spite of the numerous men and women in uniforms, anyone shipping things into Cameroon has to be on the highest state of alert to know at once when the cargo arrives. A day is enough, and one might find one's container already opened and emptied by God alone knows who. Once more, after paying the tariffs required by the state, the businessperson has to pay that expected by any customs officials he is unlucky to encounter in the process of getting his cargo out of the seaport. Sometimes, even customs officials collaborate with importers and exporters to falsify their records and so share the balance of what ought to have been paid the state. It is usually a huge relief to get one's cargo out of the seaport without having a substantial quantity stolen or damaged by reckless officials out to see how much they can make for themselves. If this is considered scary behaviour, then there is the need to visit again Cameroon's Douala International Airport.

A very small airport, likely to be confused today for a bus terminal in some countries because of the goings on there, the Douala International Airport is always crowded. One cannot help wondering upon arrival if anyone is in charge there, as chaos reigns. Corruption is written on the faces of almost every errand boy or official one encounters: from those trying to help with one's bags to those checking passengers in for their flight. For no obvious reason but the need to make money out of people, some airlines officials might begin a row over the size or weight of one's bag. The same bag one flew in with as a hand luggage without any problems is suddenly too big to serve as a hand luggage on the flight out, and one now has to pay for it to be stowed in the hold. Of course, they are hoping the passenger will edge in closer and promise to bribe them. Shamelessly, after such a promise to bribe, some direct the passenger to a contact who is easily spotted eyeing him like a hawk as at last his "heavy" bag is being tagged and loaded on the conveyor belt for boarding. As the passenger walks away, the contact immediately closes in on him to collect the money he had promised the well-dressed professional-looking airlines worker at the counter. How they get to know the exact amount in next to no time, and without radios, beats one. Then the quarantine unit collects more money from the passenger for food with which he is travelling, but the receipt they give is registering only half the amount they took from him. And these officers look at the passenger with a straight face as if doing anything else would have been the anomaly.

Next, the passenger comes face to face with the police, a unit of which department also functions as the department of immigration in Cameroon. His passport is scrutinized with displeasure written all over the officer's face; it is obvious he is the only one at the airport without any false yet seemingly authentic reason to try to cheat passengers of their money. Then he slowly goes through some collections of obviously wanted Cameroonians' pictures to see if the passenger's picture appears anywhere, or if his name is on the list before playing his trump card: "Do you have a green card?" What business does a Cameroonian policeman have with somebody's green card in Cameroon? What has a Cameroonian officer to do with a Cameroonian's odyssey in Europe, being that Cameroon, other than with France, has hardly any security agreement with any foreign nation? In any case, having shown his green card, the passenger is on his way through the last point where he is searched again behind some curtains. Shamelessly the police officer pulls out the passenger's bank notes from his pocket as if it is illegal for one to travel with any amount whatsoever, no matter how small it is. Then he declares as if it is a rule, that the passenger no longer needs the money since he is leaving the country. If the passenger is easily intimidated, that is his money gone. A travelling partner once asked an officer who did that to him what he thought he would use for paying a cab and eating upon returning to Cameroon before asking him to return his money, which he immediately did as he could sense the fumes beginning to gush out of the man's nostrils. One would think one is done with all the hassle, but then one has to be humiliated a couple more times.

Just before entering the plane, one's visa is scrutinized by officials of some Western carriers, especially Air France, as if one's only job in Cameroon, Africa, is to spend time forging visas into European countries. Who can blame these officials? All of this is because of African presidents who have destroyed their nations, causing their citizens, some of them the best qualified workers one could find anywhere, to want to leave their homelands desperately, hoping they could find some peace and stability somewhere else before they go insane.

At last in the plane comes the imperialist's final humiliation: an airhostess pretends to be apologetic for her impending behaviour, blaming it on some strange international organization's expectations, before spraying the plane with some kind of chemical agent. One gets the feeling of being sanitized, yet these same planes left Europe for Africa without a similar treatment. But of course, bugs and diseases are uniquely African. This kind of abuse is only possible because of the lack of strategic structures that ought to ensure that planes from Europe and elsewhere are sprayed before bringing in whatever to Africa, also. At last, in any case, one is glad to have left behind those mostly thieving officials at the Douala airport, even if only for the month one is going to be away.

Most Cameroonians' days in whatever European or American country they are visiting, are always tormented by sudden bouts of fear and anxiety attacks as they think of their return trip home and the impending encounter they are bound to have with those officials, the customs especially, at the Douala International Airport upon arrival. How pathetic it is to see Cameroonians returning to their own country traumatized by thoughts of what their encounter with their own authorities will be. And these are tourists and visitors just bringing back home mostly gifts for friends and family members. The meaning here is that Cameroonians receive much better treatment at foreign ports than they do in their own country and this is because of officers foraging through their property like rodents in search of food remains. They are searching for whatever they can imagine is to be sold, so they can ask the traveller to pay tariffs for the items, but which money goes into their pockets instead of to the government of Cameroon.

Literally, a Cameroonian's trip back to Cameroon from anywhere beyond the national boundaries but especially from Europe, America, and Asia is traumatizing. Those with contacts have to call home days in advance to ensure that such and such an authority with the police, the military, or the customs department itself will be at the airport to help get them past the corrupt airport officials; those without well-placed contacts just set aside money with which to bribe their way. It is interesting to hear a customs official asking a returning traveller to give him the dollars so he can go and have it exchanged into francs and then he can be paid. In fact, they have, recently, graduated into asking for their bribes in dollars and Euros mainly, since these currencies yield more when the corrupt officers later on do the exchange by themselves. Where does a genuine customs official get the time to leave his post and go about for whatever transactions other than ensuring that the appropriate tariff is paid to the state? Michela Wrong's depiction of the situation in a river port in the Congo reflects what obtains even within the Douala International Airport:

> The pulse of apprehension drummed as I stuffed my clothes back into the ageing suitcase that had chosen the river crossing between Brazzaville and Kinshasa as the moment to split at the seams, transforming me into a truly African traveller. It quickened as a sweating young British diplomat signally failed to talk our way through the red tape and a chain of hostile policemen picked through the intimacies of my luggage, deciding which bits to keep. It subsided as we emerged from our three-hour ordeal, a little the lighter, finally crossing the magic line separating the customs area from the city. (3)

One cannot help but wonder why there is an x-ray machine to scan the things of those leaving Cameroon, yet there is none to scan those returning. Such a machine, it becomes obvious after an entry into Cameroon, would eliminate the shameful foraging through people's private belongings in the name of identifying contraband or business items being imported for sale back in Cameroon. Small wonder nobody has made the recommendation that such a machine is needed. When, for example, does a custom officer in London's Heathrow, Paris' Charles de Gaulle, or Chicago's O'Hare International Airport, have the time to manually pick through a passenger's bags in search of deodorants that seem to be too many for one person's personal use so as to ask the returning citizen, or foreigner even, to pay money for items such as these so they are not confiscated and later owned by the corrupt officer?

Such a machine would have saved a colleagues' cherished briefcase, a gift from a dear friend, which a female customs officer in Douala ripped open, permanently damaging the box on its maiden trip anywhere. Were this done for genuine security concerns, it would have mattered less to this colleague, but the female custom officer believed, since she was coming from Europe, there had to be a lot in her box which she was trying to hide by claiming her keys were missing. The truth was that the chaos at the arrival terminal in the Douala airport had caused her to drop her keys as she struggled to snatch and put her arriving bags in one identifiable heap before they disappeared. How stupid it all turned out to be when the custom officer found out the suitcase contained nothing but clothing and a few gifts for which even she herself could not ask for a bribe. The box was never used again as my colleague had to use a rope to hold its contents in place in order to leave the airport without her belongings littering her tracks. Here, one has to point out in this respect that Nigerian customs officers at the Murtala Mohammed Airport in Lagos are much better off in their approach than their Cameroonian counterparts.

Nigerian customs are very proud people and do not bother themselves unless the kill is significant. Armed with nightmarish experiences from Cameroon's Douala International Airport, in August of 2007, for example, a friend visited Nigeria expecting hell from the customs officers of the airport, but he walked out with his hand luggage and a single briefcase in tow until he left the airport without any of the customs officers bothering himself to call him over and search his things. This friend was so confused he almost walked back in and up to a customs officer to volunteer information that he had just come into the country, and to ask if the officer could go through his things, of course, the way it is done in Douala, Cameroon. The friend was later to learn that travelling light was enough indication to the officers that he had just private belongings in his luggage and so they do not bother themselves with such passengers. This was commendable because in Douala, as already indicated, nothing is too small or compact to be searched. Pathetic!

Whenever an international flight is to arrive in Douala, the atmosphere at the airport is thick with tension as everyone gets ready to pounce on the travellers. Relatives and host families can be seen pacing and devising strategies to get their guests past customs, with customs officers prowling about wetting their lips in anticipation as they size the boxes emerging from the carousel. Meanwhile, black marketeers are going about eyeing those they think may be carrying dollars and euros for potential transactions. Nobody wants to make any foolish error as it could cost him all the money he could have made for the day from the arriving passengers. It is usually much easier going through the immigration police officials stamping passports since they have no way of squeezing anything out of travellers; everyone arriving has his or her documents intact. After sailing through these immigration police officers without much ado, trouble immediately slaps the passengers in their faces as they get to the baggage claim area which is usually crowded by a strange assortment of human beings with all kinds of roles to play. Once, a travelling partner was busy trying to find her bags, panic-stricken that her stuff might not have arrived with her flight, when out of sheer luck she saw a young man struggling in the distance under the weight of one of her bags with duct tape around it — the identifying factor. Angrily she stormed over to the young man to ask what he was doing with her bags. Being that this was routine, the young man was at a loss for words as with drooping lips he marvelled at this lady who was acting "strangely" because he had brought her bag to a customs officer. The officer, meanwhile, like the dwarf version of a colossus, towered over the bags with the looks of one of those colonialist hunters priding himself on having killed an African elephant during a hunt. After a barrage of words discouraging the young man from picking up other people's luggage in the future, my companion now had to deal with the hunter himself. The young man was only a retriever trained to identify and salvage particular luggage. However, my companion, a true Cameroonian, had earlier gone to work and had a team of well-placed officials waiting for her at the airport. This offended the customs officer like nothing I have ever seen, even though he did all in his power to remain calm. He was pacified with a consolation tip from one of the superior officers who had come to rescue my friend. The customs officer had in fact asked coyly for the tip, given that he was now talking to a superior military officer who freely conceded to his now humble request. Wow! But without such powerful officers, any such relief from having gone through the customs is bound to be short-lived.

On the way out of the airport, travellers are usually stopped at phony police roadblocks and asked to open their bags and show proof that they have been through customs. The policemen then begin asking passengers to pay their import tax within the city of Douala. Of course, these policemen were at the airport where they spotted vehicles that were heavily loaded with bags from international flights, and then they took off before the vehicles and trapped them on the way. Others tail the vehicle, then go past on a straight stretch and pull the vehicle over at an illegal checkpoint they have just erected. The experience with officers at the airport and its environs is, to say the least, embarrassing and humiliating.

When compared to their Western counterparts, the majority of Cameroon's customs officers are a disgrace, a pilfering bunch whose duty is to make an already difficult life a lot more miserable for their compatriots trying to survive in an already dismal economy. But, of course, they too must survive, and this would not be the case were they to depend on their salaries only. Do we remember the salary cuts and other damaging financial strategies, like the Structural Adjustment Programme (SAP), imposed on African countries by foreign monetary organizations? They virtually emasculated the citizens' economic effectiveness, leaving them acquiescent to corrupt practices, since they must survive. Even entire nations were trapped in what Nantang Jua has described as the "borrowing-repayment-rescheduling syndrome (Economic Management 42) Tatah Mentan reveals the neutering of Cameroon's economic potency by SAP:

> The implication of Cameroon's entry into the club of heavily indebted countries is that is has committed itself to being under the structural adjustment yoke for decades to come. Cameroon will be required to produce exactly the same kind of crops and raw material as it had under colonialism and to use its earnings to buy from the former masters machines and processed goods. In fact, this was the institutionalization of the neo-classic economic strategy, which combines the following elements: (a) abolition of all intervening 'distortions' in the pricing mechanisms to achieve maximization of growth for the new owners of the erstwhile state enterprises; (b) liberalization of foreign trade in order to remove incentives for inward-looking economic behaviour and to replace them with incentives for outward-looking and export-oriented economic activity; and (c) reduction of the public sector in size through

privatization of public enterprises and the surrender of as many economic tasks as possible to private foreign companies. ("Political Economy" 124/125)

The result is corruption extraordinaire, perfected and raised to disturbing levels in a country supposedly with a government in place. Hence we encounter uniformed officers in reckless abandonment extorting money from citizens and foreigners alike, to the point where some have degenerated outright into bandits — officers of the law by day and bandits by night. After all, "goat di chop for place we them tie am" (one must seize the opportunity to benefit where and when it presents), a notorious pidgin saying in this country, confirms that the customs officers, like the police and gendarmes, are only browsing where they are tethered. They must make the best of a situation out of the opportunity presented them by their uniforms and their workstations — the national borders, the seaports, and the airports in the main. Nonsense! Yet this is Cameroon under Paul Biya.

The uniform, that supposedly awe-inspiring symbol of authority, confirming one a servant of the state and, therefore, of the people, has been misused and transformed in Cameroon into a laughable badge of disgrace instead. Accordingly, uniformed officers in Cameroon, the police especially, have all kinds of insulting nicknames — *camamburuh*, *mbélé kaki*, *mange mille*, and *sans galon*, are examples. Uniformed officers, because of their nose for bribes and corrupt practices have degenerated into a nuisance instead. Who does not know that because of their corrupt practices almost every uniformed officer in Cameroon has a monetary value? They are a bunch of men and women without any worth in the eyes of the public any longer, as in them people see a bunch licensed to steal from and abuse the public instead of being the upholders of peace and order they are supposed to be. Bribed, corrupted, and lured on by the existing kleptocracy, uniformed officers in Cameroon have unwittingly been programmed against their own people whom they exploit, hurt, and kill for the flimsiest reason. Hence the state of anomy spiced by the perpetual tension between uniformed officers and the populace.

Theses uniformed citizens have degenerated into a clog in the wheel powering an equally corrupt system that is denying the people a decent standard of living in spite of how hard they toil. In Cameroon, values have been flushed out and corruption reigns, infesting nigh on the whole nation. Virtually the entire population has been transformed into addicts overdosing on corruption for a bizarre high, a temporary state of delusional satisfaction and success compared only to the wellbeing experienced by drug addicts; a high which exhilarates temporarily while destroying permanently, unless help is sought. Is it not a shame that today in Cameroon priorities are so reversed that successful frauds, thieves, corrupt officers who can display wealth now pass for heroes in the neighbourhood? One group of such men who, thanks to illegal and clandestine activities like smuggling, sponsoring armed gangs, forgery and the rest, have made much money are called *feymen* in Cameroon. These are the recent "heroes" of the SAP initiated economic crisis. "Since the mid-1990s, *feymen* or Cameroonian swindlers, who through deceit, extortion, and other unlawful practices succeed in accumulating an unimaginable fortune in a short space of time, have become the embodiment of success in Cameroon (Basile Ndjio "Intimate Strangers" 69). In the case of Cameroon, only a true patriot of a leader will be able to rehabilitate this nation by re-educating the masses: according them a sense of awareness that the welfare of a nation means the ultimate welfare of its citizens and vice versa, that offices and services can function without bribes—the raison d'être of any government of value. With this new sense of purpose, Cameroonians will then begin thinking of their country instead of their individual stomachs first, and in this way a new and thriving nation will emerge from the ashes of today, a season of anomy fired by the powers that be.

Chapter Seven
Towards a Renaissance: What must be done

The question looming large now is whether Africa must continue down this path of destruction *ad infinitum*, or can something be done to salvage what is left of the continent and her peoples? And this is an urgent question, as one is fed up with portraits ridiculing the continent because of its repertoire of socio-economic blunders, even if imposed on the regimes by their creditors, coupled with an all too often pilfering leadership that mistook colonialist plunder in Africa for the standard of leadership.

The truth is that Africa is where she is today thanks to imperialist goals, contrary to what imperialist propagandists would want the world to believe. That most African political leaders have proven themselves at best quixotic and at worst quislings by reducing themselves into puppets gyrating to foreign political rhythms is true, yet contrary to schools of thought that claim otherwise, these leaders are the fruits of imperialism in Africa. Jacob U. Gordon confirms this when he observes:

> At the conclusion of the twentieth century, the impact of colonialism still reverberates throughout the African continent. The lingering effects of its seventy-five years of domination are manifested most profoundly in Africa's current leadership problem, which remains a malignant (central) feature of the general African crisis. The evidence now available demonstrates the incontrovertible fact that the overarching influence of colonial capitalism led to a mutation of Africa's political leadership and performance that can be characterized as nothing less than contemptible. (1)

Indeed, African traditional leaders and institutions which had established effective ways of managing their peoples were not like this, not even those still around today, for where we have problems with traditional leadership today, it is obvious that corrupt modern day political leaders are in the background trying to manipulate traditional politics in favour of their selfish whims.

It is imperialist nations that imposed and continue to impose on Africa un-African values and the result is the chaos currently reigning all over the continent. Africa's problems, in the main, are consequences of imperialist activities on the continent during the colonial and postcolonial eras: their arbitrary boundaries on the continent, their assimilationist and divide and rule tactics that pitted Africans against each other while leading to cultural disintegration, their enslaving loans that get Africans states permanently indebted and so easily exploited through the mortgaging of their resources are a few examples of the Western albatross about Africa's neck. Although written about the Betsimisaraka of Madagascar, Jennifer Cole's observation is true of colonialism everywhere. She remarks that in some ways, the experience of colonization was "disruptive but manageable", but "many aspects of colonization have been assimilated, others modified, still others erased by the colonized". This notwithstanding, "some aspects of colonization were profoundly wrenching and the marks they have left run deep" (35). The city-council *askaris* found in Kenya, who according to Binyavanga Wainaina are the "most hated people in Kenya", constitute another example of "a veritable colonialist enterprise" which continues wrecking havoc on the people like the colonialists did. It is not surprising the remarkable scholar, Walter Rodney, urged Africa to establish a radical break from the international capitalist system if the continent hoped to make any progress. Africans are yet to effect that break, not with the inroads still being made on the continent by international monetary organisations, and the numerous *Francophonie* nations still clinging to the Franc CFA. African leadership, at the very least, must stand on its own two legs in order for the continent to take a stride. One is simply fed up with the West's role as wet nurse to the continent, if that is indeed what it is; a role, based on foreign political and economic theories, that ushers in one economic problem after the other, leaving Africa's children malnourished and the entire continent the laughing stock of the West. If Western nations will not genuinely cooperate with African nations, instead of imposing and dictating, then it is time Africa begins looking elsewhere for genuine cooperation.

Cameroon's problem, like most of Africa south of the Sahara, is with the leadership. The leaders of these great African nations are yet to be patriots as they take undue advantage of their people's love for peace and destroy their economies by stealing from the nation's coffers: it was done in then Zaire, it has been done in Nigeria repeatedly, it was and it is still being done in Cameroon. A study of ongoing wars in Africa will indicate that the people have had to put up with too much before engaging in war as a last resort. In the case of Cameroon, the leaders must know what it means to belong to a nation and must understand the responsibility that lies on the shoulders of such leaders. Were Cameroon's leaders true patriots, they would make their small but very rich country look like those Western countries where they love to go on vacations; where they love to go shopping; where they love to do banking; where they love to buy real estate property; and where they love to go establish their businesses from which their own people back at home cannot benefit in any way either as employees, patrons, or as investors.

Beyond Cameroon with its legacy of corrupt leadership, not many African leaders have left behind a heritage they could be proud of, as they have wasted their time, that of the citizens, and the resources of their lands by governing their countries as if they belong to somebody else. In the end, they have distanced themselves from their compatriots only for them to realize they are not even welcome in those Western countries where they had buried the stolen wealth of their native countries. What beats me is how African leaders never seem to learn. They see their predecessors dying and leaving all their stolen wealth to benefit alien shores, only for the successors to come in and do the same thing; this is plain stupid! A few suggestions as the way to commence may begin yielding positive results to these African nations rendered depressed by imperialist political and economic tunes, rhythms, and tugs, along with unpatriotic native leaders gyrating in response.

The Need for True Patriots as Leaders

African leaders must learn to be patriots, and role models to the younger generation consequently, or else get out of office before they betray their fatherland and damn their legacies forever. Consider the example of the Cameroonian governor — Mr. Oben Peter Ashu — who called other Cameroonians "settlers" in their own country, or think of the so-called Mfoundi elite in Yaounde writing and signing a ridiculous letter threatening other Cameroonians engaged in genuine nation building political activities to leave their town, by which they mean the capital city of Cameron, Yaounde, a city built, in the main, with money from the nation's treasury and the economic activities of those "foreigners" they are now threatening. But for the lawless state of the country that even gave birth to such nonsense in the first place, such disruptive politics from a leader and, above all, one supposed to be considered an elder like Oben Peter Ashu as per Africa's traditional values, is a shame; more so is the display by the Mfoundi elites as they call themselves. When elders open their mouths, wisdom is expected, not filth simply because they are trying to hold on to power. Cameroon is home to all Cameroonians, and so a Cameroonian should feel at home anywhere in Cameroon. Yet here we are losing our values for ephemeral political handouts which, in fact, are supposed to be directed towards serving instead of antagonizing the population.

If Cameroon must grow and become what she was thirty/forty years ago, then such worthless and uncalled-for divisive sentiments must not be tolerated. Cameroonians must be taught their history and made to understand that if we cannot function as one people, then we must first go back and respect the Federal constitution that was in place before Ahidjo's illegal partial administrative annexation of West Cameroon.[1] In this way only can Cameroonians respect each other, mindful of the devastating impact our colonial legacies have left on our cultural id. For Francophone regimes to continue playing ostrich to the Anglophone problem is simply ridiculous and smacks of ill will, as it is tantamount to claiming there was never a West Cameroon or a people administered by the English. Yes, there was and still is even if we are not ridiculously attached to Britain the way Francophones are to France. According to the Francophone architects of this gorgon-state, they have annexed Southern Cameroon, thereby hijacking our independence; but the government has realized its plan was a pipe dream. Even now, the situation is made more provocative as Francophone administrators, especially, continue to treat English-speaking Cameroonians with disrespect and bias, according them a second-class citizen status. It is in this light that for any educated and informed Francophone to argue that there is no Anglophone problem in Cameroon, while at the same time paradoxically attempting to downplay its seriousness by comparing the problem to tribal differences within Francophone Cameroun, amounts to a precedent that must be considered as dangerously provocative as it is misleading. It displays ignorance of one's national history while authenticating Anglophone claims to Francophone unwillingness to face the truth and solve the ongoing crisis in a civil manner. Consider someone who is supposed to be an authority like Mr. Charles Assale, the first prime minister of former East Cameroon in the days of the federation, arguing ridiculously that Anglophones are trying to secede only because of their oil rich territory. He goes on to the point of claiming that if oil wells suddenly dried up Anglophones would lose interest in their push for autonomy (Awasom). This is as disturbing as it is childish. By arguing thus, Charles Assale fails to realize that pushing for total secession is the only choice Francophone dominated regimes in Yaounde have accorded the Anglophone population. Assale's observation would have made sense were Anglophones the ones being unreasonable. As history will reveal, Anglophones have done everything for the governments in Yaounde to sit with Anglophone leaders and discuss their plight in this unfortunate union with La République du Cameroon to no avail. Had Anglophones been accepted in the reunion and treated with the respect accorded their heritage by the federal constitution, there is no way there would have been this push for outright secession. After all, Anglophones have invested as much, if not more, in this union; it must not be forgotten. Abandoning everything we have invested and seceding is a desperate move by a people who want peace, dignity, respect, and stability, qualities Francophone Cameroon has denied them. Having rejected dialogue, while still playing ostrich to the Anglophone problem by refusing to accept that there is such a thing, it is not surprising then that Anglophones want out. It is such a spirit by Francophone leaders, that led Ahmadou Ali, while Minister of Defence, to declare roguishly, or at best ignorantly, that "Cameroon has always been one, not more" (Jua 88) To dread dialogue is to fear facing facts, and so the grievances will remain to be addressed another day, if only they do not escalate into something else before then. And this is more likely the case as irresponsible Francophone leaders procrastinate in their stupor of dispassion whelped by virtual absolute power and unchallenged political malpractices along with epicurean excesses.

We are Anglophones, citizens of a former colony wrongfully denied the right to self-determination by the United Nations primarily, and now by another former colony, La République du Cameroun, and we say there is a problem. What right has a Francophone, whose leaders are oppressing Anglophones, to tell us there is no Anglophone problem in Cameroon? Even in the bible, the Egyptians did not think the Israelites they had enslaved had a problem, and it took the Almighty God Himself to twist the imperial arm before Egypt could reluctantly free His people. In view of that, it is not surprising that the Francophone oppressor cannot seem to see the problem to which the oppressed Anglophone is referring. A scholar from East Africa has emerged with a working definition of the oppressed as follows:

> A social group or groups who find themselves, or may be objectively determined to be, disadvantaged or accorded unequal, differential treatment, either because of deliberate policies or structural arrangements in (a) the family, community, country, region or world they live in, and or (b) the position they occupy in the prevailing relations of production or arrangements and, as a consequence, become especially exposed to human rights denials and abuse. (qtd. in Campbell 208)

While there are other ethnic groups in La République du Cameroun that may consider themselves victims in this light—the Bassas and the Bamilekes—that is a whole other matter within the context of the groups that make up La

République du Cameroun. Nevertheless, we as Anglophones, we as a people with an identical colonial heritage, experience conditions of oppression simply because we were not colonized by the French, but are now being forced to become Francophones while being discriminated against in our fatherland by an occupational regime, and so we talk of the Anglophone problem. As effectively summed up by Piet Konings and Francis B. Nyamnjoh, the Anglophone problem is that "...widespread feeling in this region that reunification with Francophone Cameroon in 1961 has led to a growing marginalization of the Anglophone minority in the nation-state project controlled by the Francophone political elite, endangering its cultural heritage and identity" (*Negotiating* 2).

Within West Cameroon, after solving the "La République problem", like the siblings that we are, under the same colonial parentage, we will then sit, true to our legacy of dialoguing, before the theoretical annexation of West Cameroon, to discuss, and straighten things out. Much of our problems are merely superficial, having been created by the Francophone governments of La République du Cameroun. We had few or no problems until the decision to divide and so ably exploit us was made by Francophone regimes. From West Cameroon, we became the South-West and the North-West Provinces, and now we are being made to distrust each other while La République continues its tactical exploitation of the human and natural resources of West Cameroon. They will be considered fools, those siblings who permit a stepsibling living on his own property to throw them at loggerheads with each other, and they continue fighting even as the stepsibling comes into their property and carries away their belongings. They shall be wise if they stop their disagreement temporarily, confront the "thieving stepsibling" first, as was done during the GCE crisis, and so stop him from making away with that which is theirs before returning to settle their differences. This is simple common sense. It must be remembered that Anglophone Cameroonians only thought of secession when it became clear that the Francophone leadership does not seem to understand the meaning of dialogue, the meaning of respect for a people and their culture. And this is besides the fact that everything Anglophone had been exploited to the benefit of Francophone territories mainly. This, however, is food for another venture outside the scope of this volume. However, unless the existence of problems within the fabric of the nation is urgently acknowledged and tabled for discussion by patriotic leaders with a goal towards genuine resolution and possible reconciliation, Cameroon remains another war in the making and the question to be answered is "when" not "if".

Stop the Stealing and Corruption

In other successful nations with populations about ten times and more that of Cameroon, patriotic regimes have been able to establish that it is possible for the vast majority to live their lives having more than the basic necessities for a happy life. Because one can only improve upon one's situation by striving to be like those who are better, there is the need for the leaders of Cameroon today to look back at the Ahmadou Ahidjo era and see for themselves how they have destroyed the Cameroonian nation be elevating kleptocracy to the norm instead of an unfortunate exception.

Ahidjo supported family life, for which reason there was a healthy family allowance package included in people's salaries, such that some people went on having children as a way of increasing their family's annual income. In like manner, every year, civil servants had salary increments befitting their echelons. In fact, because of how well the economy was doing, some parastatal organizations had thirteen and even fourteenth month salaries. Where was all that money coming from? Some people have thought it was from the oil revenue, which the country started earning long before the man on the streets in Cameroon knew Cameroon was exporting oil. One cannot help asking then, why, if there was oil money during Ahidjo's time, why not now during Mr. Biya's tenure when it is no longer a secret that Cameroon is exporting oil, nor has the supply slowed down?

The taxes in Cameroon were fair during Ahidjo's reign; they were such that Cameroonians could afford them, and so they were willing to pay without striking fraudulent deals that now characterize businesses and the department of taxation. Today, the idea of taxing the public is such that money is squeezed out of the hands of the poor for use by the corrupt and powerful in government. One of the latest nightmares to the people of Cameroon is the tollgate system introduced by Mr. Simon Achidi Achu when he was prime minister. Toll gates are meant to generate funds to be used in improving upon the conditions of the roads for which citizens are thus being taxed, but not so in Cameroon. The money is collected and squandered by those in power with the roads deteriorating at an alarming rate. For example, a small but strategic bridge (approximately fifty to a hundred feet in length) linking the South-West and Littoral Provinces was damaged, and it took Cameroon forever to repair it.

In fact, in Cameroon today, being appointed to a government position is an official invitation for the individual to steal from, instead of serve the nation, and interestingly nothing is done when in a blatantly obvious manner the newly appointed official begins stealing. True to this scenario, a study of all those appointed ministers in the last twenty-five years, for example, will reveal that within the first few months of their appointments, their bank accounts suddenly jumped in worth, or else they started one kind of construction project or other, which conflicts with the size of their official pay packet. It is no doubt Cameroonians now have a saying about government positions: "Chop I chop", a kind of "pilfer and let's pilfer", syndrome. This is the mentality in most African countries, especially those south of the Sahara, and this needs to stop if these governments want to regain their trust in the face of the populace in order to begin working once again as a nation with the common goal of bettering the standard of living of their citizens. Stealing government money, directly or indirectly, is now a firmly established practice in Cameroon to the point where citizens no longer realize it is a wrongdoing. Because corruption is now the norm, anyone trying to do the correct thing by serving Cameroonians without stealing or asking for bribe, can lose his job or even his life, if he persists, as his colleagues accuse him of snatching the morsel from their mouths. Charles Manga Fombad confirms this trend when he observes:

> Attempting to go against the current of corruption and graft, particularly in the Cameroonian bureaucracy, is greeted with scorn, ridicule and

sometimes ostracism. You think you alone can change the system! Prospective whistleblowers are intimidated and terrorized into silence. (360)

Most African leaders have just deteriorated into compulsive thieves who must go on stealing even if they have stashed away so much that even their great grandchildren can still go through life without working. With a certain amount of stolen wealth, these leaders could at least invest this money in some profit generating business at home which will be of help to the rest of the citizens, but no, they go on stealing from a nation they have crippled, only for them to die leaving behind billions of dollars, which no other person can withdraw, in foreign banks. What kind of mentality is this? African leaders must be patriots and have their countries at heart. If they think they are failing, they must get out and let someone else try his or her hands at leading the people. Why is it so hard for African leaders to leave power gracefully and then stay at home giving advice, since more often than not one is able to think and reason clearly when one is not directly involved? No, instead Africa's leaders must plunge their countries into war before they leave as fugitives, only to die like dogs in someone else's country.

Then there are other public servants who have held particular positions all their lives, despite their ages, as if nobody else is good enough for that position. This is typical of some uniform officers in Cameroon. Interestingly, younger soldiers who joined these fossils in the military have served and gone on retirement while these surviving dinosaurs are still in the military and earning fantastic salaries, simply for vegetating in uniform, because they belong to the administrative clique. One can only imagine what it is that makes these obsolete soldiers who have never gone on a refresher course so invaluable to the military of these African nations.

In the same manner, one person ought not to hold multiple high ranking positions for all of which he is being paid. It is not uncommon to hear in Cameroon that one person is the director of two strategic professional schools, as if he is the only one capable of managing both institutions. Alternatively, take the case of a minister who is still clinging to his former position from which he was appointed minister; this strangely, uniquely talented individual is also receiving both salaries while there are others out there with similar or better qualifications that are unemployed or underemployed.

Again, the government in Cameroon must learn to appoint high-ranking civil servants to positions they are qualified to manage. It is arguably only in Africa, and mainly Cameroon, where a man without any training in medicine or an affiliated discipline is made to head the Ministry of Health. Are we surprised then that such a person fails to see the need for hospitals to be equipped with basic needs like an x-ray machine? How is such a person to understand the concept of a medical doctor being overworked because of the number of patients he has to see in a day? Virtually impossible, because the minister spends his time gallivanting from one meeting to another earning outstation allowances, while refusing to stay in office and receive Cameroonians who need his attention. We have seen these misfits in many other ministries in Cameroon, and all it amounts to is a waste of resources as they stay in office doing nothing but earning money for going around singing political campaign songs in honour of a regime that has rendered the socio-economic life of the nation comatose. But this is understandable: it is either they sing or they are fired, and they have their families for whom to provide.

Otherwise, consider a minister with a degree in French trying to pass for a minister of Agriculture. As insane as it sounds, it even gets worse when this ignoramus does not realize his limits and so he urges a junior staff person who is an expert to work on a paper for the minister to present during an international conference of agricultural experts. Yes, after practicing it repeatedly, reading the paper may not constitute a problem, but then there is bound to be the question-answer session and then Mr. Minister's paucity of knowledge is at once noticed as it lights up like a light bulb in a dark room. The minister's ignorance dampens his once bright mien as he tries hiding behind the microphone in vain, and so an entire nation is humiliated, not because there are no experts in agriculture in this country, but simply because offices are accorded by patronage instead of merit. This is the process that has led to the transformation of many frustrated experts into human laboratories for processing urine from beer. It is no wonder they die before long from liver complications that the population is always quick to blame on witchcraft, another weapon for survival in the local armoury.

Under Ahidjo, Cameroonians used to go on study-furloughs and would return with a higher certificate. It was no big deal for them to be reclassified based on their latest certificate. Nowadays, the system has crashed such that it can be said Cameroonians are in fact being punished for going back to school and improving upon their academic and professional standing. There are numerous Cameroonians who returned with higher certificates and were sent back to continue where they left off with the same job and salary; tell me of a country that frustrates talents. Even if it is those who are jealous holding these people back, this can only be possible because there is no system in place for checks and balances. The result is that many Cameroonians who would have thought of going back to school and bettering themselves, see no need for this since the whole venture is haunted by tortuous experiences upon their return. As a result, employees prefer to stay in their present positions while numbing their intellect with unhealthy yet beckoning social activities. After all, when they drink and get drunk, for a brief moment, they forget their plight. This is how the nation destroys itself.

Tribalism, nepotism, and favouritism are some of the vices in Cameroon that must be stopped. Projects and contracts must be given to people and firms based on merit and not personal connections. Even if personal connection should come in, networking as it is called in some societies, it should be a way of linking qualified people to the authorities concerned before they compete to prove their worth in executing the project and not in corrupting the authority contracting the project. In this way, the need for accountability will become a fair weapon in the hands of government to determine if the project was being executed as requested, without the temptation of letting a poorly done or unfinished job through because a friend or consanguineous relation executed it. Thus, all those wasteful projects will become a thing of the past any time soon as money will be provided for a project based on the need for the project rather than as a way of creating room for stealing the funds. As Harford points out correctly:

> The rot starts with the government, but it afflicts the entire society. There's no point investing in a business because the government will not protect you against thieves. (So you might as well become a thief yourself.) There's no point in paying your phone bill because no court can make you pay. (So there's no point being a phone company.) There's no point setting up an import business because the customs officers will be the ones to benefit. (So the customs office is underfunded and looks even harder for bribes.) There's no point getting an education because jobs are not handed out on merit. (And in any case, you can't borrow money for school fees because the bank can't collect on the loan).

Again, Cameroonians must learn to serve instead of lord it over others. A stifling tradition all over Africa, a spill over from the colonial days, is the "big man" syndrome. It has eaten so deeply into the social fabric that people forget the need to serve instead of longing for needy citizens to worship them. From the messenger in an office to the president, they all want to be considered "big men;" poor, broke, thieves that many are, in spite of their beautiful attires and positions of power and influence. Consider trying to meet with a public servant in any office in Cameroon and the message will strike home. Take a bank for instance. One walks in to deposit one's money, which the bank is badly in need of, and some unqualified teller who got the job because she is dating the boss treats one as if one is in the bank to beg a favour from her. In a government office, one dares not approach a District Officer. One will be lucky after waiting for hours to see him, and then he treats a citizen he should be serving like dirt. What in God's name is the matter with Cameroonians? Why do we not enjoy serving people at our places of work? Why do we not enjoy bringing a smile to the face of everyone who comes our way for the day? Why do we enjoy keeping people waiting for our services which we could easily render in just a few minutes?

Even some members of the clergy are now playing "big men" too as they keep members of their congregation or parish wanting to see them for one spiritual need or the other waiting. In some cases, it is true, those waiting are there to beg for assistance of some sort, yet that is no reason to keep a person waiting; after all, is it not the clergy themselves who tell us to see our Lord Jesus Christ in each other? Equally disturbing is the fact that when, finally, they show up, they do not seem to see anything wrong with keeping somebody waiting, and so an apology is out of the question. Nowadays, with their mostly expensive cars and gadgets, many clergy members have suddenly forgotten that their primary call is to save souls, and to appear in public for who they are instead of hiding behind private attires for whatever modern reason. In the case of Catholic priests, one cannot help wondering if the Roman collar now hurts or if the dust has suddenly become too much for the dignifying cassocks that a handful love having on all the time as it should be. Acculturation is not an excuse here, for are the bishops and Cardinals in Africa not part of that doctrine? Yet how often do we see a bishop with an *agbada, boubou,* or some tropical suit with nothing to announce his vocation? Given the tide of events, there is need for us to go back to the days when one could easily tell the Blessed Mother's sons from their attire. It helped in many ways: one could easily locate a priest, even by chance, during an emergency; people were able to give them the respect they deserve; it kept them in check also as they were constantly reminded of their vocation and its expectations in the face of ever present distractions. This is not the case today that many go around looking like third class chiefs in overflowing robes that belie their oaths of obedience, poverty, and service. Hardly anyone is against acculturation as recommended by today's church, but like everything else, it has to be done within reasonable limits mindful of one's vocation. Shirts, traditional and otherwise can be fashioned to accommodate the Roman collar so our beloved priest stand out instead of hiding behind derailing and equally misleading outfits. The church has its own tradition, which should be paramount, especially for its priests, acculturation notwithstanding.

It is not only professional but also courteous that while in one's office, one should not keep anyone waiting. It is only after serving the public that one can then face whatever paper work might be waiting. How did the paper work pile up in the first place in any case? Herein lies the Cameroonian paradox, for Cameroonians are friendly people, yet in a position of power they degenerate into monsters lording it over others who need their services, services for which the government or any other employer is paying them.

Even as this is being written, a colleague's experience in his career as a teacher keeps coming to mind. One of his students from ENS Bambili, a woman well-placed by marriage as she gave him to understand subtly, politely attacked him for keeping her waiting; a thing the colleague would never do intentionally. Even then, all taken into consideration it is hoped she sees her mistake, albeit belatedly. First, she had no appointment with this colleague, and decided to show up at his house without even notifying him or trying to find out his schedule for the day. After hours teaching, this colleague hurried home to take a badly needed nap, given that he had been up most of the previous night grading students' papers, but student after student, unscheduled, kept coming to his home with school problems. He had never blamed students for this given the nature of things in ENS Bambili at the time, and so he always made sure he tried to solve their problems and send them on their way. After sleepily attending to three students, this colleague informed his children to ask anyone who showed up needing him to wait. He then went in and immediately slept off. When finally he got up, this student of his — she probably came in shortly after he retired — had been waiting. She tactfully queried him for keeping her waiting. According to this colleague, he never answered back as he tried to remain polite; it was all about her and not her teacher. What one is trying to show here is the other side of the coin, how even some well-intentioned individuals have to suffer because of the chaos now reigning in Cameroon. Even though this student left thinking she had been disrespected, the truth is she had violated every single rule of decorum between guest and host, and because she was probably a "big man's" wife, she had the audacity to complain, albeit politely. Had she a scheduled appointment it would have been a whole different matter, but this was not the case.

In the light of this episode, as basic as it sounds, Cameroonians need to begin respecting time, while developing an understanding that people have private schedules and lives to live. This in no way, however, conflicts with our communal life style, but it puts in place certain limitations as to how much one can expect of another under normal circumstances. Within our communal life-style, it is all right to visit unannounced, because these are casual visits with usually nothing at stake, and which visits could be repeated over and over if need be. But in the case of this student, this was not a casual visit; this was somebody bringing work to another during after work hours, and not where the teacher works, but to his home and without previously alerting him to it. Again, within our communal life-style, there is nothing wrong to visit and hear that the host is asleep, and then one leaves without a fight. Africans must begin taking time seriously, and stop that ridiculous excuse for lateness by claiming "African time". Being on time is being on time and so is being late; the one brings about order and the other confusion and chaos. When people cannot keep to time, they cannot be organized and this disrupts so much. Imagine those on time having to wait for late comers before an occasion can begin, instead of the occasion beginning on time so that those who show up late are embarrassed.

The Rule of Law is a Must

In Cameroon there is the law but only in theory; otherwise, at best, it works when it is applied against the downtrodden as one sees this same legal system violated on a daily basis by those in powerful government positions, by the wealthy, and even by those employed to uphold it. If this is not the case, why is it all right for a minister to shamelessly tell lies about government policies to citizens? If this is not the case, why is it okay for a policeman in uniform to take five hundred francs from a taxi driver who has broken the law by not having a fire extinguisher in his car, for example, and then letting him off without as much as a warning?

In other words, those in power and those with money are above the law in Cameroon. The members of these groups can do virtually anything and go free. Consider the case of a policeman killing a civilian for absolutely no reason other than that, fed up with officers stealing his hard-earned money through bribes that they demand, a driver drives away after a policeman sounds his whistle requiring the driver to stop. As a result, the policeman fires his gun at the car, killing the driver. After such an atrocity, it is shameful to say there is no investigation into it, and when the local population begins making plans to teach the policeman a lesson, after all true power resides with the people, the government moves the murderer in uniform to a different town, and the case, which hitherto existed only in the minds of the people, is closed.

It is not a joke to state that Cameroon today does not have an investigating unit other than a gestapo with the duty of "investigating" those supposedly inciting people against the regime. When a crime is committed, there is no specially trained unit that reports at the scene to gather information and evidence of any sort. Usually, a few out-of-shape men in uniform show up and fool around the crime scene, in the process damaging evidence that would have been cherished by true crime experts. They ask a few questions here and there, and then drive off with the body of the deceased, if there was any, and that is the end of the story as nothing is ever heard after that about the case. A glaring example is the death of over a thousand people in the Nyos area of Wum, in

Cameroon, on August 21, 1986. It was said to be carbon dioxide gas that bubbled out of Lake Nyos, killing only people and animals without destroying homes or plants. All kind of suspicion was in the air, with scientists from abroad coming in and out. However, decades after, the government of Cameroon is yet to publish an official report on what happened that led to the death of over a thousand Cameroonians, and Mr. Biya is still posing as head of state. Only in Mr. Biya's Cameroon can such colossal indifference on the part of the government be tolerated. This is not because the people as a nation do not care, but because the government has no system in place to deal with such eventualities, nor does the president himself really care.

In the same vein, recently Bate Besong, one of (Anglophone) Cameroon's leading literary icons, died in a most ghastly accident along the Douala-Yaounde death-trap of a highway, and whereas eulogies were pouring into Cameroon from all around the world, it did not occur to the president to join his compatriots in mourning, even if he was Besong's most distinguished target. It becomes more embarrassing when it is remembered that Besong died in the company of one of Cameroon's foremost Anglophone TV producers, Kwasen Gwangwa'a. Granted that because of his writings Bate Besong could have been considered an enemy of the state, and so the president celebrated rather than lament his demise, but what about the death of Gwangwa'a, the distinguished state employee, which also failed to touch the heart of Cameroon's government and so extract a eulogy from the administration? Of what use is such a government? President Bush of the United States of America did not consider himself too busy or too "big" to find time and meet with the widow of one of his escort riders who died in an accident while escorting him – one escort rider! True presidents are constant sources of consolation to their citizens, to their nations, but not African presidents who spend their time with a few in-house traitors scheming against their nations instead.

Cameroon must go back to that point in time where it used to be when nobody was above the law; Ahidjo made it possible once, and it can still be re-established. Major-General Babatunde Abdulkadir Idiagbon (Tunde Idiagbon) did it Nigeria with War Against Indiscipline (WAI) and it worked. Because of the absence of a credible police force and an equally credible legal system, chaos now reigns in Cameroon. This saying in Cameroon "I fit kill you I pay money" (I can murder anyone and pay the price in cash) best illustrates the situation of things. Even though used by people jokingly, it is the truth about life in Cameroon today. A person with the means can do anything, even murder another Cameroonian and bribe his way out. In the same manner, a rich person can have an innocent person detained in jail, even without a charge, simply because he has the money or knows the chief of police. The motive is just to show to other underlings that he is an influential person, even if his influence is based on a corrupt foundation.

Cameroonians, like other Africans, must stop thinking it is all right to use one's resources against one's fellow citizens. When the imperialists used their power and wealth against the colonized indigenes, it was because the imperialists did not belong, and it was not a secret that they were there to do just that and get as much as they could out of the people in terms of labour and raw materials. Why then is the African doing the same thing against his own people with whom he is doomed to co-exist forever? The reason is obvious: the decolonization of the African is yet to reach the masses; it is yet to be drummed into us with that same intensity with which colonial policies and ideologies were instilled into the now somewhat alienated African. This must be a blunt process introduced within our educational systems and not limited to literature students and conferences only, but aimed at the entire population; otherwise, we will continue seeing the African "naturally" trying to colonize the African in his or her ways because it was a pattern acculturated into the values of Africa during the colonial era.

Until the day, then, when Africans will return to their roots by understanding that even with today's nation-states we are still a community; that in spite of the numerous ethnic groups now forced to co-exist in that one nation, we remain a community; that elders should be elders not political truants; that anyone who breaks the law, regardless of wealth or position, will face the elders, as of old, which is exactly what our "modern" courts are supposed to be, the ongoing disarray will continue to reign, relegating Africans onto the garbage heap of the human race where others love to see them.

Intensify the Decolonization Process

For decades today there has been a lot of talking about decolonizing the African mind, but a critical look reveals that a lot more talking and writing has been done about this than drastic and equally strategic steps taken to bring about its effective realization. The truth is, fifty years, or thereabouts, after most African countries gained their independence, their freedom from the colonial yoke, the minds of their citizens are yet to be free. Without realizing it, more often than not, most Africans remain ideological victims of colonization. When one listens to numerous young Africans, undergraduates even, talking, one cannot help lamenting the sounds of colonial ideological chains jangling. At the very least, these young people (the hope of our future) are embarrassed about their Africaness; their own ways, the people they are and what their culture is all about. Of course, the white man had qualified all their physical features—their blackness, their blunt noses, and their full and firm lips—as negative; their languages—thousands of beautiful tonal languages—as uncouth sounds and at best dialects; their resource-rich countries with varying temperatures and undulating landscapes of varied and attractive flora and fauna of heavenly beauty as hot, dusty, and stinking; in fact everything African has been given negative connotations. These poisonous doctrines that blighted our dignity, our self confidence, and our respect, are still being regurgitated around Africans on a daily basis even as Africa's labour force is being exploited at home and abroad, and her natural resources processed for Western and mainly African markets. The truth then is that even with all the years gone by, along with the attendant efforts at decolonization, there is still a lot of work left to be done. The reason for these troubling results is the absence of a unified effort by Africa to decolonize the African. One has, instead, frequently encountered some Africans claiming they are higher up there upon Western established scales of racial superiority, because of the colour of their skin, or, in the case of South Africa today, resulting from the unfortunate encounter with the doctrines of apartheid that misled black

South Africans into thinking they are better than blacks from the rest of Africa. In the words of Said Adejumobi:

> Beyond mere clichés of the leadership of the ANC, and some cadres in the South African liberation movement, majority of South Africans especially the blacks do not see themselves as Africans. When they comment on Africa, they refer to "you people from Africa". The mindset created under apartheid is that Africa is a jungle, where people are beasts, hungry and hopeless. The mindset remains unchanged and South Africans especially blacks don't want to identify with this.
>
> Coming from a history of denial and deprivation, South African blacks don't want to associate with those who have a semblance of their perceived former image; those who are deprived and hopeless. They therefore see themselves differently, and far better than other Africans. They often tend to compare themselves with Europeans and Americans, with little or no African identity.

In response to this shame heaped on the African south of the Sahara by the blacks in South Africa, one can only think of the pidgin saying in Cameroon: "Ashes fire don cold dog enter sleep for there". It is like saying everyone has insulted the black man from Africa south of the Sahara until the black South African who was a victim of apartheid only yesterday, whom we struggled in so many different ways to set free, can now also claim superiority over us. It is a sad day for Africa that gave birth to such garbage. This complex must be purged for Africa to stand and walk in the centuries ahead or else she will continue crawling, as is the case today, even with all her limbs in the best working conditions and her surroundings udders to the world.

To begin with, "decolonization" is, and hitherto remains an undergraduate term. In other words, Africans, as victims of the colonial mentality, encounter that term and an understanding of the concept of colonialism, even while living it, at the level of the university mainly; hence the trudging results of efforts at decolonization. The question arises: given Africa's population, how many of our sons and daughters make it to the university where they might learn about colonialism, the effects it has on how we live our lives, how we relate to each other, how we associate with the rest of the world, and the efforts at eradicating it? So what happens to those—a significant percentage—who do not make it into universities? They never hear of the colonial mentality, let alone of the fact that it is Africa's priority to eradicate its damned impact on the continent. As a result, while a privileged few write and make speeches about decolonization at high-level meetings and conferences, the vast majority continue living it and handing it over to future generations they father and mother. The colonial mentality then must be attacked with all of Africa's might and from all angles—at home, at school, at work, at play, in church. Africans must breathe decolonization; they must be reminded every second of their lives, that human beings are born equal and that the denigration of the African was orchestrated and maintained to facilitate the exploitation of Africa's resources and her labour force. This is common knowledge to those in academe but not to the vast majority who people the streets without university education.

This new thrust at decolonization must begin at home; this is where the poisoning of the portrait of the African began. It was instilled into our parents by all means possible by colonial administrators. They took away power from traditional leaders; forced our elders to work for nothing; denied them local luxuries while imposing on them more expensive and harmful Western synthetic variations; banned our traditional rites which they damned as heathen while imposing Western rituals on us in the name of religion; abolished or diluted our legal systems, and exiled recalcitrant traditional leaders and elders, all to establish the lie that they and their ways are better. For decades these lies were injected into the African, the black man, in every way possible, and true to the nature of the human mind, they succeeded in burning it in. Africans, thus stigmatized, have, as a result, carried this "curse" and have consciously or otherwise, unwittingly passed it on for generations, while Western propaganda, growing stronger than ever, continues its proliferation of racial nonsense even until today. Shockingly, it is sometimes paraded as scientific knowledge. Consider the fact that as late as 2007, James Watson, a 79-year-old Nobel laureate praised for his contribution in DNA research told a London newspaper that tests show black Africans are not as intelligent as whites; what a legacy he hopes to bequeath posterity with his last breath.

Beyond our homes, from elementary school up to university level, programs must be designed to expose this lie, and the great achievements of Africans on the mother continent and in the diaspora made common knowledge. These lessons must have priority over Western history and literature which in numerous African schools, even until today, remain strategic subjects aiding in the perpetuation of the colonization of the African. Slogans and lines of allegiance to their integrity must be indoctrinated into African kids and elders alike, like "God save the queen" was caned into our elementary school Empire-minds of yore. At work or at play, relevant songs must teach our children and elders pride in themselves and the ways of the African, while also being taught to understand that they, as black human beings, are capable of everything humanly possible; an already established fact. Religious leaders must, from the pulpits, preach equality while debunking racist's myths upon the slightest opportunity, and so must our radio and television stations.

In like manner, there is the need for a common African language, which will unite Africans and give them a sense of belonging wherever they find themselves. Africa's fragmented linguistic landscape denies Africans the strength of unity, which though at its most basic level yet, they could muster to raise the continent to its deserved position in history. If Africans can meet anywhere and speak Swahili, Hausa, Yoruba, or Lingala, instead of the languages of other peoples, Africa would have taken the first steps towards becoming a force to reckon with. At once, Africans will feel a sense of pride and belonging which is denied them today because of the patchwork nature of their linguistic landscape and their resultant dependence on languages of colonization.[2] It is not surprising then that Africans are quick to identify along tribal lines than by their Africaness, a twist which will take precedence were they all able to converse in a common African tongue. This dream notwithstanding, furnishing Africa with an African lingua franca will be no easy task to accomplish given already existing rivalries.

These rivalries will evidently lead to different linguistic groups wanting to impose their language on others as the language of choice. However, educating the population and selecting from languages already widely in use can easily solve this problem. This suggestion may sound overly ambitious, but certainly not as far-fetched a dream as thoughts of placing a human being on the moon could have been when first conceived of. It will take decades, may be a century even, but guided by the advantages it will accord the continent, it can be realized should we apply ourselves to this dream without pessimism.

Unless Africa approaches the decolonization of the African mind with the determination that the epidemic requires, with the zeal with which colonialism was approached, Africa will remain timid, reluctant, intimidated, self-confirmed underdogs and so continue dancing in circles while being ridiculed by the main culprits of her plight. Wherever Africa was denied the opportunity because her children were considered inept, and later given equal opportunity, Africa has excelled. Where Africa has failed, a critical look will reveal Western designs, and the records can only be set right by the complete liberation of the African mind shackled especially during the colonial encounter and today still being held captive by Western propaganda. An anecdote will better illuminate my point. Upon arriving the Douala International airport some time in 2003, right out of the plane, one ran into a French family sitting there blocking the passage as they were waiting for the arrival of a dear one supposedly, but there was not a single Cameroonian in sight. Some police officer, a victim of the colonialist imposed inferiority complex, had allowed this French family to come right to the arrival terminal to receive their dear one in our country, Cameroon, but our own relatives could not enjoy that privilege in our own fatherland. They were hurdled in a group and held at bay outside, away even from the arrival area around the lone carousel. So in France this French family will be accorded much better treatment over us Cameroonians because they are in their country, and then in our country our ignorant police men and women, victims of colonialist indoctrinated inferiority complexes, will still give the French family preference over us. And so the African suffers twice: at home and away in the white man's own country. This has to stop, and only an aggressive decolonization strategy will bring about its cessation.

Human Resources

Any serious government must do all to bring back home the willing millions of qualified Cameroonians now resident in different parts of the world where their talents and qualifications are being made use of by foreign nations; this goes for the continent of Africa as a whole. That done, the government must do all to encourage positive private initiative, especially those with economic value, instead of the current stifling practices.

To start a business in Cameroon, for example, is a nightmare, given the amount of physical stamps, paper work, and cumbersome procedures expected of the individual involved, and most of the documents are plain stupid and unnecessary as all they do is take investment capital out of the hands of the prospective business owner. Furthermore, the humongous taxes expected of a fledgling venture are just incredible and are not working in favour of sprouting businesses. It is common knowledge that any serious government gives a grace period for new companies to begin maturing at least before they are charged taxes, but this is not the case in Cameroon. Even while still trying to register the company, taxes are imposed on the potential business based on an estimated turnover. When pitted against the situation in the United States as per studies by The World Bank Group on starting a business in Cameroon, the facts are alarming and indicative of a government that is not there to make life easier for its citizens. Consider the fact that while it costs an American in the United States just about $100.00 (approximately 49.800frs CFA today) to begin a business after visiting only one office building in the state (one's province in the Cameroonian setting), it costs the Cameroonian, comparatively speaking, $1,536.88 (762.000frs CFA approximately); he also has to visit about twelve different offices and he is not sure to be served the same day, unlike the American who will be served within an hour. New companies are tortured from the very beginning by corrupt taxation officials who end up not giving the money they collect to the government. The end result is the collapse of the new business effort as it crumbles within the very first couple of years because of fiscal malpractices. Are the policy maker's just plain wicked or stupid such that they cannot even realize that flourishing new businesses will come along with beautiful infrastructure and employment for millions of citizens? If it is not taxes that stifle these young companies, then those at the helm of the venture steal all the money. Africans returning home must be encouraged to bring in what they have learnt, and to introduce practices that are decent, relevant, and beneficiary to the local system.

Again, Cameroonians must be employed on merit and not because of godparents. If a person studied and has the certificates and skills to concretize his qualification for a position, then he or she should be given the job without all those ongoing fictitious excuses around today such as the ratio-wise allocation of positions to different provinces. It is these practices that have carved out a disturbingly strange destiny for Cameroon's skilled labour as victims of a tripartite fate: they either never return home to Cameroon after valuable years of studies abroad; or they return but cannot become a part of the circus Cameroon has degenerated into and so leave on self-exile, at best, if not chased away by the existing gestapo; or, last but not the least, they remain in this Gehenna of a nation, combating the situation in a brave effort to maintain their sanity as they wait for a benefactor or else drown in the filth as players in their own right. This ought not to be the situation were there a president at the head of the government who cared for his people.

The Maintenance Culture

In societies that understand the value of maintenance, each time a valuable device breaks down, it takes at most a day or two (except when parts need to be ordered), for technicians to come in, access the problem, and immediately repair the system. In Cameroon nowadays, such a breakdown would mean the end of the said device's lifespan even though it was just a few months old, and cost the nation millions of francs to acquire. This is the problem with most of those carcasses of cars, buses, tractors, bulldozers, typewriters, copiers, computers and so on, found lying all around ministries and different government or company lots in the country — wealth strewn in mud.

Cameroonians, therefore, must introduce where it was not, and reintroduce where it was, the practice of maintenance which is virtually absent in the country today. Similarly, there is dire need for an effective department that oversees the completion and maintenance of projects in the country. There are, for example, roads in the country which were literally abandoned after the foreign companies that constructed them left the country. There is no local body charged with the upkeep of these roads, even as the potholes begin appearing and increasing in size until they are deep gullies and craters. The trend in the country today is for those in charge to feel completely satisfied that a venture has taken off. Whether the venture is completed or not, strangely enough, is of no importance to them, not even the quality of the venture seems to matter. The results of this are all those uncompleted and poorly executed projects that can be found lying all over the country. There is one along Ayaba Street in Bamenda, between the Veterinary Junction and the Taxation Building, a huge building just rotting away with nobody able to tell what is going on. So many of these "ghost projects" are dotted around the country, even in Yaounde itself, and nobody is yet to be held accountable for them.

Again, consider the recently finished Bamenda-Batibo supposed trunk "A" road, a disgrace of an effort at road building. One cannot help asking if that is supposed to pass for a tarred road, and if indeed it was considered a part of the trans-African highway about which so much ado had been made from the seventies? Even for somebody's private road, the project was most shoddily executed. The truth is the Bamenda-Batibo road is some track merely painted with bitumen and nothing more. Compare it with the Fumbot-Foumban road even today, or with the Nigerian section of this trans-African highway, and the Bamenda-Batibo travesty will appear as a child's house built of a pack of cards in the face of an architect's skyscraper. Is anyone surprised, then, that even before the people could begin using the road, there were already potholes caused by raindrops? And this is not because the engineers who constructed the road are professional toddlers, no; it is because somebody who was in charge did not discharge his duties effectively for reasons that are obvious by now — corruption. Who were the engineers who approved of such a joke when it was supposedly finished? And to think of the trouble the company caused the people as they blocked and barred traffic along this road during construction, without creating side-passages for people to use in getting to their homes, because they claimed they were building a road; the people tolerated it, looking forward to the road they would have at the end, only for this substandard road to be the reward. One can already see the damage it would cause to people's vehicle when the tar begins peeling off in larger pieces, as is already the case, mindful of the fact that there is no worthwhile maintenance crew. In a nutshell, the Bamenda-Batibo road amounts to nonsense.

When Southern Cameroons was yet to join La République, standards and the maintenance culture were ingrained in the ways of the people. Every government department, for example, had its motor vehicle maintenance department where all department vehicles were repaired, and so it was easy for things to be accounted for and crosschecked. Nevertheless, that was not what the new authorities from Yaounde liked since it eliminated any chances of fraudulent claims which are rampant today. Who does not know in Cameroon that government vehicles have been abandoned as beyond repairs, whereas they are in perfect shape, only for those in control later to buy the supposedly damaged vehicle at a giveaway price? This is creativity one can describe as negative ingenuity, yet it flourishes at every level and in almost every aspect of Cameroonian life today; one of numerous ways that the government loses money as an otherwise thriving nation is made to grind to a halt by miscreants parading as faithful servants of the public. Were there maintenance units for each department, such a thing would hardly happen as the engineer in charge could easily be held responsible after such fraudulent deals are carried out and later exposed.

Other units in similar straits are hospitals, which never seem to change in terms of equipment because they cannot be maintained. A country like Cameroon is without basic medical equipment that could help devoted doctors and laboratory technicians carry out their jobs effectively, simply because even the obsolete machines in place, which could otherwise have been functioning, cannot be maintained. We know some of the equipment were donated to these facilities, the more reason why the government should treasure them and put aside funds for their upkeep. Why is it so hard for the government to determined its needs and encourage citizens to specialize in such areas? A reasonable government would have highlighted the need for maintenance engineers and put out scholarships in those areas to help with their training, but certainly not Cameroon, where even if it were done, unqualified relations to those in power would flood the programme. The venture would, from its inception, be transformed into a channel to get relative overseas where they would involve themselves in what they are interested and abandon the government project that sent them out. Such treacherous activities could still be punishable in a country that had a true government guiding it; that does not sound like Cameroon today.

Because of corruption and the want of maintenance units in the country, so much is lost in the form of infrastructure, equipment, and skilled maintenance engineers who are now serving in other parts of the world instead. The practice of maintenance, especially for a nation that does not manufacture, is one that must be revived. This is necessary, not only because it will save the country a lot of money, but also because that is the way it is supposed to be. With a government that is not interested in maintenance, the citizens themselves have become lethargic to the need for repairs except in areas that command special interest like cars which are status-symbols and so must be kept in the best possible shape at all cost. It is not surprising then that a person might be living in a house and until the day that drops of rain begin jostling with him over bedroom space, only then does he begin thinking his roof might need repairs. The result is the current state of disrepair of virtually everything in the country.

The Need to Serve

While respect for age and authority is a major and invaluable feature of our African tradition, we must eliminate the "big man" syndrome in our administrative setup. Its existence slows down procedure, thereby leading to an inefficient administrative system and a frustrated and unpatriotic work force.

After all, who is proud of a government that is not concerned about the welfare of the people? The "big man" syndrome is a gorgon that was inherited from colonial administrators and has no place in our traditional setup, which, unfortunately, is already being infected by this syndrome. The "respect" shown the "big man" is different from that shown an elder. The "big man" is in fact not respected as, more often than not, his corrupt practices and haughty disposition make him unpopular or at best notorious. He is, by all the gestures displayed by the subordinate, being stupefied and fooled into thinking the fawning citizen admires and holds him and his position in awe. This is not true, because the same fawning citizen insults the "big man" when he turns his back by questioning ridiculously: "Big man, big man, is he the one feeding me?"

Our respect for an elder, on the other hand, comes from a genuine feeling of appreciation and devotion to his age and/or his achievements in society that present him as the concerned role model that he is for his community. The respect shown the elder is not forced out of the subordinate, or used by the latter merely as a means of coaxing a favour from the elder or person in authority as is the case in the "big man" syndrome, hence its genuineness. In the same vein, Jacob U. Gordon adds: "The African philosophy of respect for elders was based upon the assumption that, all other things being equal, those who were living in the world and experiencing life before others were born should possess greater knowledge" (2). The "big man" syndrome will die out if citizens only know their rights, the services the "big man" is supposed to be performing, and that he is, in fact, there to serve and not lord it over others. This would have been the case were people able to sue such "big men" for neglect of duty and get speedy court decisions, putting these "big men" in their places by making them pay damages for their wrongdoings. But for this to happen, the administrative arms of government—the executive, the legislative, and the judiciary—must gain their autonomy so the one can check the excesses of the other.

Cameroonians, therefore, must remember to serve and not lord it over fellow citizens. There is much joy in being of assistance to someone in need; how much more so when the service one is rendering is one's job. We all need to remember, these positions are all short-lived and all you so-called "big men" will have to return to society and meet the rest of the masses. They will also accept you depending on how you treated them while you were a "big man".

Beyond just the "big man" syndrome, Africa's leaders must learn to relinquish power. It is a disturbing truth that there is something pathologically disconcerting about modern day political leaders in Africa. Beyond that threshold—the power-line—into positions of power, something in an African leader snaps. It has been said absolute power corrupts absolutely, but as evidenced in Africa, that is only the first stage before our leaders are deranged and transformed into madmen and corrupt specialists demolishing their own nations. Otherwise, why is it that even after so many years in power, during which years these leaders have destroyed the social, political, and economic framework of their nations, do they still cling to power, to the point that they unleash thugs, uniformed and otherwise, to beat up, maim, and even kill their opponents? Robert Mugabe is doing that now even as one is writing. Paul Biya of Cameroon, after twenty-six years in office, more than six continuous terms in a sane society, is also warming up to the same effect by letting out words hinting at his willingness to continue as president of Cameroon for life, which country he has already distinguished by mismanaging it into socio-economic notoriety. One has come to believe this clinging to power is mostly characteristic of parvenus and that is what most African leaders are: from the mere administrator to the president himself. The ordinary administrator is arbitrarily given power by a dictator for some strange reason like the fact that he echoes his meaningless political mantra, and the dictator was himself given power by a role model of a despotic predecessor (colonialist or otherwise) for an equally selfish reason. The parvenu suddenly finds himself thrust into a position of power, like Cameroon's Paul Biya, or else with foreign support snatches it from a precursor like Mobutu Sesse Sekou of Zaire fame. Leaders such as these are too frequently without the character to manage the power accorded them by their office: they missed out on that legalized struggling phase, which slowly grooms and thus transforms an otherwise misdirected dictator into a noble and patriotic statesman. It is during that struggling phase that the potential leader comes to terms with why he seeks change or power even, and how he will put it to use. Otherwise, absolute power overwhelms and then derails its prey as before long he begins thinking he is a god even as he misses out on the fact that he does not know what the very next second holds in store for him.

Like the Master Himself, we must all serve instead of lording it over people, for we will answer, eventually, believer or not, unfortunately, for all that we do to the least of His brethren. Yet man has spent his time preying on man instead of striving to thrive together given the abundance of the world's resources, It is in this light that one realizes sadly, that of all God's creations, mankind has failed woefully. His failure lies in the misuse of his intellect, in spite of his conscience, to excuse his indulgence in activities that pervert his will, satisfy his body, but damn his soul.

Re-Introduce Professionalism

Beyond the need to serve, especially as it relates to leaders, professionalism has to become a part of Cameroon's business culture. Africa, generally speaking, lacks the spirit of professionalism, and this is very obvious in many government and privately owned organizations. It is seen in the way the workers, from the boss down to the messengers treat members of the public. In Cameroon, like the rest of Africa, people beg, bribe, and even visit marabouts all in an effort to influence an employment decision, but when they get the job, they fail to render effective services to their clients whom they were recruited to serve. They immediately begin treating their customers like wretches in search of favours. Even the owners of businesses, whose money and livelihood is at stake, are very rude, arrogant, and have absolutely no knowledge of how to relate to their customers.

The business owner and her staff do not seem to realize that they are dependent on their customers, the public in other words, for business which then translates into revenue and their salaries subsequently. It is that "big man" syndrome again that takes control. A business owner whose business is thriving suddenly becomes arrogant, wanting people to lie down for him to walk over them. Before long, his customers abandon his business, and potential customers do not even get to approach the venture since they have heard the owner is a disrespectful idiot. The result is that the business collapses. The non-professional business owner begins accusing imaginary and usually innocent people for his business' fate, unable to realize that the lack of professionalism, on his part and that of his workers, is responsible.

Rich business owners and managers of government ventures in Africa must learn one thing—they are rich, so what? They do not pay the bills of members of the public nor do they feed them for free. Their money is *their* money, not the public's so why do they expect people to lie down for them to walk over them? It is not as if they go around just writing free cheques and distributing free money to people. So what is this bragging and arrogance about? Even if members of the public receive money from the rich, it is for services they have rendered and these rich people need these services desperately for their business to thrive. So in actual fact, the rich are the ones to go around trying to recruit the best labour they can afford. No, Africa's rich sit like demi-gods, waiting for people they need to come begging, after all, they have the money. All this, beyond the fact that the imperialist reversed priorities when dealing with Africa, is because Africa's governments have failed to create seminar sessions during which effective business management ideas are introduced and disseminated amongst a largely uneducated yet arrogant bunch of entrepreneurs. But, of course, governments can only get to the point of being able to provide such services when they are themselves stable, and this is yet to be the case in Africa.

Employers (government or private) and employees must understand the difference between doing business and rendering a favour. An employer employs workers mainly for the purpose of having services rendered, and those services must be rendered effectively or else the employee must be sacked. If this is not done, it is common knowledge that sooner or later the attitudes of bad employees become the standard for other workers and this is bound to affect the business adversely and bring about its collapse ultimately. In this light, employees must be thorough professionals, from the busboy through the manager to the director general or governor of a province or state. They were employed, given, or elected into these positions to serve the public in a professional manner, not lord it over others. These employees must stop thinking or considering their services to the public a favour. No! This is their job, along with the work for which they are being paid and without it they will be unemployed. Render these services then with dignity and respect instead of grudgingly as is the case nowadays.

It becomes obvious then that, beyond whatever qualifications made employees to deserve their jobs, there is the overwhelming need for their attitude in the face of those they serve to be professionally honed. Beyond certificates, businesses must train their employees towards, and demand professionalism from them so that their mission statement is best fulfilled, bearing in mind that at its most basic, the customer is boss, and rendering him distinguished services in return for his money is the most basic mission of any business. If this is done, then workers will go to work with the will to serve instead of the will to show off that they are employed and working for such and such a company, even while failing to produce.

In the same manner, these business ventures must look for a way of measuring production or output on the part of their staff as a way of strengthening professionalism. If a worker knows his or her production is being monitored, then he or she will sit up and behave professionally. Even the effectiveness of a customer service department can be monitored by occasionally having customers answer to survey questions about how they are being received and treated by attendant staff in a particular company. If the findings show that customers are dissatisfied, then the necessary training must be provided and if after that things still do not improve, then it is time to send workers packing and a new set recruited. In this way, staff concerned with customer services, and therefore responsible for projecting a particular image of the company out there, and this is everybody working for the enterprise, will sit up.

For this kind of service measurement practices to take place, there has to be effective division of labour within the place of work, something that is missing in most places of work in Cameroon. Because there is no effective division of labour, apparently nobody is accountable for any service other than the boss up there who, because of the poor sense of centralization, is usually unable to monitor in other parts of the company or business he is running. Unless there is effective division of labour, there can be no effective system of accountability. In successful ventures, there is no room for speculation about who is supposed to do what because of the clearly spelt out job description that is characteristic. In Cameroon, it is true that job descriptions in most government and private endeavours are vague. As a result, there are moments when several employees are doing nothing but none will volunteer to carry out a particular service for the company because he or she is waiting for the other to volunteer or for the boss to instruct somebody to do it. Job descriptions must then be provided to the smallest detail such that "A" can easily be held responsible for a failed service or "B" instead of everybody being blamed for not doing something that nobody in particular was supposed to be doing.

In like manner, taking initiative is something that needs to be rewarded instead of the worker being accused by peers of being nosy or even pushy as is the case today. These are the things to be taught workers from time to time when they are employed by any service in the public or private sector. In fact, initially, every staff who is hired should be on probation while he or she learns to do the work involved. Until it is proven that the recruit on probation has promise, only then should he or she be made permanent. This probation phase, however, should be one during which the recruit is being trained yet he or she should be on full pay. This period is not intended to be a moment of exploitation when the recruit works to death for only a percentage of his salary or nothing even, as is practiced today by some people. This is illegal exploitation of labour and should not be tolerated by the Department of Labour in any country, which department should also carry out frequent checks to ensure that workers receive fair treatment from employers. This used to be the case in Cameroon under the Ahidjo regime, but not today. One wonders if the Ministry of Labour is still functioning even, and what its functions are if it does, or better still, how it serves the abused and exploited labour force in Cameroon today when the government is, in fact, the greatest offender here.

Uphold the Ways of our Forefathers

So much about Cameroon's predicament today is because of her hybrid quality in virtually everything. Most of what Cameroonians do today, whether we like it or not, has a stamp of the colonial blight, and this is making it hard for Cameroonians to be who they really are, and so forge a future for themselves. Accordingly, there is the need for Cameroonians to be guided primarily by their own values before those acquired as a result of the colonial encounter can be given a chance. Even then, these must come in only when Cameroonians are interacting with Westerners. Where is the wisdom speaking college level English to a person who speaks only pidgin or Mungaka or Douala?

A core aspect of Cameroon's culture is respect for age and hierarchy in society. Possibly only Asian cultures can rival Africa when it comes to this; it is an aspect of our culture that Africans should be so proud of and do all to maintain. It is because of respect for age and authority that there was so much peace and order before the rat race given birth to after capitalism invaded the continent. Yet the truth is that what used to be the norm in most African cultures is today on the wane as our children see garbage on television and think it is the way of the hour. Respect for elders, for authority, and vice versa, is a *sine qua non* for a successful society in Africa. If today's African leaders had just a little bit of respect for their subjects as per our tradition, they would not do most of what they do when in office: lying, stealing, victimizing, and murdering rivals. In the days of old, when Africa was Africa, they would have been dealt with swiftly by the appropriate secret societies instead of the prejudiced methods used by today's Western legal systems even with practitioners proclaiming its neutrality and objectivity. Justice is supposed to be blind, but it is not; Western jurisprudence has eyes and it sees through its blindfold.

Decency is on the wane too, and this is very necessary for a balanced society. It is traditional for Africans to dress decently. It is for this reason that men, women, boys, and girls knew what to wear to what occasion without offending anybody. Beyond just what they had on, they knew how to walk respectfully when in the midst of their elders; the young knew how to carry themselves and how to come across when talking to an elder. Today, these enviable values are threatened as some in our societies who have been out in the West return and try behaving like Westerners (with their concept of freedom and equality) in the midst of elders. For a people to betray their culture by trying to come across as other peoples, is not only stupid and disappointing but also culturally suicidal. Africans must realize that their values are theirs only and unless they value and protect their ways like endangered species, then the destabilization which has led to unrest and on-going mismanagement in Africa is only just beginning.

We must remember that the family is one of the most valuable units in our societies and so must protect its sacredness instead of turning that relationship into a gambling game in which after a few years any former member of a spousal union can go his or her way for the flimsiest possible reason; this was not the way of Africa until recently, comparatively speaking. A family's name must remain as sacred as it used to be, and thus protected by all decent means. When we begin again studying and practicing the ways and ethical values of our cultures while highlighting the pride and moral wealth imbedded therein, then prosperity and stability will gradually set in. Otherwise, we are on a course of perdition, as tomorrow being African will mean nothing other than just a nominal expression for identification purposes only.

Cameroonians must be determined to improve upon their lot and strive towards that goal. This is the responsibility of every Cameroonian, our status in society notwithstanding, and like a spiral, we will spring back into a better lot after all. It is basic that human nature, as such, can identify that which is wrong and that which is good. It is man's will, then, to persist in doing that which is wrong. From simply denying to disrespect a fellow Cameroonian to the point of refusing to give or accept bribes, Cameroonians can make that change which this country so badly needs. Everyone, therefore, must ask himself or herself, what he or she is doing to help change the negative and equally destructive worldview now reigning in this country? People must do that which they know they are supposed to do, whether as administrators, doctors, teachers, or uniform officers; just begin today by doing that which is right as per one's office and position in society and before long one is bound to have positively affected someone else, and so that virtue will slowly but surely spread.

Meanwhile the government must work towards giving her citizens equal rights before the law, before government opportunities and facilities, as patrimonialism is today a cancer that is destroying Cameroon. Cameroonians should do all to make life easy for anyone who comes their way and not the other way round. If we can all start like this, we would go a long way. The bigger responsibility, though, is on the shoulders of the government, being that it has virtually all the resources needed to guide and lead the country out of the current socio-political wilderness in which it is stranded but has chosen instead to fuel the state of anarchy. This is the means through which leaders of government and their private associates benefit at the expense of the citizens whom they have succeed in antagonizing and placing under siege, thanks to the help of the armed forces and the overflow of heavily laced beer. It is not surprising then that Nzongola-Ntalaja observes: "Africa is full of unpatriotic leaders who seem to believe that if they cannot run a country they might as well wreck it" (17).

No pretence is made here to suggest that these ideas would completely solve Cameroon's and Africa's problems, especially without a change in mentality towards each other, the nation and continent as a whole. It is hoped, however, that one must begin from somewhere; so, consider these fledgling strides in the right direction in any case. When people begin considering and practicing some of these suggested virtues, a lot will naturally fall in place as a result, leading slowly but certainly to a better society focused on the wellbeing of the citizenry as a whole, instead of a few well placed power brokers who have transformed government into a secret society and governance into séance.

That Cameroon's socio-economic collapse, like that of the continent south of the Sahara, is dangerously chronic lies in the fact that an overwhelming percentage of those with an international background which entails experiencing diversified, and in most cases more efficient systems return home only to undress themselves of these positive foreign values and jump into the mud bath

Cameroon has degenerated into: politicians, doctors, lawyers, teachers, law officers, civil servants, all. But for the existence of a promising younger generation, the prognostics would have been dismal as otherwise the country is doomed, trapped in a powerfully vicious cycle of corruption of cyclonic propulsions that just sucks in and shreds all. Our hope is the youths of today; if they can survive the AIDS plague, they may rescue the nation from a selfish group of alienated old men and women humiliating themselves in the name of leaders. But a voice is needed to help guide the endangered youths into becoming a salvaging adult population tomorrow — the voice of the writer as the conscience of society, and the voice of God as the moral mould (despite the antithesis of its being the opiate of society); only then can there be hope.

Chapter Eight
Conclusion

After all is said and done, in terms of the "modern" state, the inability of Africans to dispose of tribalism and function as a nation remains a major obstacle in the path of progress. It is time Africans recognize the continent's predicament today. We cannot now simply dismiss the modern states put in place by imperialists and return to days before colonialism in order to begin establishing new states, kingdoms, or empires by conquering and absorbing the weak as a way of expanding. There is no room for that, given the present world order. Accordingly, while identifying and maintaining individual cultural values, since that is what a person's identity is all about, we must at least relegate the tribal mentality for the national—certainly easier said than done, yet it seems to be the main highway out of our present quagmire. Unless we begin operating as nations, we will keep building only to tear down, marking time in the path of progress. An objective constitution, a strong and independent judiciary, and a presidency with vision determined to serve rather than exploit its people can help in jumpstarting this process. This is easy to institute, provided our leaders are willing to realize that the welfare of the citizenry is the *raison d'être* of any organized society or nation, and so begin sharing power. The presidency ought to be a national and not a personal or private institution, or worse still, one that belongs to a clique. In fact, this institution must have a defined term of office, as indeed it is the case, until power hungry African leaders begin toying with the constitution.

Nobody with any sense of Africa's history can doubt the fact that the continent today is not what it would have been without her encounter with imperialist aspirations. That Africa's unique evolutionary process was forcefully halted and with extreme brutality re-directed by imperialists, is being confirmed daily—the slave trade, colonialism, neo-colonialism, and now globalization. For this reason, Africa's history can never be complete without the damaging consequences of imperialism on the continent mentioned, albeit to the chagrin of those who feel otherwise. Time has passed, and so Africans should have been able to restructure the course of their evolution, some do posit. Those who argue thus against Africa and the effects of colonialism on the continent, mindful of its chaotic present, including African scholars, are propagandist or else simply frustrated by the goings-on on the continent under kleptocracies headed by unpatriotic indigenes. As a result, these condescending and disillusioned scholars, alien and indigenous respectively, have rushed to self-destructive conclusions like the failed economic strategist who blows his brains out with a gun, or the humiliated politician who hangs himself. There would have been significant value in this claim about the continent had Africa, in all fairness, been given the honest chance to pick up from the shards of imperialist activities on the continent without persistent foreign interference. Tatah Mentan himself, despite his own frustration, agrees with me when he points out that the lack of development in Africa is caused largely by Africa's asymmetrical relationship with the imperial international system and the weak states it has fostered (*Recolonisation* 16). This asymmetrical relationship is not a concept of today, but one that was there from the very beginning of relationships between imperialists and Africa. It is for this reason that the colonial legacy remains forever relevant in the discussion of Africa's plight today, the role of mainly idiotic and/or unpatriotic leaders notwithstanding.

In keeping with imperialist goals and the lack of genuine goodwill towards Africa's progress, imperialists, after hundreds of years of slavery, immediately banded together without giving Africa a breather and divided the continent into colonies. It was with the utmost reluctance that imperialist nations parted with these colonies decades after. Even then, it was only to employ neo-colonial tactics which are today segueing into another method of socio-political subjugation and destabilization in the guise of globalization. This fact becomes glaring when it is realized that most of the current loans and aid gestures on the continent today are hypocritical, given the interest earning motive and other attendant benefits attached.

Yes, colonialism did not take place in Africa only, but it must be remembered that there are other factors which are always neglected when people argue in this way: the cultures of these different parts of the world, the nature and structure of their societies, and the degree of colonialist involvement are a few examples. Claude Ake has made this same point: "Colonialism in Africa was markedly different from the colonial experiences of the Americas, Europe, and Asia. To begin with, it was unusually statist" (1-2). Ake argues further that the colonial state redistributed land and determined who should produce what and how; it attended to the supply of labour, sometimes resorting to forced labour; it churned out administrative instruments and legislated taxes to induce the break-up of traditional social relations of production, the atomization of society, and the process of proletarianization. Even when people have pointed out that the colonialist educated Africans, it is always forgotten that colonialist goal was to ensure the supply of partially skilled labour that could provide specific services required of non-colonial subjects who were also required to remain steadfast in the performance of their often tedious and disagreeable tasks. The colonialists built roads, railways, and ports for the sole reason of facilitating the collection and exportation of commodities as well as the importation of manufactured goods. The colonial state sold commodities through commodity boards and controlled every aspect of the colonial economy meticulously (Ake 2). The goal was to maintain its power and domination and to realize the socio-political and economic objectives of colonization—subjugation and exploitation. Sounding the same note, Le Vine writes:

> There is no simple, satisfying explanation for the impetus that drove the nations of Europe to establish colonies all over the world. *There is only a complex of motives and pressures as various as the situation in which they operated*: the colonization of South America differs as much in its underlying motivations as the conquest of India by Britain differs from the European penetration and colonization of sub-Saharan Africa. *Each case presents its own patterns of cause and effect; each instance its unique characteristics.* (*The Cameroons*. 15 emphasis mine)

Yes, colonialism obtained in other parts of the world, but many factors that influenced the colonization of Africa—"...the curiosity of the first European seafarers to venture south of the Pillars of Hercules; the competition of the great trader nations for the slaves, palm oil, and gold..." from Africa; the dire "need for raw materials to feed the burgeoning European industrialization of the eighteenth and nineteenth centuries; the simple factor of rivalry for colonies and the need to keep others from getting there first; and even the less tangible factors of prestige and military security" (Le Vine, *The Cameroons* 15)—are not all found in other parts of the world, hence the peculiar nature of the causes and effects of colonization in Africa.

Interestingly, while shouting to the world that Africa should now be held responsible for her trailing in world capitalist trends, those responsible for her plight are still actively holding Africa back because of their clandestine imperialist activities on the continent often paraded as international concern, monetary loans, expatriate assistance, cooperation and the like. Is it news that African governments and leaders that have refused dancing to the patronizing and often alienating and destructive tunes of their former colonialist plunderers and other Western nations and organizations by attempting to question established patterns of economic exploitation and political interference have been destroyed by these bodies? Was that not the case with Guinea's Sekou Touré, Ghana's Kwame Nkrumah and even Patrice Lumumba of the Congo? Is that not what is happening in Côte d'Ivoire even as recently as 2004? And are the consequences of these interferences obvious? Yet some Westerners are doing all to transform Africa, especially Africa south of the Sahara, into a laughing stock by screaming out denigrating titles and headlines about the continent.

If all the hoopla about helping Africa had a genuine goal, why is it that the world continues tolerating and working with corrupt African leaders? If embargos can be placed on supposedly rogue governments for decades, leading to great suffering on the part of innocent citizens, why is it difficult to place embargos on rogue government officials only? For example, the United Nations should, after a five-year advance warning, bar rogue African leaders and their families from receiving health care and executing financial transactions in countries other than theirs. This will certainly push these leaders into providing at least one excellent hospital in their native countries, while also curbing capital flight which they have transformed into their main distinguishing preoccupation. After all, how many Africans can afford to travel overseas for medical attention? So why should heads of states, their family members, and other members of government, who are not even representative of their citizens, be allowed to enjoy these facilities while the people in the countries they are mismanaging are rotting without care? Preventing rogue African heads of states from benefiting from facilities beyond their national territories which they could have developed in their native countries but would not, can be done; yet how idiotic one feels making this suggestion, given capitalist profit-oriented trends. Africa, by all means, has the work force to manage these different facilities these treacherous presidents love visiting overseas, but corrupt regimes have led to the emigration of African experts into other parts of the world where they are putting their skills to work for the benefit of foreign nations. As a result the native countries of these experts continue deteriorating, thanks to unpatriotic leaders whose only goal is to remain in power forever even as their countries literally degenerate into nothing but a name and a chaotic population held captive by despotic wiles.

Of course, we are in a world today where might is right, and African countries are yet to gatecrash into the club of dangerous nations of the world, otherwise called "superpowers" (Powell n. pag.).[1] One cannot help wondering about the legal or official founders of this club, given that the others trying to join it are now being called gatecrashers. How is membership officially acquired so other leaders and their aspiring nations do not pass for gatecrashers? It is only natural then that with current behind-the-scene imperialist presence and activities in Africa, the continent will continue facing the problems she is experiencing today, which are preventing her from taking any step forward. After all, the consequences of colonialism, be it direct colonialism as was the case until the end of the first half of the twentieth century or indirect as it has been since the 1960s—neo-colonialism and globalisation—have been and are still devastating. It is for these reasons that only propaganda, or plain ignorance as to the working of these interferences could lead to anyone holding Africa solely or mainly responsible for the chaotic status quo on the continent, or her inability to change it even. As Jacob U. Gordon points out effectively:

> The general argument coming out of Europe in the nineteenth century (and which persists even today) is that one of the purposes of colonial rule was to 'civilize' Africans for leadership roles. However, the legacy of European colonization is one of negation of civilization and leadership. The evidence clearly shows that the colonial state was about enriching those who had access to state power, not about developing leadership. Laws were enacted to wrench rights to land, mineral resources, and trade from the hands of the powerless. Scant attention, if any, was given to infrastructural development. In fact, the legacy of colonialism in Africa may be summarized as underdevelopment, backwardness, economic domination, exploitation, violence, discrimination, and cultural bastardization. (12)

Gordon is later to conclude:

> In essence, the colonial experience endured by Africa was one of an extremely violent, undemocratic state; a parasitic and repressive military structure; inefficient and corrupt bureaucracy; spatial distortion and disarticulation; politicization of social and cultural differences; and a general legacy of lack of consultation and insensitivity; political arrogance; disrespect for cultural or traditional institution; suppression of initiative and the imposition of a foreign world view, taste and value. (13)

With Gordon's summation of the consequences of Western meddling in Africa in the name of colonialism thus presented, one feels like asking God almighty to arrest Africa's case in the face of maligning propagandist; but not yet. It is not surprising therefore that Richard Joseph observes in the landmark volume *Gaullist Africa: Cameroon Under Ahmadu Ahidjo*, that:

> Anyone wishing to analyse and understand the politics of independent Africa today will find it necessary to examine the importance of colonial factors in conditioning contemporary developments, whether this involves regional and ethnic conflict in Nigeria, the entrenchment of a property-owning bureaucratic bourgeoisie in Kenya, or the regional pressures and internal poverty bequeathed in Mozambique and Angola by European colonialism. ("France in Africa" 3)

Accordingly, the West destroyed Africa by derailing the continent from her traditional ways, thus denying her the opportunity to evolve and develop naturally. Today, the West is maintaining Africa's underdevelopment directly by deciding who becomes president in many African nations, and indirectly by imposing on the continent through international organizations, alien political and financial trends which have no basis with the realities of life on the continent. The result is that the abrupt and equally drastic nature of these alien political strategies and economic theories have impacted Africa's socio-economic landscape like tornadoes an American coastline. The way out has been for the so-called experts to continue blaming Africa for mismanaging these economic tornadoes. What Western country can reduce, in a few months, the purchasing power of its citizens by about 90% and still function? But this is virtually what the Structural Adjustment Programme did to some African states, especially in the eighties and early nineties, as salaries were arbitrarily reduced by about 80% in most cases and then the currency devalued by another 50%, and these African economies were expected to improve in the long run. Of Structural Adjustment Programmes, Kevin Shillington declares:

> Access to IMF and World Bank funds have been tied to certain sets of preconditions known as Structural Adjustment Programmes (SAPs). These 'conditionalities', applied universally, have been modelled on the practices of developed capitalist systems rather than on the specific needs and best interests of the individual African countries concerned. What were presented as solutions to underlying problems carried with them even greater problems of their own. (422)

Of the consequences of the Structural Adjustment Programmes Richard Sandbrook observes:

> In light of the controversies surrounding the evaluation of structural adjustment even in the dramatic case of Ghana, prudence dictates a circumspect judgement. Structural adjustment programmes had mixed but often disappointing results in sub-Saharan Africa in the 1980s. The international financial institutions have tried to put the best face on the adjustment record....A 1988 'Mid-Term Review' by the UN's Program of Action for African Economic Recovery and Development reached a conclusion on structural adjustment that more accurately reflects the evidence and independent evaluations: 'a handful of countries registered some improvement in their overall economic fortunes. For a slightly

greater number, there have been positive trends in certain macroeconomic indicators (higher export volumes, lower inflation rates, reduced budgetary deficits). But for a majority of African states, there has not been even a hint of recovery. (*Africa's Economic Recovery* 11)

Of course the devastating impact of these draconian strategies on the lives of the people was of no consequence to those imposing these requirements on African governments, and then we hear it every day in the West as the citizens of these African countries are ridiculed for living on $1.00 a day. Naturally, the immediate result was a frustrated and angry population as unemployment skyrocketed with governments forced to reduce the number on their payrolls. The long-term result was chaos, instead of economic improvement, as having lost their jobs and sources of income, unskilled labour and the under-qualified, in some cases, took to banditry to survive, while the qualified abandoned ship and took off to continue serving stable systems in the West, leaving Africa permanently challenged due to brain-drain. What a cycle! Yet, Africa is persistently being ridiculed for not functioning.

Interestingly, some Africans also think it is time to stop blaming the West and hold Africans fully responsible for the "mess" on the continent because yes the West started it all, but Africans have refused to change the trend. A Cameroonian, lamentably, writes keenly about the "'myth of the African will for development', that all too often is a way of obscuring local incompetence by reference to the so-called international neo-colonial plot" (Chabal and Daloz 127). Chabal and Daloz present another Cameroonian writer who asks "with a pleasantly mischievous sense of humour, whether Africa does not in reality need 'a cultural adjustment programme'". They go on to point out that according to this author's logic:

> ... the fundamental reason why the continent south of the Sahara has 'deviated' from the common developmental norm is 'African culture', the 'common core' of which includes: apathy, a large dose of fatalism, a peculiar relation to the notion of time, the insignificance of the individual in the face of the community, a tendency to 'convivial' excesses, the primacy of conflict avoidance and the weight of the 'irrational'. (128)

Chabal and Daloz conclude by pointing out that it could be argued, and with good reasons, that such generalizations are clichés. They do not hesitate to add, however, that stereotypes can be revealing. And why should they be blamed when a Cameroonian showed them the way, in the words of Achebe? With *évolués* (remember how they had to alienate themselves from their roots to qualify) present all over the place and still believing their true home is away from Africa, one can always expect anything anytime. There is incompetence, no doubt about it, in every culture, but that existing in most parts of Africa having to do with the modern state, as imported as it is, is caused by the African's inability to manage his own traditional values in the face of alien political norms. Indeed, the African may need a "cultural adjustment programme" (CAP) as the latter Cameroonian suggests, but one can only wonder the direction of the adjustment needed by Africans—becoming Westerners? Has this writer even wondered why there is the need for this CAP he/she is suggesting? These are people who think development means becoming Westernized; hence, the idea of that part of the continent south of the Sahara "deviating" from the common developmental model as it struggles to remain African. Lamentably, these people argue thus even as they witness the different nations of Africa south of the Sahara limping and staggering, all because of social, political, and economic blows from the perpetually meddling West. But again, to the *évolué*, such an argument amounts to that "myth of the African will for development" and the attendant shield of a "reference to the so-called international neo-colonial plot". Appropriately, Chabal and Daloz, point to the clichéic quality of such generalizations, even if stereotypes are revealing (128).[2] What a befitting response from Westerners to another brainwashed and alienated African duo.

Whatever the case, to take such a position against Africa south of the Sahara, as do these Cameroonians cited by Chabal and Daloz, is to have underestimated so much about the tangled nature of Africa's relations with the West. It is to mitigate the consequences of the fact that many African nations are only nominally independent as the nations that colonized them are still very much in control, even if they call it "cooperation". It is to fail to acknowledge the fact that even as Africans struggle to vote true patriots into office, puppets end up imposed or manoeuvred into power in many African countries with the connivance of Western governments. To take such a position is to fail to recognize Africa's compromised bargaining power, alienated and dependent as the continent, resultantly, is today on the West. It amounts to blaming the debris—human and otherwise—in entropic gyrations triggered by a tornado, for not halting its reckless and destructive tumbles while still under the disastrously stupefying power of the storm that generated the initial energy that set and maintained it in motion. Until the tornado spends itself, all that it has in cataclysmic shift remains helplessly victimized. The tornado that triggered Africa into this destructive spin—imperialist activities—is still gathering momentum instead. Today it goes by the name of globalization, even as it continues winnowing Africa and carting away everything of value from the continent while publicly giving the impression Africa has nothing to offer. And so, until Africa's Bastilles are stormed by a conscientized, disillusioned, and angry proletariat, triggered into action by misery this time, thereby bringing about a dislocation in the chain of capitalist grasp of Africa, the continent will continue in the Western orchestrated path of self-alienation, dependence, subservience, and ultimate destruction. This is certainly the case when it is remembered that pre-colonial traditional structures and processes, administrative, for example, simply became ineffective and subsequently eradicated as leaders were now forced to submit to colonial administrative officers than to traditionally established organs and the elite. It is obviously the case when colonial powers rejected and subsequently eliminated those traditional institutions that were incompatible with colonial goals and structures. Francis B. Nyamnjoh's observation rightly sums up the destructive consequences of imperialist activities on the continent of Africa during the colonial experience: "The history of colonialism was one of fundamental structural and institutional changes, which were not reversed at independence" (*Africa's Media* 102), hence the bastardization of the continent as it is today.

Those who can, therefore, must educate the peoples of Africa to understand that Africa's leadership today, generally speaking, has failed them. There is the need for a new breed to take over with new patriotic goals, instead of imitating the treacherous immediate-postcolonial generation of leaders by ridiculously professing themselves students of alien political oppressors masquerading as concerned allies. Africa's plight is more complex than a simple sentence blaming her for not taking control. Walter Rodney, long ago even, had a better understanding of this complexity, and so urged Africa to break away from the capitalist West, instead of accusing her for failing to improve upon her lot. It is very easy for today's scholars to continue echoing Rodney's vision of decades ago, even while lacing it with different emotional flavours—anger, frustration, and the condemnation of African heads of states for not changing the tide of events in Africa. This is *déjà vu*. Real contribution by these scholars towards progress will be made when they begin pointing out what Africans and African heads of states need to do to improve upon the dire socio-economic conditions on the continent. Rodney led the way in 1972 by recommending a clean break from Western capitalism. Ghai Dharam followed with suggestions as to how this could be done, yet there remains the need, especially today, mindful of Africa's socio-politically devastating poise, to explore further some of these suggestions in an effort to confirm, at the very least, their potential to be effective. According to Dharam, national enterprises need to replace foreign enterprises, there is the need for a massive training of required workplace skills, foreign capitalists should be replaced with local versions, the incorporation of a national element into foreign corporations in inevitable, and lastly, the growth of indigenous entrepreneurship needs to be encouraged (qtd. in Vakunta).

The most important strategy today then, is to revisit the equally important concern of how to bring about the break from the West advocated by Rodney decades ago. This is the issue that needs to be addressed, especially by those African scholars today disappointed in Africa. In the main, they have damned Africa while sounding in their condemnation as if Pharaoh had no qualms with the Israelites leaving Egypt but for the Israelites themselves who were making no endeavour towards this. We all know this was not the case. Africa's path to true independence from the West and the subsequent progress of the continent is a mined field, booby-trapped with all kinds of ideas from Western leaders and their monetary organizations passing for world relief houses instead of the cutthroat money siphoning ventures they are. The brunt of the anger of those critics frustrated and disillusioned by Africa's inability to improve upon her lot after so long should be directed towards Pharaoh and not Moses and the Islraelites whose efforts, certain flaws notwithstanding, are being blatantly thwarted by the former. Long ago, Rodney knew the problem was not in pointing out what needed to be done, but in how to go about doing what needed to be done. This is the puzzle he put in place with his recommendation, which requires figuring out.

That Africa is a complicated continent tortured by myriads of intricate problems exacerbated by the innumerable ethnicities present is a fact. Cameroon as a veritable example of this is by now obvious. Within Cameroon alone, there is the problem between the governors and the governed, there is the problem of discrimination between the Francophones and the Anglophones, and then there are intra-Francophone and the intra-Anglophone tensions. How then can an entity at war with itself flourish, yet this is what is expected of Africa even with the forces of destabilization still at work thwarting rebellions against treacherous regimes on the continent. In addition, there is the need to remember that colonialists carved and forged into existence these artificial nations rivalling each other all over Africa today.

For long Africans have hoped, because of all the seemingly altruistic gestures and talks about world bodies working for peace in the world, that help will come to them from the so-called powerful nations of the West, the imperialist nations that colonized, plundered, and exploited the continent before institutionalizing division and conflict; these nations that have always been in control of African governments and their alienating policies. The truth, however, is that this might forever remain a pipedream as even gestures along these lines have been carried out only half-heartedly at best. It remains a fact, and seemingly in keeping with capitalist norms, that Africa has been a concern to the West only in so far as it benefited the latter. As the late Claude Ake had effectively demonstrated in his book *Democracy and Development in Africa*, even when Western organizations gave the impression they wanted to help Africa, they failed to look at Africa's problems as perceived and presented by Africans who were experiencing the problems firsthand. They instead considered the problems of the continent through Western historical experiences, thereby attempting to impose on Africa's evolution, political and economic theories derived from foreign experiences incongruent with ongoing socio-cultural trends within Africa. The question remains, why do Westerners want Western theories to lead to African experiences instead of African experiences leading to African theories as it occurred in the West? Marina Ottaway is querying this trend when she writes:

> Historical studies of democratic transformations in specific countries trace enormously complicated, conflictual, socio-economic and political processes stretching over many decades, if not centuries. While such studies should be required reading for practitioners of democratic assistance as an antidote to complacency, they do not offer much help in formulating policy. Prescriptions for democratization by international donors go to the opposite extreme, envisaging a sequence of stereotyped steps that appear ludicrously simplistic when compared with the historical record. The road to democracy is seen as a linear path any country can enter as long as the will is there. The path starts with a short period of liberalization, followed by a democratic transition achieved through the holding of multi-party elections, and winds on to its final destination through a long stretch of democratic consolidation. Countries are pressed to approach democratization by focusing on mechanisms: amend the constitution, write laws on political parties, form electoral commissions, carry out civic education, hold multi-party elections. Little attention is paid to the fundamental question of whether these mechanisms address the real problems the countries face. (4-5)

Little wonder most of these approaches, in the long run have, contrary to expert prognosis within these organizations, only worsened Africa's predicament. Discussing Africa's development agenda, Claude Ake reveals that the obstacle to Africa's development is political and that it is not so much that the project has failed as that it never got started in the first place. Ake points out that while many new African governments were preoccupied with politics, there was a dearth of ideas on how to pursue development. In the end, the international development community provided the development paradigm and agenda for Africa. But Ake discloses how agendas were competing, the one over the other, to the detriment of African nations. This was the case between the Lagos Plan (1980) and the World Bank Study, *Accelerated Development*; the former which stemmed from African leaders and the latter from African governors at the World Bank and the IMF. According to Claude Ake,

> The Lagos plan was a design for restructuring African economies on two principles: self-reliance (national and collective) and self sustaining development. Restructuring for self-reliance was to entail, among other things, changing Africa's location in the existing international division of labour, changing the pattern of production from primary commodities to manufactured goods, and relying more on internal sources of raw materials, spare parts, management, finance, and technology. The pursuit of national self-reliance was to be a matter of depending more on internal demand to stimulate production and less on imported inputs. Collective self-reliance would entail collective action to reduce Africa's vulnerability to external forces, a pooling of resources, and greater inter-African trade and cooperation.
>
> The Lagos plan leans towards participative development. It takes a holistic approach in several ways: in treating agriculture and industrial development together and being methodically attentive to the effects of the one on the other, in recognizing the integral relation of the internal and external causes of the African crisis, and in seeing development as a task that must involve everyone and every sector, private and public, agriculture and industry, labour, capital, and peasantry. (23-24)

Of the *Accelerated Development* Ake writes:

> The study sees the African crisis as a production crisis in agriculture, particularly in food production. It acknowledges that external factors, especially stagflation in the industrialized countries, high energy costs, and the slow growth of trade in primary commodities, are problems for Africa. However, the emphasis is overwhelmingly on the internal causes of underdevelopment of human resources, climatic conditions and over production, and policy failures. According to the study, the remedy for Africa's ailing economies lies in giving market forces freer play to bring about dynamism and efficiency. It singles out three areas for attention.... (24)

Most interesting is the fact that African leaders considered the *Accelerated Development* not to be in their interest, for they felt it did not take into account seriously enough the international economy as a problem to Africa, with its low commodity prices, high interest rates in the West, and the debt burden. Even then, the Bretton Woods institutions and the West rejected the approach of the Lagos Plan by ignoring it instead of reorienting the economic relationship with Africa to address the programs and policies of the plan. The ultimate result is that, finding themselves without the financial means to pursue the Lagos Plan in spite of the views of the World Bank and other foreign institutions, African heads of states capitulated and were managing their countries using policies in which they did not believe themselves. Hence my observation earlier on, that the West will help only in so far as it will benefit them, thereby sealing Africa's fate as a politically and economically retarded continent par excellence.

Africans, consequently, must come up with solutions to their problems or remain the laughing stock of the world thanks to Western propaganda. Multiparty democracy which seems to be the modern day panacea for Africa's "underdevelopment" prescribed and imposed by the West, did not come from heaven. It may be working in the West, the frequent inconsistencies notwithstanding, but it has failed in Africa where all it has generated is rivalry, hatred, enmity, wars, and poverty. Marina Ottaway confirms this when she writes:

> The problem is not limited to Africa. In a growing number of countries around the world, particularly among those with the lowest levels of economic development and the weakest democratic traditions, the limits of the model transition to democracy favoured by the United States are becoming evident. Many countries have gone through the motions of democracy without developing the content. (8)

Accordingly, Claude Ake laments:

> ... democracy has been reduced to the crude simplicity of multiparty elections to the benefit of the world's most notorious autocrats, such as Daniel arap Moi of Kenya and Paul Biya of Cameroon, who are now able to parade democratic credentials without reforming their repressive regimes. (130)

In view of this failure, the need for in-depth studies to be carried out on the possibilities of introducing traditional democratic practices as a system of government in Africa today becomes more urgent.

Samuel E. Bassey felt the same, and he has presented remarkable ideas along these lines in his book *No-Party Parliamentary Democracy*. Even his title sounds familiar, for this was how many ethnic groups in Africa, with or without a single traditional leader at the helm of affairs, operated until the colonialist started eroding Africa's culture and values by imposing theirs. The Igbo of Nigeria are a good example. As effectively portrayed by the great story-teller, Chinua Achebe, the elders of Umuaro usually came together as an authentic ensemble representative of Umuaro to confront problems facing their communities—participatory democracy, in other words, as everyone was virtually included in the decision-making process through the representation of their elders. This was gerontocracy at work. This is exactly what they did when the Chief Priest of Ulu, Ezeulu, in his anger, would not eat the left over yams and so regulate the harvesting season. The yams had stayed beyond the rightful number of moons because the colonial administrator, Captain Winterbottom, had detained the Chief Priest for months, since the latter would not yield to the pressure of becoming Winterbottom's puppet administrator. The result of the administration's retaliatory step was the collapse of order in the village; a perfect epitome of the African predicament.

Yes, democracy is African, even if labelled "primitive democracy", but not party politics. After all, it has been observed that such leadership which derived from customary rules of life was referred to as "primitive democracy" not because it lacked sophistication, but because it was in place from the beginning (Gordon 1). Of the political status quo in Africa which, in the main, has simply aped the West, albeit adversely because of the consequences of conflicting values—Western and African—Richard Sandbrook observes:

> Should we be surprised that disorder, conflict and economic disarray mark the postcolonial histories of Africa's new states? State-building and nation-building have everywhere been violent and disorderly matters. In Europe through the sixteenth to the eighteenth century, monarchs, princes, lords, and parliaments fought to control and expand proto-states. Peasants and town-dwellers were embroiled in these labyrinthine wars, or independently rebelled against the exactions of ambitious and ruthless rulers. Politics then - and indeed well into the twentieth century in some regions - was a dismal tale of revolts, assassinations, pacification campaigns, and wars. Similarly, in Latin America the independence of most colonies about 1820 led to what novelist Gabriel Garcia Marquez (1970) ironically dubbed 'One Hundred Years of Solitude' - a century or more of upheaval and violence as contenders vied to capture and fortify state power. Why should the history of Africa, since independence in the 1960s, be any different? (*Closing the Circle* 1)

Especially with continuous Western meddling, one cannot help adding. Sandbrook goes on to point out that Africa's woes—mass poverty, economic stagnation, and ecological degradation—amount to the causes and consequences of political disorder that, as already established, were inherited from the colonialists. Accordingly, he recommends that "'getting politics right' is a precondition of rising prosperity as well as of the liberty, security, and services for which all people yearn" (*Closing the Circle* 1).

Africans, therefore, must stop waiting for an alien messiah and move on to get their politics right while reconstructing their values, for development does not imply becoming Westernized. True, Africans have been almost completely derailed from the ways of their ancestors, and their confidence in themselves almost fatally wounded, yet it is not too late for us to begin carving our own tracks instead of always waiting for someone else to do it for us—a residual consequence of the colonial mentality and existing Western pressures. This state of mind cannot lead to development, a process that requires change in a most revolutionary manner. After all, no one can fight another's battle better than the one himself whose fate is tied to the battle. Therefore, certain values of traditional Africa must be born again as the present circumstances indicate: in the extreme by a clean ideological break from alien nations to which Africa's problems could never be a priority, or in moderation by taking from the West that which makes sense, mindful of the ways of Africa, and ignoring the rest. In the process, African nations must work hand in hand with interested nations of the world that are willing to consider them partners instead of subordinates. This step, bold and daring as it is, must be taken now or forever Africa will remain a beggarly continent aping the activities of others in spite of all her wealth and resources, natural and human, which for generations have benefited and continue to benefit the world even as Africa and Africans are being ridiculed on the international landscape. Claude Ake confirms this reasoning when he writes:

> Development is something that people do by themselves and for themselves, or it does not happen. The people of Africa will have to empower themselves to repossess their own development, a formidable task. Only a successful struggle for repossession will finally remove the obstacles that have until now grounded the development project. (123)

For aping others and allowing ourselves to be dictated to, even today, thanks to selfish spineless leaders, we as Africans have come across as political bastards, flotsam and jetsam from the evolutionary shipwreck of humankind, the final result being that today our social and cultural integrity is on the line. Accordingly, it is sincerely disturbing that some of Christopher Hitchens' reason for admiring Tunisia is the deculturation taking place there like in most of Africa. Hitchens observes: "Tunisia is the first African state to have been accepted as an associate member of the European Union. Its Code of Personal Status was the first in the Arab World to abolish polygamy, and the veil and the burka are never seen…" (106). As ridiculous as the idea of an African nation becoming a member of the European Union is, even more devastating and absurd is the fact that in the process such a nation must devalue and alienate itself from its roots, as indicated by Hitchens. This is what makes Nyamnjoh's lament more poignant:

> Africans have thus been invited to devalue themselves, their institutions and their cultures by cultivating an uncritical empathy for Western economic, cultural and political values which are glorified beyond impeachment. They are presented as having little chance of progress as Africans or blacks and invited to intensify their assumed craving to become like the whites in Europe and North America. ("Globalisation" 7)

Fuabeh P. Fonge's corroboration of Nyamjoh's view is even more conclusive of the bastardization of a people; a predicament that is authenticated by the dysfunctionalism that reigns on the continent:

Even a casual observation would not miss noticing the fact that African cities are littered with Western-style skyscrapers, many of which house elevators that seldom work; Africa has Western-style schools which have poor writing and teaching materials and are, in many cases, miseducating rather than improving the minds and skills of the youths; there are Western-style armies which are more concerned with staging military coup d'états for private interests than with providing the common defense; Western-style police forces which have failed woefully in law enforcement; Western style jurisprudence that instead of promoting justice tends to create injustice, enmity, and animosity (unlike the traditional African system which emphasized reconciliation and the reinstatement of the guilty individual to his society); Western-style agricultural plans which have proved deficient and unproductive; and Western-style bureaucracies which have increasingly become corrupt, mediocre, and inefficient.... African nations may possess all the characteristics of modern societies, but theirs is modernization without development. (2)

This, therefore, is the bastardization of a people since they are obliged to practice the ways of others, even with dismal results, at the expense of their own.

Our academic institutions were quick to realize that it was not by studying Shakespeare or Hemingway only that one became a literary authority, and so they introduced Chinua Achebe, Ngugi wa' Thiongo, Ferdinand Oyono, Ayi Kwei Armah, and Wole Soyinka, to name a few, into the syllabi. The other institutions of Africa must follow suit before a new breed emerges that, but for the colour of their skin, will not understand what it means to be African from south of the Sahara especially. We are a people whose plight in the entire world, wherever the fruits of Africa's loins have been directly or indirectly sown, has been to struggle to prove ourselves while all else is programmed to the contrary. This is a trend that is wrong and must be halted even if by none other than by Africans themselves, Africa herself, for we are a people with a fatherland and not bastards, except for those who have chosen otherwise, for then it is their choice, and freewill is a God-given right.

We are where we are, floundering and trailing, because of the imperialist interruption of Africa's march into the horizon. This unfortunate interference was then aided by the subsequent madness displayed by African political leaders in the name of governance. As Tata Mentan confirms about today's pseudo modern state leaders:

Africa's interminable and innumerable crises all share a similar origin. Each of Africa's crises begins when someone assumes power.... The new leader then proceeds to entrench himself in office by amassing power and surreptitiously debauching all key government institutions, namely, the military, the civil service, the judiciary, the parliament, and the financial system. With all powers in his hands, he transforms the state into his personal property to benefit himself, his cronies, and tribesmen, who then proceed to plunder the national treasury with impunity....The tyrant employs a variety of tactics to decimate opposition to his rule such as cooptation, bribery, infiltration, intimidation, and 'divide and rule.'" (*Held Together By Pins* 287)

Yet Africa must free herself from the socio-economic chokehold of the West and her treacherous leaders and begin marching again, forging a path according to her needs and values instead of letting herself be dragged along in whichever direction as has been the case hitherto. If Africans are to be blamed at all for the plight of the continent today, and that will be blaming them partially only, then it will be their greedy leaders and their foolishness of clinging to power. It will be because with their hands tied by Western terms, these have condoned Western manipulation, and so have permitted themselves to swim along with, in spite of the pressure, instead of fighting against the very powerful current of Western socio-political and capitalist navigation. Otherwise, yes, imperialism, which gave birth to the monsters (in most cases), ruling Africa today, is to blame for Africa's plight, and forever will remain the dominant spice in the dish tasting of Africa's predicament at any time in history, if that history is objective, if that history is the truth.

Notes

Chapter One

[1] The need to review, in detail, Gros' remarks in his book, *Cameroon: Politics and Society in Critical Perspectives*, is because the book is a significant contribution to the portrait of Cameroon today as an aggrieved nation. It will be wrong therefore to let some of Gros' debatable remarks go unaddressed as posterity might be bound to consider them generally acceptable comments on Cameroon.

Chapter Two

[1] Even decades after, since the Germans were forced out of Cameroon, there are still many surviving German landmarks in the country. There is the old Prime Minister's Lodge in Buea, the Senior District Officer's residence in Limbe, the Bamenda Fort, and other buildings that accommodated offices. The warehouses, and even the port facilities in Tiko and then Victoria, are other great examples.

[2] Even though Britain, true of virtually all the colonialists, administered Southern Cameroons without the will to train local politicians to take over from them as a priority, the few administrative structures they had in place positioned Southern Cameroons ahead of some African nations striving for Western-styled democratic practices in an independent country. Southern Cameroons had established state institutions that made them worthy of independence: democratic maturity, constitutional government, and a stable political climate, comparatively speaking. In fact, by 1960, they had already held free and fair elections, which brought the opposition to power—Foncha took over as Premier from Endeley who had been Premier of Southern Cameroons since 1958.

[3] All else notwithstanding, given the workings of covert diplomatic operations that have been exposed today, one can confidently suggest that France and the UK reached certain agreements behind the scene. In fact, Martin Z. Njeuma has stated categorically in his paper "Reunification and Political Opportunism in the Making of Cameroon's Independence", that "the British employed much arm-twisting at the UN to line up Western and anti-communist representation to block Foncha's bid to make secession the second question in the British-inspired plebiscite".

[4] Albert Mukong was notorious to the Ahidjo regime as he fought to the very end without compromising the fact that he did not value the Ahidjo regime one bit. This was a man who believed in setting the country free from Ahidjo's schemes so much so that he spent the better years of his life, virtually, moving from one political detention camp to another—BMM (Brigades Mixtes Mobiles) torture

chambers to Mantoum, to Tchollire. Like Mandela of South Africa, Mukong sacrificed his life for the Cameroon he believed in. He was a detainee everyone respected, but not many wanted to have anything to do with him since being associated with Mukong could easily earn one a visit to the BMM.

⁵ By horizontal colonization one is referring to the colonization of a former colony by another country that was itself a colony. This situation is almost obtaining in Cameroon today but for a resilient Anglophone population which is bent, and rightfully so, to protect whatever culture is has that it acquired from its encounter with the English, just as the majority Francophone population is guarding what it acquired from the French.

⁶ To grasp the idea of "compulsory" here, one must first understand that in schools within the English-speaking parts of Cameroon, a student had the right to decide, by the time he/she was in the fourth year of secondary school, on what he or she wanted to focus: to "specialize" in the arts or in the sciences. Accordingly, a student could drop all science subjects and focus on arts subjects like history, literature, and the likes, or drop all arts subjects and focus on the science subjects like chemistry, physics, and biology. This notwithstanding, whether a student wanted to major in either the arts or the sciences, he or she still had to take and earn a pass grade in English, French, and Math before he or she could move from one to the next class in school, hence the idea of compulsory subjects.

⁷ Ntemfac Ofege, was a journalist who worked for the government Radio and Television media houses (CRTV) for some time before falling foul with the regime because of how critical he was of the system. Ofege has written a very authoritative paper titled "Founded on the Big Lie, Corruption and Mass Graves in Mbalmayo", in which he argues that the coup attempt was in fact a big lie. Ofege argues convincingly, apparently, that in reality, it was a plot by the Biya regime to dismantle the Republican Guard, which was sympathetic to Ahidjo, while also wresting total control of the sole political party in the country at the time — Cameroon National Union — whose Chairman Ahidjo was, even as he gave up the post as the nation's president to Biya.

Chapter Three

¹ The West Cameroon, Southern Cameroons before the federation, renamed its House of Assembly West Cameroon Legislative Assembly, whereas East Cameroon, formerly La République du Cameroun, changed the name of its legislature to East Cameroon Legislative Assembly.

² This is why, much later on, potentially great leaders like Peter Mafany Musonge and Ephraim Inoni could only go so far in spite of their burning desire to turn Cameroon around. In their capacity, as prime ministers, with Biya as president, they were administrative surgeons with the authority to operate only upon the lower torso of the state body whereas the real problems rested in the brain — those irresponsible high ranking members of government in Cameroon, who are above the law. It was virtually the consensus that these two were great players in a bad team.

³"Ghost towns" is an appellation accorded the empty streets all over Cameroon in 1992 when Chairman John Fru Ndi of the then darling and lone credible opposition party in the country, The social Democratic Front (SDF) called for a boycott of work and all activities that generated capital for the government. It was hoped this would force Paul Biya to dialogue with the opposition after it was believed he had rigged the presidential elections to maintain himself in office, contrary to the expectations of the nation that John Fru Ndi was the winner.

⁴This is not always the case as sometimes one is likely to confuse that hospitality which is typically African, with this colonial mentality; the truth though is that the colonial mentality is still thriving in certain quarters and is experienced from time to time.

⁵Bamenda is the capital city of the North West Province of Cameroon.

⁶ Whereas societies with a sense of purpose are doing all to curb accidents caused by drunk driving, Cameroon virtually has no government policy about this. Once in a while, half-hearted and equally poorly organized ventures called "road safety campaigns" are carried out, only for them to die down as quickly as they had started. Imagine that in Cameroon there is this incredible practice of drivers getting tipsy before starting on a four to six hour trip with overcrowded vehicles on narrow roads characterized by totally blind curves and potholes of different shapes and sizes. Drivers who begin their journey without alcohol in their veins, even those with it, stop at rest villages on the way, usually midway to their destinations, to consume alcohol before continuing. Examples of such villages from the North-West and West Provinces are Kekem on the way to the South West and Littoral Provinces, and Ndikinimiki on the way to the Centre Province and beyond. Interestingly, even the passengers do not seem to mind tipsy and drunken people driving them. All of this is because the government has done nothing to educate the public on the effects of alcohol to the brain, one's sense of judgment, and summarily one's ability to drive safely. Of course, more often than not, even if the police knew these things, the police would confuse the source of the smell of alcohol – the driver, some passengers, or from the police themselves as they are always drunk or still drinking even as they are on the road harassing passengers while claiming to be doing their job.

Chapter Four

¹Stability of the nation here means maintaining Ahidjo as head of state for as long as possible. National security, even until today, still means the safety and wellbeing of the dictator in office.

Chapter Five

¹By combination, reference is being made to one of the different disciplinary series that had been structured and put in place, by those charged with the

curriculum, to prepare students for future professions. There were arts combinations like History, English Literature, and French Literature; History, English Literature, and Economics; and so on, whereas in the sciences there were combinations like Biology, Chemistry, Physics; and Biology, Physics, Math and the likes. A student passing out of the GCE O/Level needed such a combination in the subjects he had passed or else his pass was of no use since he/she could not get into any high school series.

[2] There is the need to point out here that this demand applies only to those who followed the English system of education (mainly Anglophones) as Cameroonians with Doctorat de Troisième Cycle, at a time that this third Cycle French doctorate was being considered a Masters degree, were still being employed. Some holders of this certificate themselves knew it was not equivalent to a Ph.D and so went on to pursue their doctoral programmes, whereas others remained dishonest to themselves and went on accepting the title "doctor" from Anglophone students, thereby giving the impression they had earned Ph.Ds. Academic dishonesty is a serious offence in the world of academe. Individuals like these must emulate Mr. Nsanda Eba who stood up once in a social event in ENS Bambili to correct a student who had addressed him Dr. Eba. "I am not a doctor", the distinguished mathematician declared, "I do not have a Ph.D". Today, however, it is said that France has eliminated all these cycles in its doctoral programs and there is just one "doctorat". In this case, the year of one's "doctorat" will come in handy to determine whether the "doctorat" can be considered equivalent to a Ph.D. This ado, however, is not necessary in Cameroon where for decades before this modification by France the Doctorat de troisiem Cycle was already masquerading as a Ph.D.

[3] Qualified academics teaching in Bambili, for example, are expected to travel to Yaounde to administer the entrance exam into ENS Bambili. This is true, as ridiculous as it sounds. It is more stupefying when it realized that about 85% percent of the students trying to get into ENS Bambili do not come from Yaounde. Why then risk the lives of faculty and interviewees, by rerouting them to Yaounde for the interview into their Bambili campus? In this case, students in Bamenda have to leave Bamenda to travel to Yaounde in order to be interviewed by Bambili faculty members so they get into Bambili which is located in Bamenda. In the same vein, students from other provinces, especially the South-West, the West, and parts of Littoral which are closer to Bambili, find themselves thus ridiculously navigated by the authorities. What is painful is the fact that nothing special takes place when interviewers and interviewees get to Yaounde that makes this trip worthwhile, nothing! The point is simply that somebody cannot imagine leaving all the bribe to go to Bambili authorities alone; they want a share of it. How citizens are inconvenienced and their lives endangered does not bother them.

[4] Although the company is today called AES SONEL because it has been taken over by the giant American energy corporation AES, in this book, the name SONEL, as it was before AES took over, is maintained so that AES is not stigmatized undeservedly. AES only came in after SONEL had achieved the disastrous status described in here under a different management. AES, however, is yet to improve upon the situation even after seven years in Cameroon.

⁵*Grand Camarade* is a term of reference for Ahmadou Ahidjo that smacks of a certain bewildering nostalgia for his days as head of state. Despite his methods, Ahidjo had a personality that people sometimes can still not help admiring even after all these years.

⁶ This is an informal kind of banking system that involves groups with specific numbers of members who have a steady source of income of some sort. The *njangi* usually meets every pay period, which is once a month or whenever the members decide. These workers and/or business people decide on a set amount, which they contribute every time the group meets, and the members take turns receiving the total amount contributed. They usually cast lots to decide the order in which to take the contributed amount, which is then invested by the member.

Chapter six

¹Some people have argued that not all good candidates can pass because the available positions are distributed in percentages according to one's area of origin, a practice that Ahidjo put in place so as to ensure that every sector of the country was fairly represented in the public service. As reasonable as it sounds, to me it does not make much sense. The implication here is that even if the very intellectually equipped for a service position are from the South-West province, for example, then some of them must be left out and ill-equipped candidates from other parts of the country just given chances they do not merit so the entire nation is represented? If this were the case ever, then as a policy it is obsolete and should be abandoned. It is this kind of compartmentalization of society that encourages and leads to division and unnecessary ethnic tension. Cameroonians are Cameroonians and members of society should prove their worth to get whatever they need.

² Governor Bell Luc René who was one of the most liked governors of the province, lost all he had worked for by allowing the military to use live bullets and grenades on the populace. He, accordingly, earned the sobriquet "Bend Look Grenade".

Chapter Seven

¹One considers the process of La République's piecemeal illegal annexation of West Cameroon tentative because it is still in process, and the French-backed La République du Cameroun is cautiously striding the path put in place by Ahidjo while watching the reactions of Anglophones. Where the reaction is volatile, the regime steps back and tries another approach.

²The African Union can deliberate upon this and agree on an African language that should become a compulsory subject in our schools from the elementary level to high schools, and after that students may continue in the subject as deemed necessary. Before long, such a language will become the lingua franca of Africa, thereby sealing our oneness. Swahili is a good example of such a language.

Chapter Eight

[1] Powell calls other non Western nations trying to create their own source for atomic energy "gatecrashers" into the club of world powers, hence one wonders when this club was formed, and what it takes to become a legal member instead of a gatecrasher.

[2] This kind of reasoning as displayed by both these Cameroonians whose names Chabal and Daloz do not release, is typical of the warped mentality of some Africans encountered in the diaspora who are obviously completely out of touch with reality in their native countries. In this case, overwhelmed by the peace and calm they enjoy in another man's country, and dazed by fumes of the doctrine of making it to French "citizens" as opposed to that of remaining French "subjects", they turn around and display a blatant disconnection from their roots that smacks of "*évoluéism*".

Works Cited

Achebe, Chinua. *Arrow of God*. Garden City: Anchor, 1969.

- - -. "The Role of the Writer in a New Nation." *Nigeria Magazine* 81 (June 1964): 157-60.

Achobang, Christopher Fon. "Prof. Lambi Dispells Rumours of Resignation." *Eden* Monday 4 – Wednesday 6 Dec. 2006: 6.

Adejumobi, Said. "South Africa: Is this What We Deserve?" PAV 11, June 2008, 6/10/2008 <htp://www.panafricanvisions.com/11/features.htm>.

Ake, Claude. *Democracy and Development in Africa*. Washington, D.C.: Brookings, 1996.

Ambe, Augustine. "France and the Frenchification of Southern Cameroons." *Southern Cameroons Interim Government-in-Exile*. 6 Jan. 2008 <http://www.SouthernCameroonIG.org>.

Awasom, Nicodemus Fru. "Colonial Background to the Development of Autonomist Tendencies in Anglophone Cameroon, 1946-1961." *Journal of Third World Studies* (Spring 1998). 27 Mar. 2008 <http://findarticles.com/p/articles/mi_qa3821/is_199804/ai_n8783744/print>.

Bassey, Samuel E. *No-Party Parliamentary Democracy: The Ideal Political System for the New Age.* Indiana: Authorhouse, 2005.

Besong, Bate. "Paul Biya 23 Years After: He has Elevated Graft into Statecraft." 18 Mar. 2007 <http://www.batebesong.com/2005/1/paul_biya_23_ye.html>.

Bohannan, Paul and Philip Curtin. *Africa and Africans*. 4th ed. Prospect Heights: Waveland, 1995.

Bond, Patrick. *Looting Africa: The Economics of Exploitation*. Pietermaritzburg, Afr.: University of KwaZulu-Natal P.; London: Zed Books, 2006.

Butake, Bole. *The Rape of Michelle*. Yaounde, Afr.: Centre d'Edition et de Production Pour l'Enseignement et la Recherche, 1994.

Campbell, Horace. "Democracy, Human Rights, and Peace in Africa." *The State and Democracy in Africa*. Ed. Georges Nzongola-Ntalaja and Margaret C. Lee. 1997. Trenton: Africa World Press, Inc. 1998

Chabal, Patrick, Jean-Paschal Dalloz. *Africa Works: Disorder as Political Instrument*. The International African Institute in association with Oxford: James Currey; Bloomington: Indiana UP, 1999.

---. Introduction. *Africa Works: Disorder as Political Instrument*. By Chabal and Dalloz. xv-xxi

Chazan, Naomi et al. *Politics and Society in Contemporary Africa*. Lynne Reinner: Boulder, 1999.

Chem-Langhëë, Bongfen. "The Road to the Unitary State of Cameroon 1959-1972." *Paideuma*.1995. 19 Mar. 2007 <http://lucy.kent.ac.uk/Chilver/Paideuma>.

Chidester, David. "Atlantic Community, Atlantic World: Anti-Americanism Between Europe and Africa." *Historycooperative.org*. 5 Mar. 2008 <http://www.historycooperative.org/journals/jah/93.2/chidester.html>.

Cole, Jennifer. Introduction. *Forget Colonialism? Sacrifice and the Art of Memory in Madagascar.* By Cole. Berkley: UCP, 2001. 1-34.

Conrad, Joseph. *Heart of Darkness. Literature of the Western World: Neoclassicism Through the Modern Period.* Ed. Brian Wilkie and James Hurt. Vol. 2. 5th ed. Upper Saddle River: Prentice, 2001.

Daloz, Jean-Pascal. *Africa Works: Disorder as Political Instrument.* The International African Institute in association with Oxford: James Currey, 1999.

Diop, Boubacar Boris. "'Ivory Coast: Colonial Adventure." Trans. Donald Houman. *Le Monde Diplomatique.* Apr. 2005. 19 Oct. 2007 <http://mondediplo.com/2005/04/10diop>.

Douala, Alexandre aka Douleur. "Charter au Mali." *Fureur.* Paris, 1997

Eko, Lyombe. "The English-Language Press and the 'Anglophone Problem' in Cameroon: Group Identity, Culture, and the Politics of Nostalgia." *Journal of Third World Studies* (Spring 2003). 2 Apr. 2008 <http://findarticles.com/p/articles/mi_qa3821/is_200304/ai_n9173452/print>.

Eyinga, Abel. Appendix. *Gaullist Africa: Cameroon Under Ahmadu Ahidjo.* Ed. Richard Joseph. Enugu, Afr.: Fourth Dimension Publishers, 1978. 215-217.

Fanon, Frantz. *The Wretched of the Earth.* Harmondsworth: Penguin, 1967.

Fombad, Charles Manga. "The Dynamics of Record-breaking Endemic Corruption and Political Opportunism in Cameroon." *The Leadership Challenge in Africa: Cameroon Under Paul Biya.* Ed. John Mukum Mbaku and Joseph Takougang. Trenton: Africa World Press, 2004. 357-394.

Fonge, Fuabeh P. "Introduction." Modernization without Development in Africa: Patterns of Change and Continuity in Post-Independence Cameroonian Public Service." By Fonge. Trenton: Africa World Press, 1997. 1-18

"French Army Clash with CAR Rebels." *Eden* 29 Nov. – 4 Dec. 2006: 11.

Gordon, Jacob U. *African Leadership in the Twentieth Century: An Enduring Experiment in Democracy.* Lanham: UP of America, Inc, 2002.

Gros, Jean-Germain. ed. *Cameroon: Politics and Society in Critical Perspectives.* Lanham: UP of America, 2003.

Gros, Jean-Germain. "Cameroon in Synopsis." Gros 1-32.

---. Preface. Gros xv-xxiv.

Harford, Tim. "Why Poor Countries Are Poor: The Clues Lie on a Bumpy Road Leading to the World's Worst Library." *Reason Online.* Mar. 2006. 23 Mar. 2006 <http://reason.com/0603/fe.th.why.shtml>.

Hitchens, Christopher. "At the Desert's Edge." *Vanity Fair* 563 July 2007: 104-108.

Jing, Thomas Ayeah. "Bamileke: Friend or Foe?" *Postwatch.com.* 30 June 2004. 19 Mar. 2007 <http://www.powtwatchmagazine.com/2004/06/index.html>.

Joseph, Richard. *Gaullist Africa: Cameroon Under Ahmadu Ahidjo.* Enugu, Afr. Fourth Dimension Publishers, 1978.

---. Preface. *Gaullist Africa: Cameroon Under Ahmadu Ahidjo.* Joseph ix-iv.

---. "France in Africa." *Gaullist Africa: Cameroon Under Ahmadu Ahidjo.* Joseph 3-11

---. "The Gaullist Legacy." *Gaullist Africa: Cameroon Under Ahmadu Ahidjo.* Joseph 12-27.

Jua, Nantang. "Anglophone Political Struggles and State Responses." Gros 87-110.

---. "Economic Management in Neo-Colonial States: A Case Study of Cameroon. Research Reports no. 38/1990. Leiden: African Studies Centre, 1990.

Jua, Nantang and Piet Konings. Occupation of Public Space: Anglophone Nationalism in Cameroon. Cahiers D'études Africaines. 44, 175, (2004): 609 - 633. 24 June 2008 <http://etudesafricaines.revues.org/document4756.html?format=print>

Konings, Piet, and Francis B. Nyamnjoh. "President Paul Biya and the 'Anglophone Problem' in Cameroon." *The Leadership Challenge in Africa: Cameroon Under Paul Biya*. Ed. John Mukum Mbaku and Joseph Takougang. Trenton: Africa World Press, 2004. 191-234.

---. *Negotiating an Anglophone Identity: A Study of the Politics of Recognition and Representation in Cameroon*. Afrika-Studiecentrum Series, Vol.1. Leiden: Brill, 2003.

Konings, Piet. "'Bendskin' Drivers in Douala New Bell Neighbourhood: Masters of the Road and the City." *Crisis and creativity: Exploring the Wealth of the African Neighbourhood*. Ed. Piet Konings and Dick Foeken. Leiden: Brill, 2006. 46-65.

---. *Labour Resistance in Cameroon: Managerial Strategies & Labour Resistance in the Agro-Industrial Plantations of the Cameroon Development Corporation*. London: Currey,1993.

---. "The Post-Colonial State and Economic and Political Reforms in Cameroon." *Liberalization in the Developing World: Insitutional and Economic Changes in Latin America, Africa, and Asia*. Ed. Alex E. Fernárdez Jilberto and André Mommen. London: Routledge 1996. 244-265.

Kummer, Patricia K. *Cameroon*. New York: Children's Press (A Division of Scholastic Inc. [2004?].

Lapiro de Mbanga, "Qui N'est Rien N'a Rien." *Na You*. JPS Productions, 2001

---. "Na You." *Na You*. JPS Productions, 2001.

---. "Money For Hand Back for Ground." *Pas Argent No Love*. Haissam Records, 1985.

Le Vine, Victor. *The Cameroons from Mandate to Independence*. California: U California P Berkley, 1964.

---. Preface. Le Vine. vii-x.

---. "Ahmadu Ahidjo Revisited." Gros 33-60.

Mentan, Tatah. Preface. *With Neither Guns Nor Bullets: Recolonisation of Africa Today*. By Mentan. New Delhi: Global Media Publications. 2007. 9-13.

---. *Held together By Pins: Liberal Democracy under Siege in Africa*. Trenton: Africa World Press. 2007.

---. "Cameroon: The Political Economy of Poverty." Gros 111-130.

Morgan, W.B. and J. C. Pugh. *West Africa*. London: Methuen & Co Ltd. 1969.

Mukong, Albert. *Prisoner without a Crime*. Limbe, Afr.: Alfresco, 1985.

Murphy, Dervla. *Cameroon with Egbert*. New York: The Overlook, 1990.

Monga, Célestin. The Anthropology of Anger: Civil Society and Democracy in Africa. Trans. Linda L. Fleck & Célestin Monga. Boulder: Reinner. 1996.

Ndjio, Basile. "Carrefour de La Joie: Popular Deconstruction of the African Postcolonial Public Sphere." *Africa* 75.3 (2005): 265-294.

---. "Intimate Strangers: Neighbourhood, autochthony and the Politics of Belonging." *Crisis and creativity: Exploring the Wealth of the African Neighbourhood.* Ed. Piet Konings and Dick Foeken. Leiden: Brill, 2006. 66-87.

Ndze, Clemens. "Cry the Beloved Country." *Postwatch.com.* 30 June 2004. 18 Mar. 2007 <http://www.Postwatchmagazine.com/2005/05/cry_the_beloved.html>.

Nfor, Nfor N. *Southern Cameroons and La République du Cameroun Union: The Hidden Agenda.* Bamenda, Afr.: Unique Printers, 1994.

Ngenge, Tata Simon. The Institutional Roots of the 'Anglophone Problem' in Cameroon." Gros 61-86.

Ngwafor, Ephraim. *May Former Victoria Smile Again.* London: Institute of Third World Art and Literature, 1989.

Ngwane, George. "'Cameroon's Democratic Process: Vision 2020.'" *CODESRIA* 3-4 (2004): 20-26.

"Nobel Prize Winner Sets Off Firestorm With Comments About Blacks." *Star Tribune* Friday 19 Oct. 2007, A7.

Njeuma, Martin Z. "Reunification and Political Opportunism in the Making of Cameroon's Independence." *Perspectives on the State: From Political History to Ethnography in Cameroon. Essays for Sally Chilver.* 19 Mar.2007 <http://lucy.kent.ac.uk/Chilver/Paideuma>.

Nyamnjoh, Francis B. "For Many are Called but Few are Chosen: Globalisation and Popular Disenchantment in Africa." *African Sociological Review* 4.2 (2000): 1-31.

---. *Africa's Media: Democracy and the Politics of Belonging.* London: Zed Books, 2005.

Nzongola-Ntalaja, Georges. "The State and Democracy in Africa." *The State and Democracy in Africa.* Ed. Georges Nzongola-Ntalaja and Margaret C. Lee. 1997. Trenton: Africa World Press, Inc.1998.

Ofege, Ntemfac. "Corruption in Cameroon: A State of the Art." *Postwatch.com.* 18 Mar. 2006. 30 Mar. 2006 <http://postwatchmagazine.com/2006/02corruption_in_c_1.html>.

---. "Founded on the Big Lie, Corruption and Mass Graves in Mbalmayo." *Postwatch.com.* 15 Mar. 2007. 19 Mar. 2007 <http://www.postwatchmagazine.com2006/02/founded_on_the_html>

Ottaway, Marina. *Africa's New Leaders: Democracy or State Reconstruction?* Washington: Carnegie Endowment for international Peace, 1999.

Pio, Padre, perf. *Padre Pio, Man of God.* Dir. Paolo Damoss. Capuchin Frairs of Foggia. Nova-T S.r.l. 1999.

Powell, Bill. "A Gate Crasher in the Most Dangerous Club." *Time* 25 December 2006/1 January, 2007. n. pag.

Rodney, Walter. *How Europe Underdeveloped Africa.* Enugu, Afr.: Ikenga Publishers, 1982.

---. Preface. *How Europe Underdeveloped Africa.* By Rodney 7-8.

Sandbrook, Richard. *Closing the Circle: Democratization and Development in Africa*. Toronto: Between the Lines; New York: Zed Books Ltd, 2000.

---. *The Politics of Africa's Economic Recovery*. Cambridge UP, 1993.

Schaffer, Frederic C. *Democracy in Translation: Understanding Politics in an Unfamiliar Culture*. Ithaca: Cornel UP, 1998.

Shillington, Kevin. *History of Africa*. 2nd ed. Oxford: Macmillan, 1995.

Takougang, Joseph, and Krieger Milton. *African State and Society in the 1990s*. Colorado: Westview, 1998.

Takougang, Joseph. "The Nature of Politics in Cameroon." *The Leadership Challenge in Africa: Cameroon Under Paul Biya*. Ed. John Mukum Mbaku and Joseph Takougang. Trenton: Africa World, 2004. 67–94.

Tchop-Tchop. per. "Makalapatie (Corruption)." *Nsam Efoulan*. Dir. Emmanuel Eyengue. MC POP Music, 1999.

Thomson, Alex. *An Introduction to African Politics*. London: Routledge, 2000.

Tordoff, William. *Government and Politics in Africa*. 4th ed. Bloomington: Indiana UP, 2002.

Vakunta, Peter. "False Start in Postcolonial Africa." *PAV (PanAfrican Visions)* 8 (Mar. 2008). 4 Apr. 2008 <http://www.panafricanvisions.com/8/commentary.htm>.

Wainaina, Binyavanga. "Generation Kenya." *Vanity Fair* 563 July 2007: 84-94.

Wrong, Michela. *In the Footsteps of Mr. Kurtz*. New York: Perennial, 2002.

Zachary, G. Paschal. "The Coming Revolution in Africa." *The Wilson Quarterly* XXXII.1 (Winter 2008): 50-66.

---. "Plugging Into Africa." *CNNMONEY.COM*. 1 Nov. 2006. 31 Oct. 2006 <http://http://money.com.magazines/business2/business2_archive/2005/11/01/8362802/inde...>.

www.ingramcontent.com/pod-product-compliance
Lightning Source LLC
Chambersburg PA
CBHW021125300426
44113CB00006B/298